Terrorism and the US Drone Attacks in Pakistan

This book analyses the US drone attacks against terrorists in Pakistan to assess whether the 'pre-emptive' use of combat drones to kill terrorists is ever legally justified.

Exploring the doctrinal discourse of pre-emption vis-à-vis the US drone attacks against terrorists in Pakistan, the book shows that the debate surrounding this discourse encapsulates crucial tensions between the permission and limits of the right of self-defence. Drawing from the long history of God-given and man-made laws of war, this book employs positivism as a legal frame to explore and explain the doctrine of pre-emption and analyses the doctrine of the state's rights to self-defence as it stretches into pre-emptive or preventive use of force. The book investigates why the US chose the recourse to pre-emption through the use of combat drones in the 'war on terror' and whether there is a potential future for the pre-emption of terrorism through combat drones. The author argues that the policy to 'kill first' is easy to adopt; however, any disregard for the web of legal requirements surrounding the policy has the potential to undercut the legal claims of an armed act. The book enables the framing and analysis of such controversies in legal terms as opposed to a choice between law and policy.

An examination of the legal dilemma concerning drone warfare, this book will be of interest to academics in the fields of international relations, Asian politics, South Asian studies, and security studies, in particular, global security law, new wars, and emerging technologies of warfare.

Imdad Ullah is an Assistant Professor at the Centre for International Peace and Stability (CIPS) at the National University of Sciences and Technology (NUST), Pakistan.

Routledge Contemporary South Asia Series

130 **Identity and Marginality in India**
Settlement Experience of Afghan Migrants
Anwesha Ghosh

131 **Political Transformations in Nepal**
Dalit Inequality and Social Justice
Mom Bishwakarma

132 **Fertility, Health and Reproductive Politics**
Re-imagining Rights in India
Maya Unnithan

133 **Labour, Global Supply Chains, and the Garment Industry in South Asia**
Bangladesh After Rana Plaza
Sanchita Banerjee Saxena

134 **Ethnic Inequality in the Northeastern Indian Borderlands**
Social Structures and Symbolic Violence
Anita Lama

135 **Kashmir and the Future of South Asia**
Edited by Sugata Bose and Ayesha Jalal

136 **Bangladesh and International Law**
Edited by Mohammad Shahabuddin

137 **Terrorism and the US Drone Attacks in Pakistan**
Killing First
Imdad Ullah

For the full list of titles in the series please visit: https://www.routledge.com/Routledge-Contemporary-South-Asia-Series/book-series/RCSA

Terrorism and the US Drone Attacks in Pakistan

Killing First

Imdad Ullah

Routledge
Taylor & Francis Group
LONDON AND NEW YORK

First published 2021
by Routledge
2 Park Square, Milton Park, Abingdon, Oxon OX14 4RN

and by Routledge
605 Third Avenue, New York, NY 10017

Routledge is an imprint of the Taylor & Francis Group, an informa business

British Library Cataloguing-in-Publication Data
A catalogue record for this book is available from the British Library

Library of Congress Cataloging-in-Publication Data
A catalog record has been requested for this book

ISBN: 978-0-367-70076-8 (hbk)
ISBN: 978-0-367-70285-4 (pbk)
ISBN: 978-1-003-14548-6 (ebk)

Typeset in Times New Roman
by Deanta Global Publishing Services, Chennai, India

Contents

Acknowledgements

This book is the product of several years of research at the Willy Brandt School of Public Policy, University of Erfurt, Germany, culminating in the defence of a doctoral thesis in 2017.

It has been made possible through the financial support of the German Academic Exchange Service (DAAD) as well as the even more valued and sustained encouragement and support of my supervisor, Professor Dr Ciaran J. Burke, who was always there to guide me and give me a push in the right direction. For all his help and support, I am deeply indebted. Yet I would remiss if I do not thank Professor Dr Florian F. Hoffmann for his role and help in putting me on the right course at the beginning of this long journey. An initial push is always important and long remembered.

I also wish to specifically thank numerous persons who in one way or the other supported me, notably Professor Tariq Rehman, Dr Andrea Fleschenberg, Dr Ijaz Hussain, Dr Anja Mehr, Dr Ahmad Waqas Waheed, Dr Muhammad Rasheed, Mr Dennis Binder, Mr Ibrahim Khan, Miss Menahil Tahir, and Miss Ingrid Knapp.

Last but not the least, the love and encouragement of my family remain highly crucial for me. My mother always did everything in her power to support and encourage me. My deepest gratitude goes to my wife, Sana Fatima, whose invaluable logistical and moral support was crucial in finishing this book.

1 Why study the pre-emption of terrorism?

Self-defence is a cardinal legal right. States do not happily entrust this right to an international institution, because when a security threat looms at the borders, states don't want to leave it to an institution to interpret the rules and principles of the use of force for them. For state actors, security has primacy. It is the element that determines and ensures the existence of states. Such reluctance on the part of states to depend upon international institutions became even more discernible against the backdrop of the September 11 terrorist attacks, as these attacks brought about serious challenges for the laws governing the use of force among states.[1] Many states, such as the US, Russia, France, Israel, Turkey, and India, expressed their *will* to eradicate terrorism through pre-emptive wars. For instance, the Russian Defence Minister Sergei Ivanov laid down that pre-emptive use of force has become a compelling 'reality' in the contemporary world.[2] Former French President Jacques Chirac stressed that France is ready to launch a first strike against any state supporting terrorists to attack his country.[3] And Indian External Affairs Minister Jaswant Singh suggested that every state has the inherent right to launch pre-emptive strikes against the brewing security threats and that this right must not be limited to one state. In contemporary times, deterrence is synonymous with pre-emption, he stressed.[4] In these contexts, there seems to be an emerging understanding that if not backed by the strategy and threat of pre-emption, deterrence may lose its utility to counter terrorism.

The history of the pre-emptive use of force bears testimony to the fact that usually states justify the act under Article 51 of the United Nations (UN) Charter.[5]

1 Toni Pfanner, "Asymmetrical Warfare from the Perspective of Humanitarian Law and Humanitarian Action", *International Review of Red Cross* 87, no. 857 (2005): 149–153.

2 "Russia Not Planning to Give up Right of Pre-Emptive Strikes—Defence Minister", *BBC Intl., Rep.*, October 20, 2003, LEXIS, Individual Publications.

3 Molly Moore, "Chirac: Nuclear Response to Terrorism Is Possible", *The Washington Post*, January 20, 2006.

4 Jaswant Singh, "Every Country Has Right to Pre-Emption" *Press Trust of India,* September 30, 2002.

5 Michael J. Glennon, "The Fog of Law: Self-Defense, Inherence, and Incoherence in Article 51 of the United Nations Charter", *Harvard Journal of Law & Public Policy* 25, no. 2 (2002): 539–558.

For example, during the 1980s, the US military attacks against Haiti and Libya, as well as the Israeli military attacks against Lebanon, were sought to be justified under the self-defence framework of the UN Charter. Thus, it is important to mention here that after the September 11 terrorist attacks, the employment of pre-emptive self-defence in itself is not new. Instead, it is the elevation of the right of self-defence to the policy level which caused unease.[6] Therefore, recent claims by some states to use pre-emptive self-defence against emerging security threats and especially against international terrorists can have bearings for the legal order.[7] Potentially, it seems that states are confusing the right of self-defence—endorsed by the customary and contemporary international law—with the pre-emptive use of force—conceived and rationalised under the dictates of security and strategic calculus. For instance, the Bush administration asserted that:

> We must adapt the concept of imminent threat to the capabilities and objectives of today's adversaries. Rogue states and terrorists do not seek to attack us using conventional means. They know such attacks would fail. Instead, they rely on acts of terror and, potentially, the use of weapons of mass destructions—weapons that can be easily concealed, delivered covertly, and used without warning.[8]

In this context, moreover, the danger of the potential mix up of global terrorism, failing and failed states, and weapons of mass destruction is what necessitates the legal mechanisms regulating the use of force "among [the] states in question".[9] And yet, above all, the use of combat drones to employ lethal force is something that one needs to carefully examine for its relationship to the calculations for the need and the amount of violent force needed to neutralise a terrorist threat. It is submitted, therefore, that, in present times, various aspects of the security environment need to be studied for a better understanding of the legal frameworks governing and regulating the relationships between international law and the use of force. Concerning the case under investigation here, it is important to bear in mind that after the exercise of its right of self-defence in Afghanistan, perhaps the US government realised that it has failed to fully quell the threat of terrorism.

6 "The National Security Strategy of the United States of America", The White House, Washington, September 20, 2002. This strategy is also popularly known as the Bush Doctrine. It underlines that without waiting for the first strike, the US would employ pre-emptive self-defence to neutralise the terrorist threats.

7 Michael Reisman and Andrea Armstrong, "The Past and Future of the Claim of Pre-emptive Self-Defence", *American Journal of International Law* 100, no. 3 (2006): 526.

8 "The National Security Strategy of the United States of America", 15.

9 Anthony C. Arend, "International Law and the Pre-emptive Use of Military Force", *The Washington Quarterly* 26, no. 2 (2003): 78–97; Anne-Marie Slaughter and William Burke-White, "An International Constitutional Moment", *Harvard International Law Journal* 43, no. 1 (2002): 1–21; Robert F. Turner, "Operation Iraqi Freedom: Legal and Policy Considerations", *Harvard Journal of Law & Public Policy* 27, no. 3 (2004): 765–796; and William K. Lietzau, "Old Laws, New Wars: Jus ad Bellum in an Age of Terrorism", *Max Planck United Nations Yearbook* 8 (2004): 384–455.

Speaking in purely state security terms, the US, therefore, decided to launch the drone attacks in Pakistan and Yemen to *kill first* those terrorists planning to *harm* them in future.[10]

It is important to bear in mind that killing first or pre-emption is an elusive term. Its meaning changes with the change of the discipline in which it is studied. Normative theorists believe that an armed attack can be pre-emptive when launched to forestall 'an imminent attack on the pre-emptor'. Strategic thinkers, however, employ the term as an armed initiative undertaken to gain an edge over the enemy through a surprise first strike.[11] In international law, meanwhile, notions like anticipatory self-defence and preventive self-defence also exist along with pre-emptive self-defence. In general, all of them allude to any measure involving the use of force to forestall a security threat. In essence, however, these notions entail different meanings. For instance, anticipatory self-defence involves the use of force in advance of an armed attack. It does not, however, qualify the fact of the imminence of a security threat in terms of the time continuum. Inversely, pre-emptive self-defence includes the qualification of the imminence of an impending attack. In this context, the qualifying measures determine the tangibly hostile movements of the adversary, the embodying severity of harm, and the distance from the territorial borders.[12]

More precisely, this study explores and analyses the doctrinal discourse of pre-emption vis-à-vis the US drone attacks against terrorists in Pakistan. The debate surrounding this discourse encapsulates crucial tensions between the permission and the limits of the right of self-defence. The choice of the primary case is instructive in a sense because it is situated at the centre of the unfolding landscape of pre-emption, terrorism, and new technologies of warfare. Besides, the US used combat drones in Pakistan extensively. According to the US government, Al-Qaeda in Pakistan had a direct or indirect link to the September 11 terrorist attacks. So is the case of Al-Qaeda in Yemen. A Yemeni national was among the planners of the terrorist attacks. After the US invasion of Afghanistan, Al-Qaeda

10 It is important to highlight here that this study uses the notion of 'killing first' within the frame of pre-emptive self-defence and, at times, uses these two concepts alternately.

11 Henry Shue and David Rodin, eds., *Preemption: Military Action and Moral Justification* (New York: Oxford University Press, 2007), 2.

12 Thomas M. Franck, *Recourse to Force: State Action Against Threats and Armed Attacks* (Cambridge: Cambridge University Press, 2004), 52; Yoram Dinstein, *War, Aggression and Self-Defence*. 4th ed. (Cambridge: Cambridge University Press, 2005), 187; Malcolm N. Shaw, *International Law*. 6th ed. (Cambridge: Cambridge University Press, 2008), 1139; Ian Brownlie, *Principles of Public International Law*. 7th ed. (Oxford: Oxford University Press, 2008), 733–734; Tom Ruys, *'Armed Attacks' and Article 51 of the UN Charter: Evolutions in Customary Law and Practice* (Cambridge: Cambridge University Press, 2010), 252; Christopher C. Joyner, *International Law in the 21st Century: Rules for Global Governance* (Oxford: Roman & Littlefield Publishers, Inc., 2005), 168–169; Michael Byres, *War Law: International Law and Armed Conflict* (London: Atlantic Books, 2005), 73–75; David Rodin, *War and Self-Defence* (Oxford: Oxford University Press, 2002), 113–114; and Antonio Cassese, *International Law*. 2nd ed. (Oxford: Oxford University Press, 2005), 362–363.

leadership allegedly sneaked into Pakistan.[13] For a more methodological coherence, it is pertinent to mention here that the analysis of these cases is centred on the laws of war related to the right of individual self-defence. It seeks to neither apply nor explain bordering legal frameworks like collective self-defence, targeted killings, and intervention by invitation. More precisely, the focus of the discussion shall be on *what is permitted as a right of self-defence*. The level of analysis shall remain that of the inter-state. Principles of necessity and proportionality are discussed within the framework of *jus ad bellum*. This is achieved, especially in the case of proportionality, by employing the analogical conceptual reasoning from the *jus in bello* framework. Such reasoning, it is hoped, shall be useful to enrich the discourse of pre-emption within the realm of *jus ad bellum*.

This study is premised on *lex lata* (what the law is) rather than *lex ferenda* (what the law should be). In effect, a formalistic approach is used to explain legal interpretations. Main legal arguments find expression and orbit around the positive international law. However, Islamic and natural laws are also deployed to analyse the genesis and evolution of the discourse of pre-emption. Besides revealing the foundational value in explaining the doctrine of pre-emption, discourses of Islamic and natural laws help in putting across the crucial point that they are *less* coherent in comparison to the positive international law. That is why any application of natural or Islamic laws (of nations) to construct the primary argument becomes unreasonable here. It can debunk the *positivist* understandings and argumentations of the doctrine of pre-emption.[14] In a similar vein, it is argued that international law can in no way be a substitute for politics or policy. It is a general understanding that for international law to be 'law' proper it should "provide basis for common restraint".[15] Any failure, meanwhile, will reduce the international law to a mere tool of international political dispensation—meant to safeguard the state interests.[16] In this context, though this research inquiry touches upon the politics behind the policy decisions to initiate the 'war on terror', it does not deploy political arguments to assess the legality of such decisions.

This study, moreover, takes a 'dualistic' view of international law.[17] It asserts that international and domestic laws are different sets of the legal order. This methodological focus is imperative to generate a robust and coherent discussion. In legal

13 Sikander A. Shah, *International Law and Drone Strikes in Pakistan: The Legal and Socio-Political Aspects* (Oxon: Routledge, 2015), 1–6; Lawrence Ziring, *Pakistan: At the Crosscurrent of History* (Oxford: One World Publications, 2003), 318; and Sean D. Murphy, "The International Legality of US Military Cross-Border Operations from Afghanistan into Pakistan", *International Law Studies* 85 (2009): 109–111.

14 Jan Klabbers, *International Law* (Cambridge: Cambridge University Press, 2013), 13.

15 Richard A. Falk, *The Status of Law in International Society* (Princeton: Princeton University Press, 1970), 13.

16 Ibid.

17 For further details of this legal dichotomy in international law, see Hans Kelsen, *Principles of International Law* (New York: Reinehart & Company Inc., 1952), 290 and 551; Hans Kelsen, *General Theory of Law and State*, trans. Anders Wedberg (Cambridge: Harvard University Press, 1945), 363; James Crawford, *Brownlie's Principles of Public International Law*. 8th ed. (Oxford: Oxford University Press, 2012), 48–49.

studies, research methods guide us in assessing *where* to find the law and *how* to interpret it. To locate and explain the law proper, in this context, the study involves both the qualitative and the quantitative[18] sources of data and modes of argumentation. They help enrich the discussions within the frame of the doctrinal discourse on pre-emptive self-defence (Chapters 2 and 3). In terms of research strategy, the book is a case study[19] seeking to investigate the pre-emptive uses of drone attacks to hunt down terrorists (Chapter 5), within the overarching frame of the 'war on terror' (Chapter 4). The specific outcomes of this research are then further explicated to understand the contemporary dynamics of drone campaigns (Chapter 6).

Furthermore, it is also important to differentiate between the *case study method* and the *case method* of inquiry in any legal research. Here, a case study seeks to investigate legal issues through the application of legal doctrines and principles, whereas the case method discusses an already settled case to explain the relevant legal doctrines and principles. At the same time, a case study may also make extensive use of the case law to explain the applicable legal doctrines and principles. In the case under investigation here, there exist multiple causal mechanisms and several causal effects. Concerning the causal mechanisms, the terrorist security threat and its link to the territory of Pakistan denote the overarching cause. So is the perception of these security threats in the security calculus of the concerned state party here embodying causal effects. Now, there can be various dimensions to a research inquiry to understand the causal effects. These may include intervention by invitation, collective self-defence, self-defence, and pre-emptive self-defence. In these contexts, the choice of a particular variable over the other may be challenging for this study. It is noted, however, from an ontological perspective that social realities continue to exist despite the fact of the absence of any research inquiry to understand and explain them. The choice of theory and method may not, at times, succeed in absolutely comprehending the reality. It can, nonetheless, help in understanding and explaining the reality. In return, it helps in expanding the boundaries of knowledge.

Further on, the case study method involves the principles of "agreement" and "difference".[20] The method of *agreement* presumes that multiple variables can

18 The selection of local informants for interviews is based on their direct or indirect relevance to the damages of drone strikes. At times, these individuals are relatives of those who are dead; on other occasions, they were witnesses to the losses. Four of these individuals are based in North Waziristan, while two in South Waziristan. This proportion parallels the average of drone strikes in these regions, which almost 67 per cent in North Waziristan and 30 per cent in South Waziristan (3 per cent scattered around scores of other areas). The names and identity of informants is withheld due to safety reasons.

19 The case study method is an appropriate tool to investigate this specific issue. It can effectively make sense and enhance our deep understanding of the issue. For details, see Arch G. Woodside, *Case Study Research: Theory. Methods. Practice* (Bingley: Emerald Group Publishing Ltd., 2010), 5–6; and John Gerring, *Case Study Research: Principles and Practices* (Cambridge: Cambridge University Press, 2007), 17–18.

20 Charles C. Ragin, *The Comparative Method: Moving Beyond Qualitative and Quantitative Strategies* (Berkeley: University of California Press, 1987), 39.

cause a single effect. As explained above, however, multiple variables are causing many effects. The method of agreement, therefore, seems problematic in handling this causality understanding and explanation of the case. The method of *difference* is, thus, more appropriate in understanding the causal relationship between the different independent variables, as well as the effect of such variables. Multi-point causality links, in this context, include (i) the security threat in Pakistan and Yemen and its link to the state, (ii) the security threat posed by the terrorists in Pakistan and Yemen, (iii) the link of such a security threat to the state security of the US and its nationals abroad, and (iv) the choice of pre-emptive self-defence framework through the use of combat drones for a military intervention to neutralise such security threats.

Bibliography

Arend, Anthony C. "International Law and the Pre-emptive Use of Military Force". *The Washington Quarterly* 26, no. 2 (2003): 78–97.

Brownlie, Ian. *Principles of Public International Law*. 7th ed. Oxford: Oxford University Press, 2008.

Byres, Michael. *War Law: International Law and Armed Conflict*. London: Atlantic Books, 2005.

Cassese, Antonio. *International Law*. 2nd ed. Oxford: Oxford University Press, 2005.

Crawford, James. *Brownlie's Principles of Public International Law*. 8th ed. Oxford: Oxford University Press, 2012.

Dinstein, Yoram. *War, Aggression and Self-Defence*. 4th ed. Cambridge: Cambridge University Press, 2005.

Falk, Richard A. *The Status of Law in International Society*. Princeton, NJ: Princeton University Press, 1970.

Franck, Thomas. *Recourse to Force: State Action Against Threats and Armed Attacks*. Cambridge: Cambridge University Press, 2004.

Gerring, John. *Case Study Research: Principles and Practices*. Cambridge: Cambridge University Press, 2007.

Glennon, Michael J. "The Fog of Law: Self-Defense, Inherence, and Incoherence in Article 51 of the United Nations Charter". *Harvard Journal of Law & Public Policy* 25, no. 2 (2002): 539–558.

Joyner, Christopher C. *International Law in the 21st Century: Rules for Global Governance*. Oxford: Roman & Littlefield Publishers, Inc., 2005.

Kelsen, Hans. *General Theory of Law and State*. Translated by Anders Wedberg. Cambridge: Harvard University Press, 1945.

Kelsen, Hans. *Principles of International Law*. New York: Reinehart & Company Inc., 1952.

Klabbers, Jan. *International Law*. Cambridge: Cambridge University Press, 2013.

Lietzau, William K. "Old Laws, New Wars: Jus ad Bellum in an Age of Terrorism". *Max Planck United Nations Yearbook* 8 (2004): 384–455.

Moore, Molly. "Chirac: Nuclear Response to Terrorism is Possible". *The Washington Post*, January 20, 2006.

Murphy, Sean D. "The International Legality of US Military Cross-Border Operations from Afghanistan into Pakistan". *International Law Studies* 85 (2009): 109–139.

Pfanner, Toni. "Asymmetrical Warfare from the Perspective of Humanitarian Law and Humanitarian Action". *International Review of Red Cross* 87, no. 857 (2005): 149–174.

Ragin, Charles C. *The Comparative Method: Moving Beyond Qualitative and Quantitative Strategies*. Berkeley: University of California Press, 1987.

Reisman, Michael and Andrea Armstrong. "The Past and Future of the Claim of Pre-emptive Self-Defence". *American Journal of International Law* 100, no. 3 (2006): 525–550.

Rodin, David. *War and Self-Defence*. Oxford: Oxford University Press, 2002.

"Russia Not Planning to Give up Right of Pre-emptive, Strikes—Defence Minister". *BBC Intl., Rep.*, October 20, 2003, LEXIS, Individual Publications.

Ruys, Tom. *'Armed Attacks' and Article 51 of the UN Charter: Evolutions in Customary Law and Practice*. Cambridge: Cambridge University Press, 2010.

Shah, Sikander A. *International Law and Drone Strikes in Pakistan: The Legal and Socio-Political Aspects*. Oxon: Routledge, 2015.

Shaw, Malcolm N. *International Law*. 6th ed. Cambridge: Cambridge University Press, 2008.

Shue, Henry and David Rodin, eds. *Preemption: Military Action and Moral Justification*. New York: Oxford University Press, 2007.

Singh, Jaswant. "Every Country has Right to Preemption". *Press Trust of India*, September 30, 2002.

Slaughter, Anne-Marie and William Burke-White. "An International Constitutional Moment". *Harvard International Law Journal* 43, no. 1 (2002): 1–21.

"The National Security Strategy of the United States of America". *White House*, Washington, September 20, 2002.

Turner, Robert F. "Operation Iraqi Freedom: Legal and Policy Considerations". *Harvard Journal of Law & Public Policy* 27, no. 3 (2004): 765–796.

Woodside, Arch G. *Case Study Research: Theory, Methods, Practice*. Bingley: Emerald Group Publishing Ltd., 2010.

Ziring, Lawrence. *Pakistan: At the Crosscurrent of History*. Oxford: Oneworld Publications, 2003.

2 Discourses of pre-emptive use of force

The discourse on pre-emptive use of force embodies the study of a (legal) text in its specific (socio-political) context.[1] It assumes that every text has a history and meaning. A study of the text, therefore, along the various points of time and across different modes of conversation, such as speeches, policy statements, treaties, judgements, reports, memos, and interviews, helps to understand the construction of meanings.[2] About laws, however, it is assumed that they are written in a generalised language to make them applicable to different situations and events. Perhaps it gives way to uncertainty and indeterminacy in the legal interpretation.[3] If it is context specific, the application of law across time becomes questionable. After all, one cannot have laws for every specific situation. In the context of laws and their interpretation, therefore, one may assume that incoherence is perhaps inherent, which is nowhere more evident than in the laws of war. To explore and explain this phenomenon, this chapter aims to analyse different discourses on the laws of war and those related to pre-emptive self-defence.

It is presumed that a basic understanding of international relations is constructed through the study of state actions over a certain period of time where international law helps in regulating these relations. Thus, international law remains in a permanent struggle to emancipate itself from the clutches of sociology and politics as it continues to face questions about its role as an explanatory as well as a regulatory tool in realising the normative ideals of international order. These questions stem, most of the time, out of the incoherent theoretical foundations of international law. Attempts to explain and base the law on concrete theoretical foundations, therefore, led to the enactment of a legal discourse *between* the sociological and the political contents.[4] It helped in upholding the law as a

1 Brian Paltridge, *Discourse Analysis: An Introduction* (London: Continuum, 2006), 3. For the detailed study of the history and evolution of discourse analysis, see Malcolm Coulthart, *An Introduction to Discourse Analysis*. 2nd ed. (New York: Routledge, 2014); and James P. Gee, *An Introduction to Discourse Analysis: Theory and Method*. 3rd ed. (New York: Routledge, 2010).

2 Nicola Woods, *Describing Discourse: A Practical Guide to Discourse Analysis* (London: Hodder Headline Group, 2006), x–xi.

3 Ibid., 86.

4 Martti Koskeniemmi, *From Apology to Utopia: The Structure of International Legal Argument* (Cambridge: Cambridge University Press, 2005), 1.

separate species of scientific knowledge and in safeguarding against attacks from its once tributary disciplines. Yet, when the legal scholarship on the boundaries of the law as a discipline remains a work in progress, tensions between *theory* and *doctrine* continue to nag at the roots of this branch of scientific knowledge. The situation becomes even more complex when studying a doctrine informing the non-legal discourses in comparison to studying the legal ones. Anyhow, in the case of a discourse deploying a doctrine to study theory, the distinction between theory and doctrine becomes somewhat irrelevant.[5] Such is the case of this theoretical inquiry into the doctrinal discourse of pre-emption. To explain it, the following discussions try to locate the place of pre-emption in three different theoretical discourses, i.e., natural, Islamic, and positive laws of nations. The primary objective behind this exercise is to identify and explain a more appropriate theoretical discourse to guide this study, as well as to analyse the trajectory of the evolution of pre-emption.

Natural law (of nations)

Natural law[6] has its origin in the birth of the history of legal ideas.[7] Referring to the primacy of these unwritten yet explicit laws, Socrates underlines that God prepares these laws for men.[8] Thus, Divinity is the causative factor here. Such a law, moreover, proclaims to be the same at all times and for all men.[9] This is because it is based on nature, where 'rational design' remains a permanent feature in its functioning everywhere.[10] Natural law, in this context, is based on those laws which are not found in "unsettled Opinions" but, rather, are present in the "innate Sentiments of the Mind".[11] Athenians and Romans, therefore, could have

5 Ibid., 2.

6 For a detailed philosophical and legal history of the idea of natural law, see Frederick Pollock, "The History of the Law of Nature: A Preliminary Study", *Colombia Law Review* 1, no. 1 (1901): 11–32; Frederick Pollock, "The History of the Law of Nature: A Preliminary Study. Second Article", *Colombia Law Review* 2, no. 3 (1902): 131–143; Brian Bix, "Natural Law", in *A Companion to Philosophy of Law and Legal Theory*, ed. Dennis Patterson. 2nd ed. (West Sussex: Blackwell Publishing Ltd., 2010), 211–227; James Mackintosh, *A Discourse on the Study of Law of Nature and Nations* (Boston: Pratt and Company, 1843); Henry S. Maine, *Ancient Law* (London: John Murray, 1907), 48–114; John Finnis, *Natural Law and Natural Rights*. 2nd ed. (Oxford: Oxford University Press, 2011), 23–49; and Jean-Jacques Burlamaqui, *The Principles of Natural and Political Law*, trans. Thomas Nugent, ed. Peter Korkman (Indianapolis: Liberty Fund, 2006), 125–192.

7 Jose P. Egido, "Natural Law", in *Encyclopaedia of Public International Law*, ed. Rudolf Bernhardt, Vol. 7 (Amsterdam: Elsevier Science Publishers, 1984), 344.

8 Quoted in William Orton, "The Sources of Natural Law", *International Journal of Ethics* 36, no. 2 (1926): 152.

9 Aristotle, *Rhetoric*, Book I, Chapter 10, trans. William R. Roberts (Mineola: Dover Publication, Inc., 2004), 37–38.

10 Pollock, "The History of the Law of Nature: A Preliminary Study", 12.

11 Quoted in Hugo Grotius, *The Rights of War and Peace*, Book I, ed. Richard Tuck (Indianapolis: Liberty Fund Inc., 2005), 966–967.

different laws.[12] Natural law is, moreover, deeply embedded into human nature, and its basic principles are immutable, for

> human nature as a whole is one, although multiple regarding its parts. Therefore, either there is only one precept of the natural law because of the unity of the whole or there are many precepts because of the many parts of human nature.[13]

In this context, however, the plurality of precepts does not mean a plurality of natural law, as such. Inversely, the plurality of precepts emphasises the singularity of natural law.[14] Although there can be multiple "precepts of the natural law", they all have a singular foundation.[15]

In these contexts, we may assume that the insistence of early theorists on the unity of natural law is mainly due to their belief in this law as a kind of eternal law.[16] Natural law is a process "through which [a] human being participate[s] in eternal law".[17] Since the root of an eternal law is one idea, it is maintained that natural law cannot be plural.[18] In the context of war, natural law establishes that "we should do and seek good, and shun evil".[19] This primary precept breeds "all the other precepts of the natural law".[20] In this backdrop, one may assume that due to its focus on the goodness of human character, natural law summons the moral nature of humans.[21] In addition to divinity, human nature thus becomes the secondary source of natural law. It is 'natural reason' which helps to establish the fact of the primacy of the divine source in natural laws by translating it

12 Robert N. Wilkin, "Cicero: Oracle of Natural Law", *The Classical Journal* 44, no. 8 (1949): 454. Here Brian Bix notes that the reference to 'natural' in Greeks and Romans' legal discourses does not specify its certain meaning: like whether they used the term to locate laws in human nature, its derivation through human faculties, or can be found in physical order governed by the nature, or in all three. For details, see Bix, "Natural Law", 212.

13 Thomas Aquinas, *Treatise on Law*, trans. Richard J. Regan (Indianapolis: Hackett Publishing Company, Inc., 2000), 34.

14 Michael Zuckert, "The Fullness of Being: Thomas Aquinas and the Modern Critique of Natural Law", *The Review of Politics* 69, no. 1 (2007): 34.

15 Aquinas, *Treatise on Law*, 36; and James B. Scott, ed., *Selections from Three Works of Francisco Suarez*, trans. Gwladys L. Williams, Ammi Brown, and John Waldron (Oxford: The Clarendon Press, 1944), 223.

16 Zuckert, "The Fullness of Being: Thomas Aquinas and the Modern Critique of Natural Law", 35.

17 Kinga T. Szabo, *Anticipatory Action in Self-Defense: Essence and Limits under International Law* (The Hague: T.M.C Asser Press, 2011), 40; and Jose P. Egido, "Natural Law", in *Encyclopaedia of Public International Law*, ed. Bernhardt, Vol. 7, 345.

18 Zuckert, "The Fullness of Being: Thomas Aquinas and the Modern Critique of Natural Law", 35.

19 Aquinas, *Treatise on Law*, 36.

20 Ibid., 36. Spanish jurist Francisco Suarez also corresponds to these basic principles of natural law. For details, see Scott, ed., *Selections from Three Works of Francisco Suarez*, 211. Moreover, Thomas Hobbes also underlines that seeking peace is the first among the fundamental laws of the nature. For details, see William Molesworth, ed., *The English Works of Thomas Hobbes*, Vol. 3 (London: John Bohn, 1839), 117.

21 Zuckert, "The Fullness of Being: Thomas Aquinas and the Modern Critique of Natural Law", 42.

into reality through the objective interpretation of any law.[22] Further on, within the discourse of natural law, Spanish Dominican theologians played an important role in enhancing the argument on the origin of natural law and in making it more relevant to the essence of the law. For instance, Francisco de Vitoria, illustrating the importance of human reason, argues that humans are superior among all creatures. Their ability to employ reason in organising and regulating their conduct, therefore, is unparallel. In this context, to make the law relevant to changing circumstances, it is imperative that "the rule of conduct should change with changing conditions".[23] In such situations, however, the reason alone cannot fully deduce the law. To bridge this gap, revelations (Commands of God) contribute to set the contents of natural law.[24] Thus, divine law and human reason are sources of natural law.[25] Building upon the works of Greek and Roman theorists, Spanish theologians established that "the natural law is a single law with respect to all times and every condition of human nature".[26] Human nature, not a specific state of human nature, can determine such a law.[27] It consists of those principles which most of the people at "different times and places unanimously affirm" and these principles are 'self-evident'.[28] Indeed the basic principles do not change with time and place. Therefore, they can be set down in a 'systematic form'.[29]

Unlike his predecessors, Hugo Grotius believes in the fundamental role of humans in determining as well as establishing natural law.[30] He liberated the law from the shackles of divine attributes and put it into the folds of human reason.[31] He based and built his argumentation by employing theological argumentations.[32]

22 Pollock, "The History of the Law of Nature: A Preliminary Study", 18.

23 James B. Scott, *The Spanish Origin of International Law: Francisco de Vitoria and His Law of Nations* (Oxford: The Clarendon Press, 1934), 165.

24 Ibid., 166.

25 Scott, ed., *Selections from Three Works of Francisco Suarez*, 187–217; James B. Scott, *The Catholic Conception of International Law* (Washington: Georgetown University Press, 1934), 138; and David Kennedy, "Primitive Legal Scholarship", *Harvard International Law Journal* 27, no. 1 (1986): 19.

26 Scott, ed., *Selections from Three Works of Francisco Suarez*, 222; and Egido, "Natural Law", 347.

27 Scott, ed., *Selections from Three Works of Francisco Suarez*, 222.

28 Grotius, *The Rights of War and Peace*, Book I, 111–112.

29 George G. Wilson, "Grotius: Law of War and Peace", *American Journal of International Law* 35, no. 2 (1941): 218.

30 Steven Forde, "Hugo Grotius on Ethics and War", *American Political Science Review* 92, no. 3 (1998): 644.

31 Benedict Kingsbury, "The International Legal Order", *Institute for International Law and Justice Working Paper*, no. 1 (2003): 26; Egido, "Natural Law", 346; Cornelius F. Murphy, Jr., "The Grotian Vision of World Order", *American Journal of International Law* 76, no. 3 (1982): 486; and Edgar Bodenheimer, "The Natural-Law Doctrine before the Tribunal of Science: A Reply to Hans Kelsen", *The Western Political Quarterly* 3, no. 3 (1950): 338.

32 Grotius, *The Rights of War and Peace*, Book I, 79–92; Szabo, *Anticipatory Action in Self-Defense: Essence and Limits under International Law*, 49; Joan-Pau Rubies, "Hugo Grotius's Dissertation on the Origin of American Peoples and the Use of Comparative Methods", *Journal of the History of Ideas* 52, no. 2 (1991): 222; Charles G. Fenwick, *International Law*. 2nd ed. (London: D. Appleton-Century Company, 1934), 50–51; and Arthur Nussbaum, *A Concise History of the Law of Nations* (New York: The Macmillan Company, 1947), 2.

For him, due to its divine roots, natural law is free of those dictates which find a place only in the deistic mind, not in the secular one. Therefore, he established that even with His 'infinite' powers, God Himself cannot change such a law.[33] Perhaps this radical *relocation* was meant to free the law from the divine roots and to underscore that the law is evident in the frame and functioning of nature. As even when one cannot see and feel God, one can look around and experience nature in all its manifestations.

Building upon the roots of secular discourse, the later-day jurists put down the scientifically elaborated theoretical foundations.[34] For example, applying the rationalism of Grotius, Pufendorf suggests that through human reason, one can discover the authority behind natural law. The dictates of reason which justify the duty to submission before one's authority are as follows:

> [I]f he has conferred exceptional benefits on him; if it is evident that he wishes the other well and can look out for him better than he can for himself; if at the same time he actually claims direction for him; and, finally, if the other party has finally submitted to him and accepted his direction.[35]

The application of 'light of reason', therefore, helps to conclude that the author of natural law is, in fact, the 'author of the universe'.[36] We see, thus, that the discourse, which was once set up with its conception of deity, entered the Christian theological sphere and culminated in scientific underpinnings. Despite the fact of this long journey, spanning over millenniums, the sovereign authority in natural law has not changed. This fact of primacy, in return, grants natural law an essential status of law.

Being the foundational theory, natural law helped deduce and enact the law of nations. To extract the law of nations from natural law, the expression of such a law in customs is necessary. If a custom fails to conform to the contours of natural law, it cannot gain the status of the law of nations.[37] Affirming the

33 Grotius, *The Rights of War and Peace*, Book I, 155; Marek St. Korowicz, *Introduction to International Law* (The Hague: MartinusNijhoff, 1959), 32; and Josef L. Kunz, "Natural-Law Thinking in the Modern Science of International Law", *American Journal of International Law* 55, no. 4 (1961): 951–952.

34 Pufendorf produced his famous works against the backdrop of winding down of 30 years of religious wars (1618–1648) in Europe and the terribly destructive role played by the religion in it. Thus, to reconstruct the existent state of affairs among states and appeal more to the social nature of humans, he laid down the foundations of relations among states on the basis of 'sociality' and explained this new thesis through the prism of natural law. For details, see Editor's Introduction in Samuel Pufendorf, *On the Duty of Man and Citizen According to Natural Law*, Book I, trans. Michael Silverthorne, ed. James Tully (Cambridge: Cambridge University Press, 1991), xiv–xxxvii.

35 Ibid., 28.

36 Ibid.

37 Scott, *The Spanish Origin of International Law: Francisco de Vitoria and His Law of Nations*, 164.

status of customs, Thomas Aquinas underlined that those customs which are contrary to natural laws cannot gain the status of law.[38] This emphasis establishes the importance of the customary practice of an idea before it is made a necessary part of the law of nations. Likewise, the manifest will of most states to submit before such a law also affirms the status and fact of the natural law of nations.[39] And the very fact of their vast acceptance, in this context, amounts to the level of (state) consent.[40] Perhaps such a focus on customs illustrates and institutes the universal appeal of law and its normative value across the cultural and ideological divides.

Right of self-defence

It is a common belief that "nature has endowed every species of living creature[s] with the instinct of self-preservation, of avoiding what seems likely to cause injury".[41] Self-preservation, thus, underpins the natural law discourse on the use of force. The defence of one's faith also amounts to self-preservation.[42] It is important to note here that the religious dictates set the roots of natural law in self-defence. It happened when wars were waged over differences in religious belief (believer vs. non-believer). These were also transformational times because the idea of the state, as we know it today, was taking root in Europe.[43] Building upon these abstract ideas, the founders of natural law further expanded the boundaries of the law and set down the principles of resorting to war in the backdrop of the arrival of Spaniards in the Americas. The Spanish conquests of Native America, as well as the treatment of local Indians, raised many moral and legal questions.[44]

38 Aquinas, *Treatise on Law*, 66.

39 Scott, *The Spanish Origin of International Law: Francisco de Vitoria and His Law of Nations*, 172.

40 Murphy, "The Grotian Vision of World Order", 496; and John P. Doyle, "Francisco Suarez on the Law of Nations", in *Religion and International Law*, ed. Mark W. Janis and Carolyn Evans (The Hague: Martin Nijhoff Publishers, 1999), 107.

41 Cicero, *De Officiis*, Book 1, trans. Walter Miller (London: William Heinemann Ltd., 1913), 13.

42 Quoted in Szabo, *Anticipatory Action in Self-Defense: Essence and Limits under International Law*, 40.

43 Wolfgang Preiser, "Ancient Times to 1648", in *Encyclopaedia of Public International Law*, ed. Bernhardt, 147; and Leo Gross, "The Peace Westphalia, 1648–1948", *American Journal of International Law* 42, no. 1 (1948): 30.

44 Scott, *The Catholic Conception of International Law*, vi. For further details, see chapter "On the Indians Recently Discovered", in Scott, *The Spanish Origin of International Law*, 94–162; Richard Waswo, "The Formation of Natural Law to Justify Colonialism, 1539–1689", *New Literary History* 27, no. 4 (1996): 743–759; Antony Anghie, "The Evolution of International Law: Colonial and Postcolonial Realities", *Third World Quarterly* 27, no. 5 (2006): 742–744; and Preiser, "Ancient Times to 1648", 151–152. Further emphasising the point, Robert Kann notes that "the new law was established not only at the time of the discovery of the New World, but its establishment was largely due to this fact". Robert Kann, "The Law of Nations and the Conduct of War in the Early Times of the Standing Army", *The Journal of Politics* 6, no. 1 (1944): 78.

This evolving socio-political environment[45] and the humanitarian issues emerging out of the indiscriminate use of force under the guise of economic and religious expediency paved the way for the modern law of nations.

According to the Spanish theologians, the Spaniards had the right of preaching, commerce, and passage through the Native American lands under natural law. In this instance, any kind of local obstruction gives the Spaniards the right to resort to force.[46] Likewise, the use of force is also lawful to defend the lives of the locals converted to Christianity. This principle corresponds to the long-held religious decree to defend the new converts. Besides, the natural law permits to take up arms to safeguard innocent people against tyrannical local laws, such as human sacrifices and "the killing in other ways of un-condemned people for cannibalistic purposes".[47] Similarly, Grotius also argued to end the persecution of Christians for their belief. Any sort of Christian persecution, maintains Grotius, is liable to be punished by those sharing the same religion. He termed it the "innocent Self Defence".[48] In modern times, this norm is transposed into the body of positive law though not as a norm with ideological but secular underpinnings, sanctioning the use of force by a state to defend its nationals abroad.

States, like individuals, also seek self-preservation and attempt to avoid injury. They employ force to ward off any security threat endangering their survival. Security threat perception, in this context, concerns cognition, wherein past experiences, the present condition of existence, and evolving circumstances shape the cognitive ability informing the threat perception. To respond to the security threats to survival, natural law theorists laid down the principles on the use of force in self-defence. Romans believed that violent force can be used to avenge injustice.[49] And therefore, the initiation of war is meant to exact punishment for

45 For a detailed description of the socio-political realities of the New World, see Colin M. Maclachlan, *Spain's Empire in The New World: The Role of Ideas in Institutional and Social Change* (Berkley: University of California Press, 1988); Patricia Seed, "'Are These Not Also Men?': The Indians' Humanity and Capacity for Spanish Civilization", *Journal of Latin American Studies* 25, no. 3 (1993): 629–652; Lewis Hanke, "The Dawn of Conscience in America: Spanish Experiments and Experiences with Indian in the New World", *Proceedings of the American Philosophical Society* 107, no. 2 (1963): 83–92; Fred M. Kimmey, "Christianity and Indian Lands", *Ethnohistory* 7, no. 1 (1960): 44–60; and Fernando Gomez, "Francisco de Vitoria in 1934, After and Before", *Modern Language Notes* 117, no. 2 (2002): 365–405.

46 Scott, *The Catholic Conception of International Law*, 29; Korowicz, *Introduction to International Law*, 31. Also, see David Kennedy, "Primitive Legal Scholarship", *Harvard International Law Journal* 27, no. 1 (1986): 23; Josef L. Kunz, "Bellum Justum and Bellum Legale", *American Journal of International Law* 45, no. 3 (1951): 532; and Natsu T. Saito, "Colonial Presumptions: The War on Terror and the Roots of American Exceptionalism", *Georgetown Journal of Law & Modern Critical Race Perspectives* 67, no. 1 (2008): 82.

47 Scott, *The Catholic Conception of International Law*, 29–30; Scott, *The Spanish Origin of International Law*, 131; and Szabo, *Anticipatory Action in Self-Defense: Essence and Limits under International Law*, 45–46.

48 Grotius, *The Rights of War and Peace*, Book I, 1044–1045.

49 Quoted in Hans Kelsen, *Principles of International Law* (New York: Reinehart & Company Inc., 1952), 34.

a past crime.[50] In this context, injustice also involves theft of property.[51] Other forms of injuries may also include the denial of "common commercial rights" such as transit and "grave injury to one's reputation and honor".[52]

To fulfil the larger objective of security, natural law theorists subscribe to collective self-defence. War can be waged, they assert, "in favour of those who are oppressed and suffer wrong".[53] Collective self-defence, in this context, also includes the security of allies and friends, as the Romans justified wars to defend their allies.[54] The Spaniards also endorsed this practice. They never questioned the legitimacy of the use of force in defence of allies or friends.[55] However, Grotius does not provide blanket approval. A state intervening on behalf of its ally, he suggests, should make sure that the cause of the war is just.[56] For a just cause, however, one can wage war to assist friends even without any formal treaty, he asserts.[57]

In these contexts, one can assume that natural law discourse emphasises harmony among states, which, in return, is an outcome of the responsible conduct of states. Any failure to uphold this basic principle of mutual conduct may lead to the recourse to self-defence. A state, moreover, is also responsible for the conduct of its subjects. Remedial recourse may be adopted in instances where subjects of a state have committed a crime against another state, and the host state failed to satisfy the demands of redress. In a similar vein, resort to arms in self-defence by a state is justifiable when the opposing state is harbouring the nationals of another state who have committed a crime against the former.[58] It is, thus, maintained that the concept of injury in natural law invoking the right to self-defence involves not only the acts of a state but also the actions of its nationals.

Pre-emptive self-defence

Though contemporary Europe was rife with various kinds of wars justified under economic, and religious rights, the founders of natural law did not support the legitimacy of such uses of force. For example, Francisco Suarez argues that

50 Scott, *The Spanish Origin of International Law: Francisco de Vitoria and His Law of Nations*, 201–204; Kennedy, "Primitive Legal Scholarship", 23; and Anthony Pagden and Jeremy Lawrence, eds., *Francisco De Vitoria: Political Writings* (Cambridge: Cambridge University Press, 1991), 297–298.

51 Quoted in Scott, *The Spanish Origin of International Law*, 233.

52 The injury, in this context, should have been caused against the Prince or his subjects. For details, see Scott, ed., *Selections from Three Works of Francisco Suarez*, 817; and Scott, *The Catholic Conception of International Law*, 449–450.

53 Scott, *The Spanish Origin of International Law*, 284.

54 Scott, *The Catholic Conception of International Law*, 31.

55 Scott, ed., *Selections from Three Works of Francisco Suarez*, 817; and Scott, *The Catholic Conception of International Law*, 450.

56 Grotius, *The Rights of War and Peace*, Book II, 837–838.

57 Ibid., Book I, 1156.

58 Pufendorf, *On the Duty of Man and Citizen According to Natural Law*, Book II, 170.

pre-emptive wars out of economic and religious motives are aggressive wars. He, however, underlines that a pre-emptive war can be undertaken to neutralise an impending security threat. Though it is evil, it is an evil that is "a right and [that is] necessary", he asserts.[59] The necessity of such a war stems out of the need "to ward off acts of injustice and to hold enemies in check. Nor would it be possible, without these wars, for states to be maintained in peace".[60] Besides, Grotius also backs pre-emptive wars to "lawfully prevent an insult which seems to threaten a state, even if the threat is not upon the state and rather lies at a distance".[61] He also justifies the use of force to take on an enemy that has accumulated excessive power and expressed its motives to inflict injury.[62] One can read this permission, however, in view of the norm of self-preservation, the appeal of which seems obvious, at times, when boundaries of politics, law, and religion were blurred. The intention and capability to project them thus become the marker to justify force in pre-emption.

Moreover, in the context of this systemisation of legal arguments, one can assume that Grotius, being a rationalist as well as a naturalist, was comfortable with a more expansive meaning of self-defence.[63] When one takes into account contemporary history, they can understand the primary reason for the birth of this right in the legal mind of Grotius, as offensive wars were a common norm then.[64] Further on, though, on the face of it, Pufendorf's treatment of self-defence looks as if he is not justifying pre-emptive wars, an analysis of his legal reasoning for continuing a defensive war to the point that the adversary promises not to repeat past mistakes does seem to be morphing into pre-emptive self-defence. It is because the aggrieved state, through this approach, adopts recourse to the optimal level of neutralising a future security threat.[65] To conclude, it is argued that out of the instincts of survival and self-preservation, the right of self-defence to the level of pre-emption forms an important part of the natural law discourse. As explained above, though legal scholars at times take expansive and restrictive positions around this right, these discussions inform more about the political and security circumstances of a decision to take the recourse to war. In principle, pre-emption is an essential legal element of the natural law of nations.

59 Scott, ed., *Selections from Three Works of Francisco Suarez*, 803.

60 Ibid., 804. Also, see Herfried Münkler, *The New Wars*, trans. Patrick Camiller (Cambridge: Polity Press, 2005), 63. This is also called a 'defensive warfare of preventive character', for details, see Kann, "The Law of Nations and the Conduct of War in the Early Times of the Standing Army", 84.

61 Grotius, *The Rights of War and Peace*, Book II, 416–417.

62 Ibid., 1102.

63 Szabo, *Anticipatory Action in Self-Defense: Essence and Limits under International Law*, 51.

64 Grotius frequently cites the history of Greek and Roman ideas of natural law on war to prove his point about any legal question of the contemporary world. For further details, see Benjamin Straumann, "Ancient Caesarian Lawyers in a State of Nature: Roman Tradition and Natural Rights in Hugo Grotius's De iurepraedae", *Political Theory* 34, no. 3 (2006): 331.

65 Pufendorf, *On the Duty of Man and Citizen According to Natural Law*, Book II, 168.

Islamic law (of nations)

Islam claims to be the last among the monotheistic religions with universal appeal. Its teachings are therefore timeless.[66] It sought to transform the contemporary Arab world in numerous ways. Despite claims of originality, it embodies the socio-political organising principles and customs of the pre-Islamic world.[67] The Commands of God narrate these principles.[68] In terms of its legal understanding, the content of Qur'anic revelations does not essentially conform to the modern sense of the law. Instead, it consists of teachings encompassing a set of ideas dealing with the different aspects of human conduct. In a pure legalistic sense, "only some eighty verses refer to legal topics" and doubts prevail even about their legal sanction as obligation or permission.[69]

Sharia consists of revelations and their expression through the words and deeds of Prophet Muhammad (PBUH).[70] In a literal sense, *sharia* stands for 'way to water'. In its grandiose context, however, it is rather the only sure path to survival, which God sets and wants His believers to choose for their salvation.[71] It is an absolutely 'rigid and immutable system' of public order and not "susceptible to

66 Majid Khadduri, *War and Peace in the Law of Islam* (Baltimore: The Johns Hopkins Press, 1955), 17; and Gamal M. Badr, "A Survey of Islamic International Law", in *Religion and International Law*, ed. Mark W. Janis and Carolyn Evans (The Hague: Martin Nijhoff Publishers, 1999), 95.

67 Explaining the customary nature of Islamic law, Joseph Schacht underlines that 'the rule of two witnesses' in Islamic law was part of pre-Islamic order and tradition of justice. For details, see Schacht, *An Introduction to Islamic Law* (Oxford: Oxford University Press, 1982), 9. Similarly, Islamic law also corresponds to the pre-Islamic norm of 'non-aggression' during four months. Moreover, for the detailed understanding of the genesis and the context of Islamic law, see Joseph Schacht, *The Origins of Muhammadan Jurisprudence* (Oxford: Oxford University Press, 1950); and Majid Khadduri and Herbert J. Liebesny, eds., *Law in the Middle East: Origin and Development of Islamic Law* (Washington, DC: The Middle East Institute, 1955); Muhammad Hamidullah, *Introduction to Islam* (Paris: Centre CulturelIslamique, 1969), 134; Khadduri, *War and Peace in the Law of Islam*, 19–22; Edward J. Jurji, "Islamic Law in Operation", *The American Journal of Semitic Language and Literatures* 57, no. 1 (1940): 32–49; Patricia Crone, *Roman, Provincial and Islamic Law: The Origins of the Islamic Patronate* (Cambridge: Cambridge University Press, 1987); and David Pearl, *A Textbook on Muslim Law* (London: Croom Helm Ltd., 1979).

68 Hamidullah also mentions the sanctity of the earlier Commands of God in the form of revelations as a source of Islamic law, which were sent to earlier prophets and were in some ways part of the contemporary customs before the arrival of Islam. For details, see Hamidullah, *Introduction to Islam*, 134. Also, in Quran, God says:

Lo! We did reveal the Torah, wherein is guidance and a light, by which the Prophets who surrendered (unto Allah) judged the Jews. (Q.5:44)

And We prescribed for them therein: The life for the life, and an eye for the eye, and the nose for the nose, and the ear for the ear, and the tooth for the tooth, and for wounds retaliation. (Q.5:45)

All the translations from the Qur'an are based on the work of *The Meaning of the Glorious Qur'an*, trans. Marmudake Pickthall, 1930, accessed January 2, 2020, http://www.khayma.com/librarians/call2islaam/quran/pickthall/

69 David Pearl, *A Textbook on Muslim Law* (London: Croom Helm Ltd., 1979), 1.

70 In Islamic traditions (PBUH) stands for 'peace be upon him' and, therefore, in subsequent mentions of the Prophet Muhammad, the mention of this reference will be taken as normal.

71 Hunt Janin and Andre Kahlmeyer, *Islamic Law: The Sharia from Muhammad's Time to the Present* (London: McFarland & Company, Inc. Publishers, 2007), 1.

modification by any legislative authority".[72] The *sharia* denotes "a systematic but an *uncodified* law".[73] It is systematic as it involves legal doctrines and institutions and uncodified because there is no single authoritative book that describes it in its entirety.[74] In its broader understanding, however, *sharia* comprises all religious and legal norms, sources, and methods of interpretation.[75] Due to the fact of their cohabitation in the Qur'an, initially there was no distinction between 'law' and 'religion'.[76] It was due to the emergence of the Muslim intellectuals of *sharia* law that the gradual separation of the law from the religion took place.[77] Among these, Sunni jurist Abu Al-Hasan Al-Ash`ri, for example, emphasises the role of setting down different methods for deducing and interpreting the legal contents from the theological ones.[78] Similarly, stressing upon the larger objectives of the *sharia* laws rather than sticking to their mere wordings, Ab-Ishaq al-Shatibi lays down that for any meaningful interpretation of the Islamic laws, it is important to appreciate the overarching purpose of their revelations.[79]

Concerning the sources of *sharia*, God is the sole law-giver. The Qur'an contains His laws, which are translated through the actions of Prophet Muhammad, called *sunnah*,[80] as well as his sayings called *hadith*.[81] To stress upon obedience, God emphasises in the Qur'an: "O ye Faithful, obey God and the Apostle and those set in command amongst you".[82] In hierarchical order, Commands of God and deeds of the Prophet characterise the primary textual sources of the *sharia* law.[83] The death of Prophet Muhammad, however, brought an end to revelations.

72 Noel J. Coulson, *A History of Islamic Law* (Edinburgh: Edinburgh University Press, 1964), 5. Also, see Hamidullah, *Introduction to Islam*, 129–130; David F. Forte, *Studies in Islamic Law* (Maryland: Austin and Winfield, Publishers, 1999), 16; and Hamilton A. Gibb, *Mohammednasim: An Historical Survey*. 2nd ed. (New York: Oxford University Press, 1962), 90–99. Unlike *sharia*, *Fiqh*, a part of the former (Islamic legal juristic based on human knowledge and reason), is flexible and it can adapt to the circumstances, but again living within the parameters set by the Divine Law.

73 Janin and Kahlmeyer, *Islamic Law: The Sharia from Muhammad's Time to the Present*, 3.

74 Ibid.

75 Mathias Rohe, *Islamic Law in Past and Present*, trans. Gwendolin Goldbloom (Leiden, Boston: Brill Publisher, 2014), 10.

76 Gibb, *Mohammednasim: An Historical Survey*, 89.

77 Ibid., 90.

78 Rohe, *Islamic Law in Past and Present*, 15–16. For more details of different early era Muslim jurists and their methods of interpretation of law, see ibid., 16–20.

79 Ibid., 18–19.

80 The term *sunnah* was commonly used in pre-Islamic Arabic world to denote the customary law and in its literal sense it was meant to conduct. For details, see Khadduri, *War and Peace in the Law of Islam*, 29.

81 Majid Khadduri, "Islam and the Modern Law of Nations", *American Journal of International Law* 50, no. 2 (1956): 358; and Himalton A. Gibb, "Constitutional Organization", in *Law in the Middle East: Origin and Development of Islamic Law*, ed. Khadduri and Liebesny, 3–4.

82 Q.4:62.

83 Khadduri, *The Islamic Conception of Justice*, 3. Also, inside the mainstream Shi'a school of thought the Qur'an and the *sunnah* are authoritative sources of the law, but the selection of *sunnah* is subject to the participation of any imam recognised by the Shi'a. Also, ijma is part of contextual sources of law and it is only acceptable when imam himself takes part in it. For further details,

And thus, also to *sunnah*: one of the two major sources of law. After this, Islamic law incorporated Islamic *jus natural* and Arabian *jus gentium*.[84] Within two hundred years of the death of the Prophet, Islam had spread to various parts of Europe, Africa, and Persia. In such a context, the need to develop and expand the law to deal with new subjects of Islamic polity led to the addition of two new sources of law.[85] These include 'consensus' and 'reasoning'. Through them, Islamic legal jurists sought to interpret as well as explain the Commands of God and the deeds of Prophet Muhammad to address a certain legal issue.[86] These sources are also called the contextual sources of law,[87] whereas the body of law comprising these sources is called *fiqh*.

Muslims are the primary subject of *sharia*. The other part of this law deals with non-Muslims and is called *siyar* (the plural of *sirah*, which means conduct),

---

see Khadduri, *War and Peace in the Law of Islam*, 41; Javaid Rehman, *Islamic State Practices, International Law and the Threats from Terrorism: A Critique of the 'Clash of Civilizations' in the New World Order* (Oxford: Hart Publishing, 2005), 11–13; Sherman A. Jackson, "Jihad and the Modern World", *Journal of Islamic Law and Culture* 7, no. 1 (2002): 1–25; and Richard C. Martin, "The Religious Foundations of War, Peace and Statecraft in Islam", in *Just War and Jihad: Historical and Theoretical Perspectives on War and Peace in Western and Islamic Traditions*, ed. John Kelsay and James T. Johnson (New York: Greenwood Press, 1991), 100–102.

84 Khadduri, *War and Peace in the Law of Islam*, 27.

85 The prominent Muslim jurists in the majority Sunni-Hanafi school of thought and responsible for outlining the basic foundations of these sources of Islamic law include Abu Hanifa, Ibn Abu Alyla, al-Awza'I, Abu Yusuf, and Muhammad ibn al-Hasan al-Shaybani.

86 Furthermore, some rules of Islamic law of nations can be found in treaties between Muslims and non-Muslims and 'the official instructions' of the Muslim caliphs to the field commanders and governors. For further details, see Majid Khadduri, *War and Peace in the Law of Islam*, 202–222. Also, see Wael B. Hallaq, *A History of Islamic Legal Theories* (Cambridge: Cambridge University Press, 1997), 1; John Burton, *The Sources of Islamic Law* (Edinburgh: Edinburgh University Press, 1990); Rehman, *Islamic State Practices, International Law and the Threats from Terrorism: A Critique of the 'Clash of Civilizations' in the New World Order*, 14–15; and Shaheen S. Ali and Javaid Rehman, "The Concept of *Jihad* in Islamic International Law", *Journal of Conflict and Security Law* 10, no. 3 (2005): 321–343; Moreover, renowned Islamic legal scholar Majid Khadduri equates the sources of the Islamic law of nations with the sources of the modern law of nations. According to the statute of the International Court of Justice, the sources of modern law of nations include 'agreement, custom, reason and authority'. Likewise, inside Islamic law of nations, Qur'anic sources represent authority, the *sunnah* is just like customs, and the rules laid down in treaties with non-Muslims are agreements and opinions of the Islamic caliphs and jurists based on 'legal reasoning' and 'analogy' amount to reason. For details, see Khadduri, "International Law", in *Law in the Middle East: Origin and Development of Islamic Law*, ed. Khadduri and Liebesny, 352–353. But, Christopher Ford conflicts the Khadduri's view regarding the unanimity of sources between modern international law and Islamic law of nations. Ford believes that the fundamental difference between sources of two laws is of secular and theological roots. For details, see Christopher A. Ford, "Siyar-rization and its Discontents: International Law and Islam's Constitutional Crisis", in *International Law and Islamic Law*, ed. Mashood A. Baderin (Hampshire: Ashgate Publishing Company, 2008).

87 I categorise these sources as contextual sources of the Islamic law because Islamic legal jurists interpreted the Commands of God and deeds of the Prophet in the backdrop of the evolving socio-political environment.

or, in the modern sense of legal categorisation, the Islamic law of nations.[88] It is not a different body of the law with separate sources; instead, it is an essential part of the main body. Initially, the scope of Islamic law of nations was temporary because Islam had the vision of world domination. In that case, the Islamic law of nations would have been redundant.[89] However, later, to regulate relations between Muslim and non-Muslims polities, the status of Islamic law changed from temporary to permanent.[90] The Islamic law of nations, deriving its legitimacy from an absolute God, followed the traditions of ancient Roman and medieval Christian laws, wherein the concept of state was an imperial entity.[91] Race or class does not determine the basis of a community of people (*ummah*)[92] living within the bounds of such a state. Instead, it affirms its belief in one God and allegiance to His Prophet. Any use of force for the safety and security of this community ought to find expression in the Commands of God and teachings of His Prophet.

Right of self-defence

In the pre-Islamic era, tribes formed the biggest units of social and political organisation. An individual, therefore, was not important until and unless he or she affirmed allegiance to a tribe. The public order within and among tribes was regulated through 'unwritten rules' or customs. A feud between two individuals of different tribes could lead to the collective use of force.[93] A formal peace settlement culminating in a written agreement was, otherwise, a determinant of peace. Understandably, thus, in the absence of any peace agreement, 'state of war' was 'state of nature'.[94] Before Islam, Arabs were divided into tribes along

88 Majid Khadduri, *The Islamic Conception of Justice* (Baltimore and London: The Johns Hopkins University Press, 1984), 164; and Khadduri, *War and Peace in the Law of Islam*, 1955.

89 Khadduri, *War and Peace in the Law of Islam*, 44; and Ubaidullah F. Falahi, *Islamic Polity and Orientalists* (Aligarh: Institute of Islamic Studies, 2002), 88.

90 Ibid., 44–45.

91 Khadduri, "International Law", 350; Khadduri, *War and Peace in the Law of Islam*, 45; and Khadduri, *The Islamic Conception of Justice*, 3.

92 The principal notion of political organisation in Islam revolves around the concept of 'totality of individuals' that is *ummah*.

93 Coulson, *A History of Islamic Law*, 9.

94 Khadduri, *War and Peace in the Law of Islam*, 53–54. Elaborating the warlike character and its causes in the contemporary Arab world, Quincy Wright underlines that given the fact of the warm climate and the defenceless terrain, Arabs had fully developed the warlike and aggressive character to sustain through the existent realities. For details, see Quincy Wright, *A Study of War* (Chicago: The University of Chicago Press, 1942), 63–64. Likewise, renowned English jurist Maine notes that self-preservation was the most fundamental concern for the ancient communities, which is why they always strived for the maintenance of equilibrium, and thus, settling of civil strife through the war was the norm in these societies. For details, see Maine, *Ancient Law*, 46. Also, see Ballis, *The Legal Position of War*, 40–44; Fred M. Donner, "The Sources of Islamic Conceptions of War", in *Just War and Jihad: Historical and Theoretical Perspectives on War and Peace*

ancestral lineages, rather than any political orientation,[95] but Islam transcended the existent ancestral bounds and ascribed a separate identity to its followers: the Muslims.

The tribal struggle for survival, therefore, morphed into a war between Muslims and non-Muslims, where *jihad* sets the legal framework to define and explain the contours of the use of force framework. In this context, sometimes, the use of words such as *harb* (war) and *qital* (killing) also embodies violent struggle. The literal meaning of the Arabic word *jihad* is "struggle, striving, or exertion".[96] It has both private and public connotations. Given its private subtext, it means to strive to achieve salvation or personal fulfilment.[97] And its public meanings include carrying out struggle in the path of Allah to spread His Message through tongue, deed, or sword.[98] Accentuating the 'armed-struggle', the Qur'an emphasises: "Make ready for them all thou canst of (armed) force and of horses tethered, that thereby ye may dismay the enemy of Allah and your enemy, and others beside them whom ye know not".[99] This verse highlights the value of permanent preparedness for war when 'state of war' is a common norm. In this context, some Islamic jurists argue that the normative value of the persistent conflict helped to "develop a spirit of self-reliance, courage, and co-operation among the members of a single tribe".[100] In effect, it created an atmosphere of perpetual war in the local

---

in Western and Islamic Traditions, ed. John Kelsay and James T. Johnson (New York: Greenwood Press, 1991), 34–35; Fred M. Donner, *Muhammad and the Believers: At the Origins of Islam* (Cambridge, London: Harvard University Press, 2010); Niaz A. Shah, *Islamic Law and the Law of Armed Conflict: The Armed Conflict in Pakistan* (New York: Routledge, 2011), 31–32; Richard Bell, *Introduction to the Qur'an* (Edinburgh: Edinburgh University Press, 1953), 6. Moreover, God underscores this point in the Qur'an: "Have they not seen that We have appointed a sanctuary (from violence), while mankind is ravaged all around them" (29:67).

95 Shah, *Islamic Law and the Law of Armed Conflict*, 31. For a detailed description of the social, political, and economic order of the pre-Islamic Arabic world, see Fred M. Donner, *The Early Islamic Conquests* (Princeton: Princeton University Press, 1981), 11–49; Donner, *Muhammad and the Believers: At the Origins of Islam.*

96 Q. 2:218, Q. 4: 95, and Q. 22:78. Also, see Oliver Leamann, ed., *The Qur'an: An Encyclopaedia* (London: Routledge, 2006), 331.

97 The Qur'an underlines: "He who exerts himself, exerts only for his own soul" (Q. 29:5). Meanwhile, Abdul Noorani has labelled the private aspect of *jihad* as 'spiritual' and public as 'physical'. For details, see Noorani, *Islam and Jihad: Prejudice Versus Reality* (London: Zed Books, 2003), 43.

98 The Qur'an says: "Ye should believe in Allah and His messenger, and should strive for the cause of Allah with your wealth and lives. This is better for ye, if ye did but know" (Q. 61:11). Moreover, Islamic legal scholars have laid down four kinds of the *jihad* and these include *jihad* by heart, by the tongue, by hands, and by the sword. For further details of these concepts, see Khadduri, *War and Peace in the Law of Islam*, 56–57; Gabriel Palmer-Fernandez, ed., *Encyclopaedia of Religion and War* (New York: Routledge, 2004), 234–235; and Ella Landau-Tasseron, "Jihad", in *Jihad and Martyrdom: Critical Concepts in Islamic Studies*, ed. David Cook (London: Routledge, 2010), 5–6.

99 Q. 8:60.

100 Quoted in Khadduri, *War and Peace in the Law of Islam*, 62.

communities,[101] whereas the military prowess determined as well as guaranteed the self-preservation of Muslims.

To standardise the laws of war, Islam introduced the 'juridical and doctrinal' character. Religion thus emerged as the base of violence perpetration.[102] Like natural law, Islamic law of nations also subscribes to the divine sanction.[103] To institutionalise and contextualise the laws of war, classical Islamic legal jurists introduced two categories: *dar al-Islam*[104] (the abode of Islam) and *dar al-Harb*[105] (the abode of war). This division strengthened the belief that a permanent state of war exists between Muslims and non-Muslims.[106] To negotiate this reality and justify the use of force, the Islamic law of nations introduces numerous legal principles. The status and role of these legal principles depend upon the methodology one chooses for their interpretation. For instance, the interpretive methodology of progression emphasises that since the Qur'an was gradually revealed, the content of each revelation, therefore, addresses a specific issue. During the Meccan period (AD 610–622), the focus of the Qur'anic Message was to lay down the primary foundations of faith.[107] The nature of the Message, however, changed from private to public during the Medinan period (AD 622–632).[108]

'Abrogation', on the other hand, stresses that the Qur'an was revealed in a 'chronological order'.[109] Once the final Command concerning an issue arrives,

101 William. C. Watt, *Muhammad at Medina* (Oxford: Oxford University Press, 1977), 78 and 144; and Niaz A. Shah, *Islamic Law and the Law of Armed Conflict: The Armed Conflict in Pakistan* (New York: Routledge, 2011), 31–32.

102 Khadduri, *War and Peace in the Law of Islam*, 63.

103 Thomas Sizgorich, "Sanctified Violence: Monotheist Militancy as the Tie That Bound Christian Rome and Islam", *Journal of the American Academy of Religion* 77, no. 4 (2009): 895–921; and Fazul Rahman, *Major Themes of the Qur'an* (Minneapolis: Bibliotheca Islamica, 1980), 63–64.

104 Khadduri, *War and Peace in the Law of Islam*, 155–161; and Manoucher Parvin and Maurie Sommer, "Dar al-Islam: The Evolution of Muslim Territoriality and its Implication for Conflict Resolution in the Middle East", *International Journal of Middle East Studies* 11, no. 1 (1980): 1–21.

105 Khadduri, *War and Peace in the Law of Islam*, 170–174.

106 Asma Afsaruddin, "Views of *Jihad* Throughout History", in *International Law and Islamic Law*, ed. Mashood A. Baderin (Hampshire: Ashgate Publishing Company, 2008), 99; Stephen C. Neff, *War and the Law of Nations* (Cambridge: Cambridge University Press, 2005), 41–42. According to Fred M. Donner, these concepts entered into the Islamic legal history in AD late eighth century, at a time, when the limits of the stretch of Islamic conquests were tested by the powerful Western Roman Empire. For details, see Donner, "The Sources of Islamic Conceptions of War", 50. On the contrary, there is no such division present in Qur'anic texts. While Quran refers this division as 'House of Faith (*Dar al-Iman*) and House of Disbelief (*Dar al-Kufr*)', see Richard Bonney, *Jihad: From Quran to bin Laden* (New York: Palgrave Macmillan, 2004), 8.

107 Q. 42:40–43. Ella Landau-Tasseron explains two more interpretive techniques for the Qur'anic text: assignation and specification. For details, see Landau-Tasseron, "Jihad", in *Jihad and Martyrdom: Critical Concepts in Islamic Studies*, ed. Cook, 9.

108 Bonney, *Jihad from Quran to bin Laden*, 22–24: and Leaman, *The Quran: An Encyclopaedia*, 687–689.

109 Jane D. McAuliffe, ed., *The Cambridge Companion to Qur'an* (Cambridge: Cambridge University Press, 2006), 3.

the previous ones become redundant.[110] As God asserts: "Such of Our revelations as We abrogate or cause to be forgotten, we bring (in place) one better or the like thereof. Knowest thou not that Allah is Able to do all things"?[111] But it is important to mention that such an approach, at times, leads to divisiveness. For instance, those Islamic jurists who follow the abrogation believed that the arrival of the verse, "Then, when the sacred months have passed, slay the idolaters wherever ye find them",[112] effectively annulled the previous commands related to the use of force.[113] Indeed, such an interpretation becomes a free pass to wage a permanent war.

Moreover, the verses contradict each other[114] because of the varying contexts of the revelations and the relative growth of military prowess. For instance, in Mecca, Muslims were not permitted to fight even in self-defence. But in Medina, the Message changed altogether. This change underscores the fact of transformation of the socio-political context: from a scattered community to the formal state.[115] Hence, God commands: "[S]anction is given unto those who fight because they have been wronged, and Allah is indeed able to give them victory".[116] To qualify the Message, God orders to fight for avenging the injustice meted out to "[T]hose who have been driven from their homes unjustly only because they said: Our Lord is Allah".[117] These verses are the first ones concerning the use of force. These were revealed during the first year of the Prophet's migration to Medina. A

110 Palmer-Fernandez, ed., *Encyclopaedia of Religion and War*, 235–236; Abdullah Saeed, *Interpreting the Qur'an: Towards a Contemporary Approach* (London: Routledge, 2006), 77–89; Leamann, ed., *The Qur'an: An Encyclopaedia*, 5–6; Akhtar, *The Quran and the Secular Mind*, 209; Bonney, *Jihad: From Quran to bin Laden*, 24–32; and Landau-Tasseron, "Jihad", in *Jihad and Martyrdom: Critical Concepts in Islamic Studies*, ed. Cook, 9–12. Moreover, Firestone in his remarkable study on *jihad* and its place in the Qur'an and the *sunnah* does not fully subscribe to the interpretive methodology of abrogation and 'evolutionary theory of war', and explains the scale of differences among classical Islamic jurists over the historical and topical nature of Qur'anic revelations. For further details, see Reuven Firestone, *Jihad: The Origin of Holy War in Islam* (Oxford: Oxford University Press, 1999).

111 Q. 2:106.

112 Q. 9:5.

113 According to some estimates this particular verse has abrogated almost 114 or in some cases more than that related to the conception of the *jihad*. For details, see McAuliffe, ed., *The Cambridge Companion to Qur'an*, 187–188; Leaman, *The Quran: An Encyclopaedia*, 5; and Bonney, *Jihad from Quran to bin Laden*, 23–24.

114 Firestone, *Jihad: The Origin of Holy War in Islam*, 64. Also, Michael Bonner explains that there lies immanent conflict in the Qur'anic text dealing with the warfare. He underlines that although the text is 'vivid and memorable' when taken in part, but once read as a whole it contradicts itself. This is why, the Qur'anic text is subject to so much controversy, stemming out of the method and approach, one adopts for its interpretation. For details, see Michael Bonner, *Jihad in Islamic History: Doctrines and Practice* (Princeton: Princeton University Press, 2006), 20–34.

115 In 622 A.D., the Prophet Muhammad had settled in Medina and announced the formation of the first Islamic state. Therefore, once the status of Muslim polity was settled, the Qur'an permitted the Muslims to fight. This command also underlines the importance of first establishing the legitimate polity, which will be the source of propagation and control of violence in the following years.

116 Q. 22:39.

117 Q. 22:40.

contextual analysis[118] suggests that God permitted the Prophet to fight those who forced Muslims out of their homes in Mecca only for the reason that they worship God.[119] Besides laying down the general rule for recourse to arms in self-defence, in essence, the sanction for the use of violence here has a retrospective effect.

The first command is appropriated into the justifications for resorting to war according to the Arab norms,[120] as well as into the Christian conception of 'just war'.[121] This message slowly becomes more coherent and pronounced, as God orders, "[F]ight in the way of Allah against those who fight you, but begin not hostilities. Lo! Allah loveth not aggressors".[122] This kind of war is only permitted against infidels or pagans. The permission, therefore, cannot be interpreted to attack non-Muslims such as the People of the Book (Jews, Christians, Zoroastrians, etc.).[123] Perhaps, the objective behind this qualification was to punish those who harmed Muslims during the Meccan period. This qualification also underlines the pragmatism of the law-giver as well as the essence of the *graduated* Message of the Qur'an. In practice, the Prophet conformed when he commanded: "Fight in the name of Allah and in the way of Allah; fight only those who disbelieve in Allah".[124] Thus, it can be argued that self-defence emerges as the sole justification to wage war.

To internalise the customary norm of defence of ideological brethren, the next stage of commands permitted the use of force in collective self-defence.[125] The

118 For a detailed analysis of the Qur'anic text and its historical context, see Angelika Neuwirth, Nicolai Sinai, and Michael Marx, eds., *The Quran in Context: Historical and Literary Investigations into the Qura'nic Milieu* (Leiden: Brill, 2010); Saeed, *Interpreting the Qur'an: Towards a Contemporary Approach*; and Salwa S. El-Awa, *Textual Relations in the Qur'an: Relevance, Coherence and Structure* (London: Routledge, 2006).

119 Rudolph Peters, *Jihad in Medieval and Modern Islam: The Chapter on Jihad from Averroes Legal Handbook "Bidayat al-Mujtahid" and the Treatise "Koran and Fighting" by the Late Shaykh of Azhar Mahmud Shaltut* (Leiden: E.J. Brill, 1977), 45; Niaz A. Shah, *Self-Defense in Islamic and International Law: Assessing Al-Qaeda and the Invasion of Iraq* (New York: Palgrave Macmillan, 2008), 15–16. Discussing the concept of war in Islam, Qamaruddin Khan subscribes to the persistently moderate notion among Islamic legal jurists through the ages. He believes that the Qur'an only permits the spread of Islam through preaching (*da'wah*) and grants the permission to launch a war only in self-defence or self-protection. For details, see Qamaruddin Khan, *The Political Thought of Ibn Taymiyah* (Islamabad: Islamic Research Center, 1973), 157–158; and Hilmi M. Zawati, *Is Jihad a Just War? War, Peace and Human Rights under Islamic and Public International Law* (Lewiston: Edwin Mellen, 2001), 12.

120 Firestone, *Jihad: The Origin of Holy War in Islam*, 91.

121 Leamann, ed., *The Qur'an: An Encyclopaedia*, 688–689. For the detailed description and evolution of this conception of warfare, see Joachim von Elbe, "The Evolution of the Concept of the Just War in International Law", *American Journal of International Law* 33, no. 4 (1939): 665–688.

122 Q. 2:190.

123 Quoted in Muhammad ibn al-Hasan al-Shaybani, *Kitab Al-Siyar Al-Saghir*, trans. Mahmood A. Ghazi (Islamabad: Islamic Research Center, 1998), 35. According to the legal theory of the Shi'a sect for waging *jihad* non-believers are the people against whom *jihad* should be launched, rather the believers, who disobey the imam. For further details, see Khadduri, *War and Peace in the Law of Islam*, 66–68.

124 al-Shaybani, *Kitab Al-Siyar Al-Saghir*, 43.

125 Ibid., 15–16. Also, see Niaz A Shah, "The Use of Force under Islamic Law", *European Journal of International Law* 24, no. 1 (2013): 345.

objective was to safeguard those Muslims living among non-believers, where they were persecuted just because of their belief. God thus commands:

> [H]ow should ye not fight for the cause of Allah and of the feeble among men and of the women and the children who are crying: Our Lord! Bring us forth from this town of which the people are oppressors! Oh, give us from Thy presence from some protecting friend! Oh, give us from Thy presence some defender![126]

In these circumstances, waging war becomes a duty to avenge individual as well as collective injury.

Pre-emptive self-defence

Muslims are one nation, and non-Muslims are their 'potential enemy'.[127] This realisation needs to be assessed in the context of the strength and spread of Islam. As the message and scope of the Qur'anic revelations changed with regard to Muslims' prowess; it started transmitting comprehensive purpose of Islam.[128] As God commands, "And Fight not with them at the Inviolable Place of Worship until they first attack you there, but if they attack you (there) then slay them. Such is the reward of disbelievers".[129] This is one of the 'sword verses' where the message is *quite* offensive in nature. In chronological order, this verse follows the verse (2:190) and permits recourse to arms in pre-emptive self-defence[130] to avert *imminent* persecution and to realise the purpose of propagation of Islam.[131]

Furthermore, the nature of the Message becomes even more expansive. As God commands,

> [F]ight against such of those who have been given the Scripture as believe not in Allah and the Last Day, and forbid not which the Allah hath forbidden by His messenger, and follow not the religion of truth, until they pay the tribute readily, being brought low.[132]

126 Q. 4:75.

127 Peters, *Jihad in Medieval and Modern Islam*, 4. Also, Allah emphasises in Quran:

"O ye who believe! Take not the Jews and Christians as friends. They are friends one to another. He among you taketh them for friends is (one) of them. Lo! Allah guideth not wrongdoing folk" (5:51).

The context of the revelation of this verse is the time when Muslims were establishing themselves in Medina after migration from Mecca. At that time Muslims were afraid of the strength of Meccan and wanted to strike deals with Christians and Jews tribes living in and around Medina to confront the hostile Meccans. In this situation, God through this verse cautions the Muslims that Christians and Jews cannot be their protectors (friends). For details, see Leamann, ed., *The Qur'an: An Encyclopaedia*, 679–682.

128 Bonney, *Jihad: From Quran to bin Laden*, 23; and Shah, "The Use of Force under Islamic Law", 346.

129 Q. 2:191.

130 Firestone, *Jihad: The Origin of Holy War in Islam*, 55.

131 Leamann, ed., *The Qur'an: An Encyclopaedia*, 690.

132 Q. 9:29.

After this command, the Prophet invited non-Muslims to Islam. And in the case of refusal, tribute money or *jizyah* was demanded.[133] This command may be read in the context of the accumulation of vast power. To further expand their influence, Muslims were permitted to collect protection tax or head money from non-Muslims.[134] It also ascribes to the customary practice where, in the absence of any peace agreement, a weaker tribe pays 'head money' to the stronger for protection.[135]

In these contexts, Islamic law compels Muslims to ink agreements with non-Muslims. However, it calls upon them to quit any agreement based on the mere perception of treachery. "And if thou fearest treachery from any folks, then throw to them [their treaty] fairly. Lo! Allah loveth not treacherous", commands God.[136] This verse was revealed when Muslims had consolidated their state.[137] It, therefore, orders Muslims to fight those who break the terms of an agreement or have hostile intentions.[138] Based on this, one may, perhaps, assume that war is permitted on the basis of mere hostile intentions. Some Islamic jurists, however, correspond to the *restrictive* message of such verses. Islam does not permit offensive wars, they note.[139] And so, one needs to put commands into their proper socio-political context to better understand the law on the use of force.[140] The verses in

133 Leamann, ed., *The Qur'an: An Encyclopaedia*, 690; and Firestone, *Jihad: The Origin of Holy War in Islam*, 63.

134 The context of revelation of this verse is the expedition towards Tabuk. The Prophet Muhammad came to know through sources that the Byzantines (Romans) were planning to attack Arabia and therefore, the Prophet marched towards Tabuk to take on enemies pre-emptively. The rumours proved wrong once the Prophet reached the borders. But the Prophet made agreements with the local non-Muslim tribes because they agreed to pay protection money. For details, see Shah, "The Use of Force under Islamic Law", 349. Also, see Andrew F. March and Naz K. Modirzadeh, "Ambivalent Universalism? Jus ad Bellum in Modern Islamic Legal Discourse", *European Journal of International Law* 24, no. 1 (2013): 371.

135 Shah, *Self-Defense in Islamic and International Law: Assessing Al-Qaeda and the Invasion of Iraq*, 20.

136 Q. 8:58.

137 For a detailed description and chronology of consolidation of power by the Prophet Muhammad, see Donner, *The Early Islamic Conquests*, 51–82.

138 Shah, *Self-Defense in Islamic and International Law*, 20.

139 Sohail H. Hashmi, "Interpreting the Islamic Ethics of War and Peace", in *Islamic Political Ethics, Civil Society, Pluralism and Conflict*, ed. Sohail. H. Hashmi (Princeton, NJ: Princeton University Press, 2002), 205. Also, see Abdulaziz Sachedina, "The Development of Jihad in Islamic Revelation and History", in *Cross, Crescent and Sword: The Justification and Limitation of War in Western and Islamic Traditions*, ed. James T. Johnson and John Kelsay (Westport: Greenwood Press, 1990), 35–50; Shah, *Self-Defense in Islamic and International Law: Assessing Al-Qaeda and the Invasion of Iraq*, 17.

140 Firestone calls such a genre of interpretation 'occasions of revelations'. He emphasises that Qura'nic revelations must be seen in their historical context. Following this rule, he divides the Qura'nic legislation about the war in four phases: non-confrontation, defensive fighting, fighting within existent Arabic scriptures (customary raids), and all-out offensive war. For details, Reuven Firestone, "Disparity and Resolution in the Qura'nic Teachings on War", in *Jihad and Martyrdom*, ed. Cook, 14–31.

chapter nine are among the last commands related to *jihad* in lieu of the relative power of Muslims, which could sustain aggressive conduct. Hence, they superseded the earlier commands in the Qur'an.[141] Moreover, the application of 'abrogation' makes sense in the context of the evolving political environment where the expansion of the Muslim empire was underway.[142]

One can assume that out of strength the use of force entails an expansive undercurrent. Indeed, it perfectly aligns with contemporary norms. Aggressive use of force, thus, forms part of the Islamic legal discourse.[143] For instance, the war between the Muslims and the Meccans at Badr (AD 624) is a classic example of pre-emption where Muslims confronted an *imminent* security threat.[144] This war, however, does not provide a certain framework to assess the legality of the context of imminence. Instead, it corresponds to the customary norms of initiating pre-emptive self-defence on the basis of hostility, relative strength, and the absence of any formal peace agreement. Likewise, Muslim conquests of the Byzantine and Persian territories are also examples of pre-emption based on the perceived hostility of the enemy.[145]

It is submitted that the Islamic legal discourse does not set out elaborative rules of war *per se*. It, instead, provides a set of crude ideas, which are left to interpretation. For a meaningful interpretation, however, one needs to appreciate the historical context of the origin and development of the discourse.[146] Similar to natural law, Islamic discourse on the use of force also suffers the dilemma of political and cultural interpretations of theological texts, which in turn gives birth to many moral questions.[147] It is a fact that Islam does not have uniformity in views about 'religious import', especially related to the law and its interpretations.[148] Interpretations of Islamic law thus display a fixation with the text, ignor-

141 Leaman, ed., *The Qur'an: An Encyclopaedia*, 5–6.

142 Bonney, *Jihad from Quran to bin Laden*, 24–25.

143 Khadduri, *War and Peace in the Law of Islam*, 51–54; and March and Modirzadeh, "Ambivalent Universalism? Jus ad Bellum in Modern Islamic Legal Discourse", 367–389.

144 Shah, *Self-Defense in Islamic and International Law: Assessing Al-Qaeda and the Invasion of Iraq*, 21, 165 and 166; and Muhammad M. Al-A 'Zami, *The History of the Qur'anic Text: From Revelation to Compilation* (Leicester: UK Islamic Academy, 2003), 32–33. Similarly, the Prophet Muhammad led pre-emptive military expeditions against Jewish tribes in Khaybar and northern Hijaz and Christian tribes in Najran to subjugate them. These tribes were traditionally close allies of Meccans, who were staunch enemies of the Prophet Muhammad. For details, Donner, *The Early Islamic Conquests*, 76–77; Donner, *Muhammad and the Believers: At the Origins of Islam*, 93; McAuliffe, ed., *The Cambridge Companion to the Qur'an*, 29; and Bonner, *Jihad in Islamic History*, 40.

145 Ann E. Mayer, "War and Peace in the Islamic Tradition and International Law", in *Just War and Jihad: Historical and Theoretical Perspectives on War and Peace in Western and Islamic Traditions*, ed. John Kelsay and James T. Johnson (New York: Greenwood Press, 1991), 204.

146 Donner, "The Sources of Islamic Conceptions of War", 34.

147 Sizgorich, "Sanctified Violence: Monotheist Militancy as the Tie That Bound Christian Rome and Islam".

148 Reuven Firestone, *Jihad: The Origin of Holy War in Islam* (Oxford: Oxford University Press, 1999), 14.

ing the context.[149] A close reading of Islamic texts suggests that they not only 'passively' address the unfolding events but 'actively' reshape the discourse. They command Muslims to take into account the socio-political realities and lay down the legal order to conduct relations with non-Muslims.[150] In sum, the Islamic law sanctions that, once threatened, Muslims should not wait too long to strike the first blow.

Positive international law

During the seventeenth century, human reason took the centre stage for creating and interpreting laws; positive law took birth out of this shift.[151] Such a law, however, got the first written expression as *jus positivum* during the medieval ages.[152] These were also the times when the concept of territorial states emerged in Europe.[153] Later, a full transition to the nation-state necessitated the transformation of legal principles to organise and govern the relations among the nation-states. Here, secular notions, such as state sovereignty and equality, displaced the role of religious precepts in law making. This presents a stark contrast with natural law, as "something is positive because it has been deliberately laid down, imposed or enacted—as opposed to what arises spontaneously by custom or nature".[154] In essence, positive law portrays descriptive and normative values. Due to these characteristics, at times, it may lack "intrinsic moral necessity".[155] Perhaps, in this context, a "law is positive in the sense that its source is an authoritative imposition by a legislator, and the law is positive in the sense that its content lacks necessary moral force".[156]

149 Bassam Tibi, "John Kelsay and 'Sharia Reasoning' in Just War in Islam: An Appreciation and a Few Propositions", *Journal of Church and State* 53, no. 1 (2011): 9.

150 Neuwirth, Sinai and Marx, eds., *The Quran in Context: Historical and Literary Investigations into the Qura'nic Milieu*, 430.

151 For the detailed discussion of philosophical origin and evolution of positive law, see James B. Murphy, *The Philosophy of Positive Law* (New Haven: Yale University Press, 2005), 1–50; Hans Kelsen, *Pure Theory of Law*, trans. Max Knight (Berkeley: University of California Press, 1970); Jules L. Coleman and Brian Leiter, "Legal Positivism", in *A Companion to Philosophy of Law and Legal Theory*, ed. Dennis Patterson. 2nd ed. (West Sussex: Blackwell Publishing Ltd., 2010), 228–248. According to Han J. Morgenthau, the philosophy of positive law takes into account only the observable facets of state-behaviour, which are then enacted through treaties and interpreted by the courts, and in the process; it throws all other manifestations for forming laws: such as ethics, psychology and sociology out of the window. For details, see Morgenthau, "Positivism, Functionalism and International Law", *American Journal of International Law* 34, no. 2 (1940): 261.

152 Roberto Ago, "Positive Law and International Law", *American Journal of International Law* 51, no. 4 (1975): 602.

153 Nussbaum, *A Concise History of the Law of Nations*, 52; Malcolm N. Shaw, "Territory in International Law", *Netherlands Yearbook of International Law* 13 (1982): 62.

154 Murphy, *The Philosophy of Positive Law*, 5; and Roberto Ago, "Positivism", in *Encyclopaedia of Public International Law*, ed. Bernhardt, 385.

155 Murphy, *The Philosophy of Positive Law*, 5.

156 Ibid., 81.

The primary principle underpinning such a law is the will to contribute towards the 'happiness and perfection' of others. This task cannot be fulfilled through one's duty to oneself—that is, through seeking one's own 'happiness and perfection'. The second principle is the freedom and liberty of states.[157] States are equal, and thus, the power or weakness of a state does not make any difference in the dispensation of obligations and enjoyment of rights.[158] Moreover, unlike natural and Islamic laws, where God remains the sovereign power, positive law regards the state as the source of sovereignty. It consists of voluntary, conventional, and customary laws. And overall, state consent is the basic requirement for a law to take effect.[159] The voluntary law stems from 'presumed consent', the conventional form of 'expressing consent' are treaties and agreements. The customary law underpins the 'tacit consent' of states. It is expressed through the willingness of states to follow the authoritative customs for orderly conduct of relations among states.[160]

In these contexts, it is also worth mentioning that the role of scientific methods was crucial to displacing the role of deity in creating laws.[161] Therefrom, the focus shifted towards the 'bottom-up' approach as opposed to the 'top-down' in the derivation and formulation of legal rules to fix the status and scope of rights and duties.[162] The objective was to make the law 'pragmatic' as well as align it with 'the immediate needs' of the contemporary world.[163] Positive law, therefore, is an effect of different law-creating facts: customs, legislation, and treaties. At

157 Emer de Vattel, *The Law of Nations*, Book I, ed. Bela Kapossy and Richard Whatmore (Indianapolis: Liberty Fund, Inc., 2008), 73–74.

158 Further explicating the point, Emer de Vattel underscores that "a dwarf is as much a man as a giant; a small republic is no less a sovereign state than the most powerful kingdom". For details, see Vattel, *The Law of Nations*, 75. Hans Kelsen also subscribes to this principle of sovereignty among states. For details, see Kelsen, *Pure Theory of Law*, 334–335.

159 Roberto Ago also maintains that the concept of positive law stems from the will of the state. He underlines that positivism is 'mere State voluntarism'. Ago, "Positivism", 386.

160 Vattel, *The Law of Nations*, Book I, 78. Dutch jurist Cornelius van Bynkershoek underlines that positive law is principally based on the consent of states where customs and treaties are the manifestations of this consent. Quoted in Francis L. Oppenheim, *International Law: A Treatise*. Vol. 1. 2nd ed. (London: Longman, Greens and Co., 1912), 98.

161 For a detailed discussion on the contemporary state-system and its impact and role in shaping the law (positive law), see Martti Koskenniemi, "The Legacy of the Nineteenth Century", in *Routledge Handbook of International Law*, ed. David Armstrong (London: Routledge, 2009), 141–153; Shaw, *International Law*, 72–98; Arnulf B. Lorca, "Universal International Law: Nineteenth-Century Histories of Imposition and Appropriation", *Harvard International Law Journal* 51, no. 2 (2010): 486–502.

162 Neff, *War and the Law of Nations*, Book II, 170.

163 Ibid. Moreover, John Finnis describes the positive law as a law, which has "variability and relativity to time, place, and polity, its admixture of human error and immorality, its radical dependence on human creativity". Finnis, "The Truth in Legal Positivism", in *The Autonomy of Law: Essays on Legal Positivism*, ed. Robert P. George (London: Clarendon Press, 1996), 195. For understanding the role of state practice in forming customary and treaty law, see Michael Byres, *Custom, Power and the Power of Rules: International Relations and Customary International Law* (Cambridge: Cambridge University Press, 2003), 35–43.

a broader level, customs are the outcome of the common practice among states, across different periods of time and space, without any prior intention of their law-making effects. By contrast, legislation is *deliberately* carried by institutions to lay down the rules to regulate the behaviour of subjects. On the other hand, treaties take birth as a result of the conscious attempt of contracting parties to set down certain legal principles to prosecute rights and duties. In contrast to customs, legislation and treaties are 'centralised' organs of law making. It is maintained that norms established through customs form customary law. Such norms have precedence over rules laid down through legislation and treaties. It is, therefore, implied that a law contrary to customs cannot stand the test of the force of law.[164] It is inimitable since, unlike individuals, states behave differently. To contain the "caprice and blind impetuosity" of a single person at the helm of affairs, organising principles are laid down among them through treaties.[165] And therefore, the rules which find manifestation in treaties and customs form the principal sources of positive law.[166] This shift in the formulation of laws makes them certain as a social fact as well as consensual in appeal.

Right of self-defence

Positive laws instilled a stark realisation among states that peaceful co-existence can be an outcome of the principles of sovereignty and equality of states,[167] where a state shall be the source of sovereign power.[168] Initially, these laws were set down on the basis of normative practices to seek self-preservation. An attempt to endanger the self-preservation of a state thus amounts to an injury. And the right to redress such an injury is called the right to security.[169] It is noteworthy that

164 Kelsen, *Principles of International Law*, 307–310; and Shaw, *International Law*, 131.

165 Vattel, *The Law of Nations*, Book I, 15.

166 Kelsen, *Pure Theory of Law*, 232. Hans Kelsen maintains that international law derived out of customs "is still in the stage of a primitive system of law" and it is broadly speaking decentralised. Hans Kelsen, *The Legal Process and International Order* (London: Constable & Co. Ltd., 1935), 14.

167 John Baylis, Steve Simth, and Patricia Owens, *The Globalization of World Politics*. 2nd ed. (Oxford: Oxford University Press, 2001), 43; Korowicz, *Introduction to International Law*, 39; Fenwick, *International Law*, 18–19; Friedrich Kratochwil, "Legal Theory and International Law", in *Routledge Handbook of International Law*, ed. David Armstrong (London: Routledge, 2009), 59–60; Leo Gross, "The Peace Westphalia, 1648-1948", *American Journal of International Law* 42, no. 1 (1948): 20–41; and Alfred Vagts and Detlev F. Vagts, "The Balance of Power in International Law: The History of an Idea", *American Journal of International Law* 73, no. 4 (1979): 555–580.

168 For details, see Fenwick, *International Law*, 17–31.

169 Vattel, *The Law of Nations*, Book II, 288. David Kennedy illustrates that the year 1648 effectively served as a melting pot, because of its importance in laying rest the natural law and shaping the positive law. He underlines a fundamental question arising out of this very era: "How can there be law among sovereigns when sovereignty, by definition admits no higher authority?" For details, see David Kennedy, "International Law and the Nineteenth Century: History of an Illusion", *Quinnipiac Law Review* 17, no. 99 (1997): 112–114.

positive law does not endorse the principle of resorting to war in defence of the laws of nature,[170] although it does correspond to the recourse to the use of force to end persecutions. States can put together a coalition against a state involved in inhuman treatments.[171] Moreover, the resort to arms is "permissible only against a violation of international law", which can include "forcible deprivation of life, liberty, and other goods, notably economic values".[172]

Positive law, however, cautions a state against initiating the use of force on the basis of 'vague and uncertain suspicions'.[173] Any punishment, moreover, must not exceed the limits of a lawful right of self-defence and must be proportionate to the injury.[174] In treaty law, the Covenant of the League of Nations was the first legal instrument to establish and protect the right of self-defence. The Covenant emphasised the peaceful settlement of disputes among the states. Nonetheless, in cases where the adjudication of disputes fails to reach a pacific settlement, states were permitted to resort to arms in self-defence under Article 15, paragraph 7, "for the maintenance of right and justice".[175] The Covenant did not succeed much in changing the legal course of resorting to arms. Instead, it affirmed the veracity of treaty law "as an institution of international law in the traditional positivist sense".[176] Subsequently, taking a clue from the framework of the Covenant, the Treaty of Locarno of 1925 also attempted to regulate the use of force in self-defence among various European states. Article 2 (1) of the Treaty lays down that the use of force to settle disputes among the contracting parties is only permissible in the event of 'legitimate defence'.[177] In these contexts, one can see a certain transition in the 'use of force' discourse, where self-defence moves towards the centre, and states may adopt it to redress the injury.

In terms of their practical utility, however, these norms did not go too far, as humanity witnessed the worst kind of carnage during the first half of the twentieth century. After this, states once more came together to regulate the use of force[178]

170 Moreover, Vattel scolds those natural law jurists who supported the legality of Europeans to subjugate the American nations in the fifteenth and sixteenth centuries under the pretext of defending the laws of nature, such as the disrespect towards parents and eating of human flesh. Vattel, *The Law of Nations*, Book II, 265.

171 Oppenheim, *International Law: A Treatise*, Vol. 1, 180.

172 Kelsen, *Pure Theory of Law*, 322.

173 Vattel, *The Law of Nations*, Book II, 289.

174 Ibid., 459.

175 Malcolm D. Evans, ed., *International Law Documents*. 7th ed. (Oxford: Oxford University Press, 2006), 5; Hans Kelsen, "Collective Security and Collective Self-Defense under the Charter of the United Nations", *American Journal of International Law* 42, no. 4 (1948): 787; and Neff, *War and the Law of Nations*, 290.

176 Neff, *War and the Law of Nations*, 293.

177 "Treaty of Mutual Guarantee between Germany, Belgium, France, Great Britain, and Italy", Locarno, October 16, 1925 (The Locarno Pact), accessed January 22, 2020, http://avalon.law.yale.edu/20th_century/locarno_001.asp

178 David Kennedy sets this demarcation to differentiate the laws of resorting to war (*jus ad bellum*) and laws of conduct of war (*jus in bello*). He terms the former as 'laws of war' and letter as 'laws in war'. David Kennedy, *Of War and Law* (Princeton: Princeton University Press, 2006).

and to chart out the future course for peaceful co-existence.[179] As an effect, Article 51 of the UN Charter came into being as an embodiment of the legal instrument to set the right of self-defence as well as guide the use of force among states. It establishes that

> [N]othing in the present Charter shall impair the inherent right of individual or collective self-defence if an armed attack occurs against a Member of the UN until the Security Council has taken the measures to maintain international peace and security.[180]

By roping in various norms in one sentence, it thrashes out the rules of the use of force within the frames of the legal, philosophical, and customary history of the laws of war. In this context, however, it is pertinent to mention that the right to resort to force in self-defence flows out of the primitive right of self-help.[181] In fact, the right to interpret, to ascertain, the fact that a state is attacked, and the decision to invoke the right to war, rests with the victim state until the time the UN Security Council intervenes.[182] This attempt to incorporate self-defence in the Charter led to a 'self-defence revolution';[183] it essentially "marked the full emergence of self-defence to the front and centre of the international stage, as a kind of all-purpose unilateral justifications to resort to armed force".[184]

The condition of 'armed attack', which was for the first time set inside Article 51, also found its way into the various regional treaties. For example, Article VII of the American Treaty on Pacific Settlement specifies that in the event of 'armed attack', state parties may lawfully embrace the recourse to force as enshrined and permitted by the UN Charter.[185] Likewise, Article 18 of the Charter of the

179 Stephen Neff believes that the UN Charter—crafted by the world leaders and legal experts—was "an urgent response to local and immediate demands and conditions rather than an expression of eternal verities". For details, see Neff, *War and the Law of Nations*, 317.

180 Ingo von Münch and Andreas Buske, eds., *International Law: The Essential Treaties and Other Relevant Documents* (Berlin: Walter de Gruyter, 1985), 11.

181 Hans Kelsen notes that international law is "primarily primitive legal order—as is evidenced among other ways by its complete lack of a particular organ charged with the application of legal norms to a concrete instance". He maintains that according to primitive order, "the individual whose legally protected interests have been violated is himself authorized by the legal order to proceed against the wrongdoer". And thus, the order based on this practice is called self-help. Kelsen, *General Theory of Law and State*, trans. Anders Wedberg (Cambridge, Massachusetts: Harvard University Press, 1949), 338–339. Also, see Kelsen, *The Legal Process and International Order*, 14; and Yoram Dinstein, "International Law as a Primitive Legal System", *New York University Journal of International Law and Politics* 19 (1986–1987): 1 and 12.

182 Kelsen, "Collective Security and Collective Self-Defense under the Charter of the United Nations", 791–792. Thomas M. Franck also subscribes to this contention, and maintains that as a result of these interpretations "the Charter text is always evolving". Franck, *Recourse to Force: State Action against Threats and Armed Attacks* (Cambridge: Cambridge University Press, 2004), 7.

183 Neff, *War and the Law of Nations*, 315.

184 Ibid.

185 "American Treaty on Pacific Settlement", Bogota, 1948, accessed January 6, 2020, http://avalon.law.yale.edu/20th_century/intam09.asp

Organization of American States (OAS) also binds the state parties not to resort to arms except in case of an armed attack as well as for the prosecution of the right of self-defence "in accordance with existing treaties".[186] This is also the case in Article 3, paragraphs 2, 3, and 4, of the Inter-American Treaty of Reciprocal Assistance, which establishes the right to resort to arms in self-defence to ward off an armed attack.[187]

Further on, conforming to the broader discourse on the use of force, positive law also protects the right of collective self-defence. For instance, a state may rightfully resort to war in defence of a neighbouring state, which is "unjustly attacked by a powerful enemy who threatens to oppress it".[188] The intervening state can avail this right even in the absence of any alliance with the aggrieved state.[189] The reason behind this intervention is to counter 'an ambitious monarch' who is battering others to accumulate power unjustly.[190] Perhaps, a state may also form a coalition to suppress a state which is "ever ready to injure others, to traverse their designs, and to excite domestic disturbances in its dominions".[191] In these contexts, we can assume that such wars correspond to the customary right of collective self-defence, as well as an established norm in Islamic and natural law discourses to pull up arms, collectively, against an aggressor. Meanwhile, the treaty law also set down this legal principle for the lawful resort to arms in collective self-defence. For example, the Covenant of the League of Nations formally instituted this right, wherein Article 16 establishes that an attack against any member state authorises the League to form a coalition of other member states to initiate military action against the offending state.[192] Later, the UN Charter also set down this principle in Article 51 by sanctioning the right of "individual and collective self-defence" against an aggressor. Article 51 thus emerged as "the main pillar of the law of self-defence in all its forms, individual and collective".[193] Articles 41 and 42, moreover, also laid down the principle of collective self-defence in instances where the Security Council is apprised of any unlawful use of force. These provisions, in this context, stipulate that after the failure of peaceful means of dispute settlement, the Security Council can "call upon the Members of the UN to take punitive action against the belligerent, threatening global peace and security".[194]

186 "Charter of the Organization of American State", Bogota, 1948, accessed January 6, 2020, http://avalon.law.yale.edu/20th_century/decad062.asp

187 "Inter-American Reciprocal Assistance", Rio de Janeiro, 1947, accessed January 6, 2020, http://avalon.law.yale.edu/20th_century/decad061.asp

188 Vattel, *The Law of Nations*, Book II, 263.

189 Ibid.

190 Ibid.

191 Ibid., 289.

192 Evans, *International Law Documents*, 5.

193 Dinstein, *War, Aggression and Self-Defence*. 4th ed. 177.

194 Münch and Buske, eds., *International Law: The Essential Treaties and Other Relevant Documents*, 10. For a detailed discussion of the intent of the Charter framers for incorporating collective self-defence mechanisms and the history of its application, see Franck, *Recourse to Force: State Action against Threats and Armed Attacks*, 21–31.

Likewise, various regional legal instruments also protected the right of collective self-defence. For example, Article 5 (f) of the OAS Charter establishes the right of collective self-defence by underlining that aggression against any member state shall be treated as an act of aggression against all members.[195] Similarly, the Inter-American Treaty of Reciprocal Assistance, in Article 3 (2), also subscribes to the right of collective self-defence and argues that the right, in such a context, shall help to address the injustice.[196] Furthermore, Article 5 of the North Atlantic Treaty Organization (NATO), in affirming consistency with Article 51 of the UN Charter, also affirms the right of collective self-defence.[197] Based on the aforementioned evidence, we can argue that the instrumentalisation of collective self-defence not only established the primacy of this norm but also helped in stabilising the right of self-defence. In the process, the positivist discourse succeeded in squeezing out the norm of self-preservation from the realm of self-defence. Self-defence, thus, moves to the centre of the laws of war.

Pre-emptive self-defence

Pre-emption in natural and Islamic law discourses symbolises the aggressive use of force and, thus, finds it hard to establish itself as a certain and separate doctrine with its own contours and explanatory norms. In positive law, however, it is relatively better established and explained. As in it, a state can invoke the right to resort to armed force to counter an adversary aggrandising power with expressed intentions to cause harm. In such circumstances, the decision to use force rests with the threatened state. It can demand explanations from the adversary for the hostile behaviour. And in the absence of any security guarantee, it may resort to using force in pre-emption.[198] Customary laws also institute this norm. A feud between the United States and British state officials, famously known as the *Caroline criteria*, helped to set down the related principles of pre-emption, wherein it was laid down that a state can use force to ward off a security threat which is "instant, over-whelming, leaving no choice of means, and no moment of deliberation".[199]

195 "Charter of the Organization of American State", 1948.

196 "Inter-American Treaty of Reciprocal Assistance", 1947.

197 "North Atlantic Treaty Organization", Washington DC, April 4, 1949, accessed January 6, 2020, http://avalon.law.yale.edu/20th_century/nato.asp

198 Vattel, *The Law of Nations*, Book III, 492 and 499. James L. Brierly also subscribes to this principle of self-defence and supports the use of force in the face of an 'actual or threatened' attack. Brierly, *The Law of Nations: An Introduction to the International Law of Peace* (Oxford: The Clarendon Press, 1928), 157.

199 Werner Meng, "The Caroline", in *Encyclopaedia of Public International Law*, ed. Bernhardt, Vol. 3, 81. Meanwhile, Ian Brownlie believes that although the formula set by Webster contributed in laying down the fundamentals of anticipatory self-defence, it made no difference in lifting up the idea to the level of a formal 'legal doctrine'. It is because 'self-defence was then regarded either as synonymous with self-preservation or as a particular instance of it'. Brownlie, *Principles of Public International Law*. 7th ed. (Oxford: Oxford University Press, 2008), 734.

Taking into account the customary practice of pre-emption, Article 51 of the UN Charter emphasises "[N]othing in the present Charter shall impair the *inherent right* of individual or collective self-defence if an armed attack occurs".[200] Indeed, the UN Charter underscored the vitality of the customary law emerging out of the centuries' old state practice. However, this endeavour to marry customary and treaty laws does not prove to be seamless as there exists a difference of opinion among legal scholars when locating the nature and character of this customary norm in the treaty law.[201] For example, it is sometimes suggested that the doctrine of pre-emption transmitted through the *Caroline criteria* is only justifiable in the event of reprisal rather than in war. But any pre-emptive armed measure can be deployed under Article 51 to confront an irrevocable hostile movement of the adversary.[202] Thus, positivists accept the admissibility of pre-emption to address an imminent security threat.[203]

However, the influx of modern destructive weapons and tactics, such as nuclear weapons, terrorism, and cyber threats made the interpretation and application of pre-emption challenging.[204] After all, in these situations *too much wait* for an attack to happen can potentially undermine the survival of a state.[205] It is therefore emphasised that "no law—and certainly not Article 51—should be interpreted" to compel states to suffer the deadly first blow for availing the right of self-defence.[206] To sum up, one can safely assume that undoubtedly, unlike Islamic and natural laws, positive law succeeded in stabilising the discourse on self-defence. It, however, cannot be ignored that new security threats like terrorism and cyber-attacks pose a serious challenge to the stability of pre-emption.

Rationalising the choice of explanatory discourse

Within the doctrinal contours of pre-emption, one may argue that self-preservation reigns supreme in Islamic and natural legal discourses. In positive international law, however, it establishes itself as a rather implicit element. To further build on this argument, the following discussions address this incongruence, compare different legal discourses, and thrash out arguments for the choice of a certain legal discourse to structure, as well as guide this research inquiry. In effect, the

200 "Charter of the United Nations", San Francisco, June 26, 1945, accessed December 11, 2020, https://www.un.org/en/charter-united-nations/ (emphasis added).

201 These differences are thoroughly explained in the chapter below.

202 Dinstein, *War, Aggression and Self-Defence*. 4th ed., 187 and 191.

203 Shaw, *International Law*, 1139. Yoram Dinstein calls this form of self-defence 'interceptive self-defence' and underscores its permissibility under the UN Charter framework, regulating the use of force. Dinstein, *War, Aggression and Self-Defence*. 4th ed., 191.

204 Shaw, *International Law*, 1138; and Franck, *Recourse to Force: State Action Against Threats and Armed Attacks*, 7 and 50.

205 Derek W. Bowett, *Self-Defence in International Law* (Manchester: Manchester University Press, 1958), 118–192.

206 Franck, *Recourse to Force: State Action against Threats and Armed Attacks*, 98; and Neff, *War and the Law of Nations*, 329.

weaknesses and strengths of the respective theories in studying the doctrinal discourse are then highlighted.

As explained above, the study of the legal discourse of the use of force across different legal traditions underlines that resort to arms entails various justifications. These are, in fact, most of the time, woven around the notions of self-preservation, survival, self-help, and self-protection. In this context, Greeks and Romans attacked the neighbours to fulfil the dictates of the civilisational project.[207] As a political fact, they aggrandised power out of these military interventions that are otherwise justified under the norm of self-preservation and perfection of civilisation. The notion of perfection, in this context, was to civilise the people of occupied territories. The arrival of Christianity and Islam provided such political justifications a religious cover. In effect, the discourse on the use of force saw the theoretical overstretch of self-defence from a legitimate right to an arbitrary duty.

Later, the evolution of the natural law discourse did acknowledge the equality of states (Christians and non-Christians).[208] This transition was the consequence of practical necessities, for the overriding role of the religious clerics, in locating and interpreting legal precepts out of religious texts, had caused enormous bloodshed in the Middle Ages. Subsequently, the *Renaissance* and *Reformation* took hold in fifteenth-century Europe. It gave birth to the classical age of law of nations—[209] dominated and driven by the natural law theorists. The Islamic law, especially dealing with the use of force did not develop during all these centuries because it remained under the influence of the political dictates of the empire-building project, which did not permit human reason to interpret and shape the legal discourse. Inversely, the religio-political movements in Europe not only freed the natural law from the clutches of religion but also gave way to scientific methods of inquiry, thus providing the basis for *positivism*. Indeed, this shift displaced the dominant role of religion from the political affairs of the state, eventually giving birth to positive international law. The scientific tradition of empiricism and secular traditions of sovereignty and equality among states provided a basis for this law.

In varying degrees, all three legal discourses subscribe to the pre-emption. Despite getting an expansive treatment within the discourses of natural and Islamic laws, it finds quite a qualified sanction inside the positive law. Perhaps, the reason for this clear division on the position of law on pre-emption has again very much

207 Both Greek and Roman empires treated the inhabitants out of their respective territories as uncivilised and barbarians, who needed to be brought under subjugation to seek perfection of the empire through the neutralisation of threat posed by these barbarians.

208 Doyle, "Francisco Suarez on the Law of Nations", 112.

209 Charles Covell, *The Law of Nations in Political Though: A Critical Survey from Vitoria to Hegel* (Hampshire: Palgrave Macmillan, 2009), 2. David Kennedy classifies the period from 1648 to 1900 and from 1900 to 1980 as traditional and modern periods of the development of international law, respectively, whereas this study treats this period from 1480 to 1648 as the classical age. He also regards the natural law scholars of the traditional age as the 'founders' of modern international law. Kennedy, "Primitive Legal Scholarship", 5.

Table 2.1 Discourses on the use of force as laid down in positive, natural, and Islamic legal traditions.

Use of force	*Natural law*	*Islamic law*	*Positive law*
Self-defence	To avenge an injury or loss of property, to defend the laws of nature, and to end religious persecution	To avenge an injury and to end religious persecution of Muslim communities in non-Muslim jurisdictions	To punish an already launched armed attack and to end crimes against humanity
Pre-emptive self-defence	Against an imminent threat, to take out any threat hindering the spread of Christianity and civilised values, and to address economic injustices	Against potential enemies of Islam preparing to wage war against the Islamic community and to curb threats to the propagation of Islam and its values	In instances arising out of the necessity of self-defence, purely out of violent intentions, but calls for strict standards of proportionality of counter armed measures

to do with the sources and scope of the respective legal theories. Islam claims to be the last among divine religions, and that is why, perhaps, the law-giver is transmitting final and comprehensive commands to equip the Islamic legal armoury with all possible tools to defend and aggressively spread the Message of God. In contrast to this, we see that the sixteenth-century natural law theorists attributed their legal reasoning for pre-emption to commands. The seventeenth-century jurists, however, diverged from this path and did not support the idea of the use of pre-emptive force to spread the religion.

This transition within natural law discourse resulted in setting an abstract principle of 'imminence'. Subsequently, this rudimentary norm did find an elaborated manifestation in positive law. As in the middle of the nineteenth century, the US Secretary of State Webster laid down the procedural requirements of 'necessity and proportionality' for the lawful execution of the right of self-defence in the face of an imminent attack.[210] This later became the guiding principle in interpreting the doctrine of pre-emption within the framework of the UN Charter. Table 2.1 shows the difference in treatment of the use of force in self-defence and pre-emptive self-defence across the three legal traditions.

A comparison of the discourse on the use of force across these legal traditions, moreover, underlines the fact that laws of nations based on Divine Commands sanction the use of force in pre-emption as a sacred duty. A difference in religious

210 Details are included in Chapter 3.

belief can be an important reason behind this permission, forming and providing the basis for going after an adversary having a different religious belief who may be conspiring to attack soon. One may find explicit legal commands setting out these principles in the Islamic law of nations. However, there is no difference among adherents of different religions when it comes to practice. Further on, a close reading of the evolution of divine laws and man-made laws underscores the point that God, as a law-giver, transmits pragmatic commands and rules of violent engagement. For example, He never permits the use of force, even in self-defence, when a religious community is weak. But the permission is granted, even for the offensive wars once it has accumulated power. The divine law thus provides full-circle permission for resorting to arms: from survival to self-preservation, and to perfection, which may be sought through the expansion of territories and amassing wealth.[211] On the contrary, man-made laws, which include positive law, as well as parts of natural law, place focus on political equality and the sovereignty of states. They promote the role of practical human reason that is expressed and enacted through customs and treaties.

Such an emerging discourse underlines the fact of changes in the formation of community units, that is, from vast empires to nation-states.[212] This shift in the conception and formulation of laws regulating the use of force, therefore, arose out of practical necessity, which in return, resulted in transforming the basic source of law: from sovereign (God) to sovereign (state). In the process, theologically oriented institutions were replaced with political institutions for enacting and interpreting laws. The content of laws within these discourses also underscores the difference in the scope and aim of respective sovereigns: it is the expansive use of force, in the case of God, and moderately justifiable, in the case of a state. Eventually, no other justification but violent harm amounts to an injury, which can unlock the use of violent means to defend oneself. Further on, these discussions also underscore another salient point, that is, the content of these laws is very much based on abstract ideas. Their interpretation to justify the use of force, thus, shall remain a subject of intense discussions and debates. This is not surprising when we deal with the use of force as an issue directly linked to the survival of states. The fact of abstraction, in this context, speaks to the requirements of practicability and generalisability—the objective of any legal construct. One can assume, however, that in comparison to natural and Islamic laws, positive law is certainly more elaborative and tangible.

In the backdrop of these discussions, it is concluded that the positive law, based on customs relevant to the use of force and treaty law, shall better explain

211 For details, see the use of force in Islamic law above.

212 This seismic shift was the cause as well as the effect of the divergence in the course of laws of war in Europe in the immediate aftermath of the bloodiest religious wars (1618–1648), culminating in the Treaty of Westphalia. This treaty proved a harbinger of a new Europe, an embodiment of nation-states, assembled on the basis of nationality rather than religion. For detail, see Gross, "The Peace Westphalia, 1648-1948", 20–41; and Kennedy, "International Law and the Nineteenth Century: History of an Illusion", 112–114.

and evaluate the doctrinal legal discourse on pre-emption concerning the US drone attacks in Pakistan and Yemen. In this context, the study of the treaty law is vital because the US claims that its recourse to combat drones is supported by the right of self-defence under Article 51. It is also assumed that the UN Charter is an epitome of centuries' old state practice as well as consent—forming the basic sources of positive international law. In addition to this, parties to the conflict may also be assumed to not be abiding by the Islamic and natural laws of nations due to their different religious orientations and subsequent interpretive dissonance.

Summary

This chapter explained the discourse on the use of force in pre-emption within different legal traditions: Islamic law, natural law, and positive international law. More precisely, it traced the conceptual genealogy, the evolution of legal reasoning, and the current status of the doctrine of pre-emption. For this, the journey through Islamic law and natural law frameworks was necessary as well as helpful in understanding that in one form or the other, the doctrine of pre-emption was an important element of legal corpse and reasoning in other traditions. Although positive international law, in this backdrop, helped in stabilising and crystallising the doctrine, for its fuller appreciation one cannot overlook the importance of the contribution of God-given laws and their later-day reason-driven explanations.

Bibliography

Afsaruddin, Asma. "Views of *Jihad* Throughout History". In *International Law and Islamic Law*. Edited by Mashood A. Baderin, 97–101. Hampshire: Ashgate Publishing Company, 2008.

Ago, Roberto. "Positive Law and International Law". *American Journal of International Law* 51, no. 4 (1957): 691–733.

Ago, Roberto. "Positivism". In *Encyclopaedia of Public International Law*. Vol. 7. Edited by Rüdolf Bernhardt, 385–392. Amsterdam: Elsevier Science Publishers, 1984.

Al-A 'Zami, Muhammad M. *The History of the Qur'anic Text: From Revelation to Compilation*. Leicester: UK Islamic Academy, 2003.

al-Shaybani, Muhammad ibn al-Hasan. *Kitab Al-Siyar Al-Saghir*. Translated by Mahmood Ahmed Ghazi. Islamabad: Islamic Research Center, 1998.

Ali, Shaheen Sardar and Javaid Rehman. "The Concept of *Jihad* in Islamic International Law". *Journal of Conflict and Security Law* 10, no. 3 (2005): 321–343.

"American Treaty on Pacific Settlement". Bogota, 1948. Accessed January 6, 2020, http://avalon.law.yale.edu/20th_century/intam09.asp.

Anghie, Antony. "The Evolution of International Law: Colonial and Postcolonial Realities." *Third World Quarterly* 27, no. 5 (2006): 739–772.

Aquinas, Thomas. *Treatise on Law*. Translated by Richard J. Regan. Indianapolis: Hackett Publishing Company, Inc., 2000.

Aristotle. *Rhetoric*. Book I. Translated by William R. Roberts. Mineola: Dover Publication, Inc., 2004.

Badr, Gamal M. "A Survey of Islamic International Law". In *Religion and International Law*. Edited by Mark W. Janis and Carolyn Evans, 95–102. The Hague: Martin Nijhoff Publishers, 1999.

Ballis, William. *The Legal Position of War: Changes in its Practice and Theory from Plato to Vattel*. The Hague: Martinus Nijhoff, 1937.

Baylis, John, Steve Simth, and Patricia Owens. *The Globalization of World Politics*. 2nd ed. Oxford: Oxford University Press, 2001.

Bell, Richard. *Introduction to the Qur'an*. Edinburgh: Edinburgh University Press, 1953.

Bix, Brian. "Natural Law". In *A Companion to Philosophy of Law and Legal Theory*. 2nd ed. Edited by Dennis Patterson, 211–227. West Sussex: Blackwell Publishing Ltd., 2010.

Bodenheimer, Edgar "The Natural-Law Doctrine before the Tribunal of Science: A Reply to Hans Kelsen". *The Western Political Quarterly* 3, no. 3 (1950): 335–363.

Bonner, Michael. *Jihad in Islamic History: Doctrines and Practice*. Princeton: Princeton University Press, 2006.

Bonney, Richard. *Jihad: From Quran to bin Laden*. New York: Palgrave Macmillan, 2004.

Bowett, Derek W. *Self-Defence in International Law*. Manchester: Manchester University Press, 1958.

Brierly, James L. *The Law of Nations: An Introduction to the International Law of Peace*. Oxford: The Clarendon Press, 1928.

Burlamaqui, Jean-Jacques. *The Principles of Natural and Politic Law*. Translated by Thomas Nugent. Edited by Peter Korkman. Indianapolis: Liberty Fund, 2006.

Burton, John. *The Sources of Islamic Law*. Edinburgh: Edinburgh University Press, 1990.

Byres, Michael. *Custom, Power and the Power of Rules: International Relations and Customary International Law*. Cambridge: Cambridge University Press, 2003.

"Charter of the United Nations". San Francisco, June 26, 1945. Accessed January 20, 2020, https://www.un.org/en/charter-united-nations/.

Cicero. *De Officiis*. Book 1. Translated by Walter Miller. London: William Heinemann Ltd., 1913.

Coleman, Jules L. and Brian Leiter. "Legal Positivism". In *A Companion to Philosophy of Law and Legal Theory*. 2nd ed. Edited by Dennis Patterson, 228–248. West Sussex: Blackwell Publishing Ltd., 2010.

Coulson, Noel J. *A History of Islamic Law*. Edinburgh: Edinburgh University Press, 1964.

Coulthart, Malcolm. *An Introduction to Discourse Analysis*. 2nd ed. New York: Routledge, 2014.

Covell, Charles. *The Law of Nations in Political Though: A Critical Survey from Vitoria to Hegel*. Hampshire: Palgrave Macmillan, 2009.

Crone, Patricia. *Roman, Provincial and Islamic Law: The Origins of the Islamic Patronate*. Cambridge: Cambridge University Press, 1987.

Dinstein, Yoram. "International Law as a Primitive Legal System". *New York University Journal of International Law and Politics* 19 (1986–7): 1–19.

Donner, Fred M. *The Early Islamic Conquests*. Princeton: Princeton University Press, 1981.

Donner, Fred M. "The Sources of Islamic Conceptions of War". In *Just War and Jihad: Historical and Theoretical Perspectives on War and Peace in Western and Islamic Traditions*. Edited by John Kelsay and James T. Johnson, 31–69. Westport: Greenwood Press, 1991.

Donner, Fred M. *Muhammad and the Believers: At the Origins of Islam*. Cambridge: Harvard University Press, 2010.

Doyle, John P. "Francisco Suarez on the Law of Nations". In *Religion and International Law*. Edited by Mark W. Janis and Carolyn Evans, 103–120. The Hague: Martin Nijhoff Publishers, 1999.

Egido, Jose P. "Natural Law". In *Encyclopaedia of Public International Law*. Vol. 7. Edited by Rüdolf Bernhardt, 344–349. Amsterdam: Elsevier Science Publishers, 1984.

El-Awa, Salwa M. S. *Textual Relations in the Qur'an: Relevance, Coherence and Structure*. London: Routledge, 2006.

Evans, Malcolm D. ed. *International Law Documents*. 7th ed. Oxford: Oxford University Press, 2006.

Falahi, Ubaidullah F. *Islamic Polity and Orientalists*. Aligarh: Institute of Islamic Studies, 2002.

Fenwick, Charles G. *International Law*. 2nd ed. New York: D. Appleton-Century Company, 1934.

Finnis, John. "The Truth in Legal Positivism". In *The Autonomy of Law: Essays on Legal Positivism*. Edited by Robert P. George, 195–214. London: Clarendon Press, 1996.

Finnis, John. *Natural Law & Natural Rights*. 2nd ed. Oxford: Oxford University Press, 2011.

Firestone, Reuven. *Jihad: The Origin of Holy War in Islam*. Oxford: Oxford University Press, 1999.

Ford, Christopher A. "Siyar-rization and its Discontents: International Law and Islam's Constitutional Crisis". In *International Law and Islamic Law*. Edited by Mashood A. Baderin, 27–49. Hampshire: Ashgate Publishing Company, 2008.

Forde, Steven. "Hugo Grotius on Ethics and War". *American Political Science Review* 92, no. 3 (1998): 639–648.

Forte, David F. *Studies in Islamic Law*. Maryland: Austin and Winfield, Publishers, 1999.

Franck, Thomas. *Recourse to Force: State Action Against Threats and Armed Attacks*. Cambridge: Cambridge University Press, 2004.

Gee, James P. *An Introduction to Discourse Analysis: Theory and Method*. 3rd ed. New York: Routledge, 2010.

Gibb, Hamilton A. *Mohammednasim: An Historical Survey*. 2nd ed. New York: Oxford University Press, 1962.

Gibb, Himalton A. R. "Constitutional Organization". In *Law in the Middle East: Origin and Development of Islamic Law*. Edited by Majid Khadduri and Herbert J. Liebesny, 3–27. Washington, DC: The Middle East Institute, 1955.

Gomez, Fernando. "Francisco de Vitoria in 1934, After and Before". *Modern Language Notes* 117, no. 2 (2002): 365–405.

Gross, Leo "The Peace Westphalia, 1648–1948". *American Journal of International Law* 42, no. 1 (1948): 20–41.

Grotius, Hugo. *The Rights of War and Peace*. Book I. Edited by Richard Tuck. Indianapolis: Liberty Fund Inc., 2005.

Grotius, Hugo. *The Rights of War and Peace*. Book II. Edited by Richard Tuck. Indianapolis: Liberty Fund Inc., 2005.

Grotius, Hugo. *The Rights of War and Peace*. Book III. Edited by Richard Tuck. Indianapolis: Liberty Fund Inc., 2005.

Hallaq, Wael B. *A History of Islamic Legal Theories*. Cambridge: Cambridge University Press, 1997.

Hamidullah, Muhammad. *Introduction to Islam*. Paris: Centre Culturel Islamique, 1969.

Hanke, Lewis. "The Dawn of Conscience in America: Spanish Experiments and Experiences with Indian in the New World". *Proceedings of the American Philosophical Society* 107, no. 2 (1963): 83–92.

Hashmi, Sohail H. "Interpreting the Islamic Ethics of War and Peace". In *Islamic Political Ethics, Civil Society, Pluralism and Conflict*. Edited by Sohail H. Hashmi, 194–216. Princeton: Princeton University Press, 2002.

Hunt, Janin and Andre Kahlmeyer, *Islamic Law: The Sharia from Muhammad's Time to the Present*. London: McFarland & Company, Inc. Publishers, 2007.

"Inter-American Reciprocal Assistance". Rio de Janeiro, 1947. Accessed January 6, 2020, http://avalon.law.yale.edu/20th_century/decad061.asp.

Jackson, Sherman A. "Jihad and the Modern World". *Journal of Islamic Law and Culture* 7 (2002): 1–25.

Jurji, Edward J. "Islamic Law in Operation". *The American Journal of Semitic Language and Literatures* 57, no. 1 (1940): 32–49.

Kann, Robert. "The Law of Nations and the Conduct of War in the Early Times of the Standing Army". *The Journal of Politics* 6, no. 1 (1944): 77–105.

Kelsen, Hans. *The Legal Process and International Order*. London: Constable & Co. Ltd., 1935.

Kelsen, Hans. *General Theory of Law and State*. Translated by Anders Wedberg. Cambridge: Harvard University Press, 1945.

Kelsen, Hans. "Collective Security and Collective Self-Defense under the Charter of the United Nations". *American Journal of International Law* 42, no. 4 (1948): 783–796.

Kelsen, Hans. *Principles of International Law*. New York: Reinehart & Company Inc., 1952.

Kelsen, Hans. *Pure Theory of Law*. Translated by Max Knight. Berkeley: University of California Press, 1970.

Kennedy, David. "Primitive Legal Scholarship". *Harvard International Law Journal* 27, no. 1 (1986): 1–98.

Kennedy, David. "International Law and the Nineteenth Century: History of an Illusion". *Quinnipiac Law Review* 17, no. 99 (1997): 99–136.

Kennedy, David. *Of War and Law*. Princeton: Princeton University Press, 2006.

Khadduri, Majid. *War and Peace in the Law of Islam*. Baltimore: The Johns Hopkins Press, 1955.

Khadduri, Majid. "Islam and the Modern Law of Nations". *American Journal of International Law* 50, no. 2 (1956): 358–372.

Khadduri, Majid. *The Islamic Conception of Justice*. Baltimore: The Johns Hopkins University Press, 1984.

Khadduri, Majid and Herbert J. Liebesny, eds. *Law in the Middle East: Origin and Development of Islamic Law*. Washington, DC: The Middle East Institute, 1955.

Khan, Qamaruddin. *The Political Thought of Ibn Taymiyah*. Islamabad: Islamic Research Center, 1973.

Kimmey, Fred M. "Christianity and Indian Lands". *Ethnohistory* 7, no. 1 (1960): 44–60.

Kingsbury, Benedict. "The International Legal Order". Institute of International Law & Justice Working Paper, New York University Law School, 2003/1: 1–30.

Korowicz, Marek S. *Introduction to International Law*. The Hague: Martinus Nijhoff, 1959.

Koskeniemmi, Martti. *From Apology to Utopia: The Structure of International Legal Argument*. Cambridge: Cambridge University Press, 2005.

Koskenniemi, Martti. "The Legacy of the Nineteenth Century". In *Routledge Handbook of International Law*. Edited by David Armstrong, 141–153. London: Routledge, 2009.

Kratochwil, Friedrich. "Legal Theory and International Law". In *Routledge Handbook of International Law*. Edited by David Armstrong, 55–67. London: Routledge, 2009.

Kunz, Josef L. "Bellum Justum and Bellum Legale". *American Journal of International Law* 45, no. 3 (1951): 528–534.

Kunz, Josef L. "Natural-Law Thinking in the Modern Science of International Law". *American Journal of International Law* 55, no. 4 (1961): 951–958.

Landau-Tasseron, Ella. "Jihad". In *Jihad and Martyrdom: Critical Concepts in Islamic Studies*. Edited by David Cook, 17–37. London: Routledge, 2010.

Leamann, Oliver, ed. *The Qur'an: An Encyclopaedia*. London: Routledge, 2006.

Lorca, Arnulf B. "Universal International Law: Nineteenth-Century Histories of Imposition and Appropriation". *Harvard International Law Journal* 51, no. 2 (2010): 486–502.

Mackintosh, James. *A Discourse on the Study of Law of Nature and Nations*. Boston: Pratt and Company, 1843.

Maclachlan, Colin M. *Spain's Empire in The New World: The Role of Ideas in Institutional and Social Change*. Berkley: University of California Press, 1988.

Maine, Henry S. *Ancient Law*. London: John Murray, 1907.

March, Andrew F. and Naz K. Modirzadeh. "Ambivalent Universalism? Jus ad Bellum in Modern Islamic Legal Discourse". *European Journal of International Law* 24, no. 1 (2013): 367–389.

Martin, Richard C. "The Religious Foundations of War, Peace and Statecraft in Islam". In *Just War and Jihad: Historical and Theoretical Perspectives on War and Peace in Western and Islamic Traditions*. Edited by James T. Johnson and John Kelsay, 91–119. New York: Greenwood Press, 1991.

Mayer, Elizabeth A. "War and Peace in the Islamic Tradition and International Law". In *Just War and Jihad: Historical and Theoretical Perspectives on War and Peace in Western and Islamic Traditions*. Edited by James T. Johnson and John Kelsay, 195–226. New York: Greenwood Press, 1991.

McAuliffe, Jane D., ed. *The Cambridge Companion to the Qur'an*. Cambridge: Cambridge University Press, 2006.

Meng, Werner. "The Caroline". In *Encyclopaedia of Public International Law*. Vol. 3. Edited by Rüdolf Bernhardt, 81–82. Amsterdam: Elsevier Science Publishers, 1984.

Molesworth, William, ed. *The English Works of Thomas Hobbes*. Vol. 3. London: John Bohn, 1839.

Morgenthau, Han J. "Positivism, Functionalism and International Law". *American Journal of International Law* 34, no. 2 (1940): 260–284.

Münkler, Herfried. *The New Wars*. Translated by Patrick Camiller. Cambridge: Polity Press, 2005.

Murphy, Jr. Cornelius F. "The Grotian Vision of World Order". *American Journal of International Law* 76, no. 3 (July 1982): 477–498.

Murphy, James B. *The Philosophy of Positive Law*. New Haven: Yale University Press, 2005.

Neff, Stephen C. *War and the Law of Nations*. Cambridge: Cambridge University Press, 2005.

Neuwirth, Angelika, Nicolai Sinai, and Michael Marx, eds. *The Quran in Context: Historical and Literary Investigations into the Qura'nic Milieu*. Leiden: Brill, 2010.

Noorani, Abdul G. *Islam and Jihad*. London: Zed Books, 2003.

"North Atlantic Treaty Organization". Washington DC, April 4, 1949. Accessed January 6, 2020, http://avalon.law.yale.edu/20th_century/nato.asp.

Nussbaum, Arthur. *A Concise History of the Law of Nations*. New York: The Macmillan Company, 1947.

Oppenheim, Francis L. *International Law: A Treatise*. Vol. 1. 2nd ed. London: Longman, Greens and Co. 1912.

Orton, William. "The Sources of Natural Law". *International Journal of Ethics* 36, no. 2 (1926): 147–161.

Pagden, Anthony and Jeremy Lawrence, eds. *Francisco De Vitoria: Political Writings*. Cambridge: Cambridge University Press, 1991.

Palmer-Fernandez, Gabriel, ed. *Encyclopaedia of Religion and War*. New York: Routledge, 2004.

Paltridge, Brian. *Discourse Analysis: An Introduction*. London: Continuum, 2006.

Parvin, Manoucher and Maurie Sommer. "Dar al-Islam: The Evolution of Muslim Territoriality and its Implication for Conflict Resolution in the Middle East". *International Journal of Middle East Studies*11, no. 1 (1980): 1–21.

Pearl, David. *A Textbook on Muslim Law*. London: Croom Helm Ltd., 1979.

Peters, Rudolph. *Jihad in Medieval and Modern Islam: The Chapter on Jihad from Averroes Legal Handbook "Bidayat al-Mujtahid" and the Treatise "Koran and Fighting" by the Late Shaykh of Azhar Mahmud Shaltut*. Leiden: E.J. Brill, 1977.

Pollock, Frederick. "The History of the Law of Nature: A Preliminary Study". *Colombia Law Review* 1, no. 1 (1901): 11–32.

Pollock, Frederick. "The History of the Law of Nature: A Preliminary Study. Second Article". *Colombia Law Review* 2, no. 3 (1902): 131–143.

Preiser, Wolfgang. "Ancient Times to 1648". In *Encyclopaedia of Public International Law*. Vol. 7. Edited by Rüdolf Bernhardt, 132–159. Amsterdam: Elsevier Science Publishers, 1984.

Pufendorf, Samuel. *On the Duty of Man and Citizen According to Natural Law*. Book I. Translated by Michael Silverthorne. Edited by James Tully. Cambridge: Cambridge University Press, 1991.

Rahman, Fazul. *Major Themes of the Qur'an*. Minneapolis: Bibliotheca Islamica, 1980.

Rehman, Javaid. *Islamic State Practices, International Law and the Threats from Terrorism: A Critique of the 'Clash of Civilizations' in the New World Order*. Oxford: Hart Publishing, 2005.

Reuven, Firestone, "Disparity and Resolution in the Qura'nic Teachings on War". In *Jihad and Martyrdom: Critical Concepts in Islamic Studies*. Edited by David Cook, 113–132. London: Routledge, 2010:

Rohe, Mathias. *Islamic Law in Past and Present*. Translated by Gwendolin Goldbloom. Leiden: Brill Publisher, 2014.

Rubies, Joan-Pau. "Hugo Grotius's Dissertation on the Origin of American Peoples and the Use of Comparative Methods". *Journal of the History of Ideas* 52, no. 2 (1991): 221–244.

Sachedina, Abdulaziz. "The Development of Jihad in Islamic Revelation and History". In *Cross, Crescent and Sword: The Justification and Limitation of War in Western and Islamic Traditions*. Edited by James T. Johnson and John Kelsay, 35–50. Westport: Greenwood Press, 1990.

Saeed, Abdullah. *Interpreting the Qur'an: Towards a Contemporary Approach*. London: Routledge, 2006.

Saito, Natsu T. “Colonial Presumptions: The War on Terror and the Roots of American Exceptionalism”. *Georgetown Journal of Law & Modern Critical Race Perspectives* 67, no. 1 (2008): 67–113.

Schacht, Joseph. *The Origins of Muhammadan Jurisprudence*. Oxford: Oxford University Press, 1950.

Schacht, Joseph. *An Introduction to Islamic Law*. Oxford: Oxford University Press, 1982.

Scott, James B. *The Catholic Conception of International Law*. Washington: Georgetown University Press, 1934.

Scott, James B. *The Spanish Origin of International Law: Francisco de Vitoria and His Law of Nations*. Oxford: The Clarendon Press, 1934.

Scott, James B., ed. *Selections from Three Works of Francisco Suarez*. Translated by Gwladys L. Williams, Ammi Brown, and John Waldron. Oxford: The Clarendon Press, 1944.

Seed, Patricia. “Are These Not Also Men?: The Indians’ Humanity and Capacity for Spanish Civilization”. *Journal of Latin American Studies* 25, no. 3 (1993): 629–652.

Shah, Niaz A. “The Use of Force under Islamic Law”. *European Journal of International Law* 24, no. 1 (2013): 343–365.

Shah, Niaz A. *Islamic Law and the Law of Armed Conflict: The Armed Conflict in Pakistan*. New York: Routledge, 2011.

Shah, Niaz A. *Self-Defence in Islamic and International Law: Assessing Al-Qaeda and the Invasion of Iraq*. New York: Palgrave Macmillan, 2008.

Shaw, Malcolm N. “Territory in International Law”. *Netherlands Yearbook of International Law* 13 (1982): 61–90.

Sizgorich, Thomas. “Sanctified Violence: Monotheist Militancy as the Tie That Bound Christian Rome and Islam”. *Journal of the American Academy of Religion* 77, no. 4 (2009): 895–921.

Straumann, Benjamin. “Ancient Caesarian Lawyers in a State of Nature: Roman Tradition and Natural Rights in Hugo Grotius’s De iure Praedae”. *Political Theory* 34, no. 3 (2006): 328–350.

Szabo, Kinga T. *Anticipatory Action in Self-Defence: Essence and Limits under International Law*. The Hague: T.M.C Asser Press, 2011.

The Meaning of the Glorious Qur’an. Translated by Marmudake Pickthall, 1930. Accessed January 20, 2020, http://www.khayma.com/librarians/call2islaam/quran/pickthall/

Tibi, Bassam. “John Kelsay and “Sharia Reasoning” in Just War in Islam: An Appreciation and a Few Propositions”. *Journal of Church and State* 53, no. 1 (2011): 1–23.

“Treaty of Mutual Guarantee between Germany, Belgium, France, Great Britain, and Italy”. Locarno, October 16, 1925 (The Locarno Pact). Accessed January 20, 2020, http://avalon.law.yale.edu/20th_century/locarno_001.asp.

Vagts, Alfred and Detlev F. Vagts. “The Balance of Power in International Law: The History of an Idea”. *American Journal of International Law* 73, no. 4 (1979): 555–580.

Vattel, Emer de. *The Law of Nations*. Book I. Edited by Bela Kapossy and Richard Whatmore. Indianapolis: Liberty Fund, Inc., 2008.

von Elbe, Joachim. “The Evolution of the Concept of the Just War in International Law”. *American Journal of International Law* 33, no. 4 (1939): 665–688.

von Münch, Ingo and Andreas Buske, eds. *International Law: The Essential Treaties and Other Relevant Documents*. Berlin: Walter de Gruyter, 1985.

Waswo, Richard. “The Formation of Natural Law to Justify Colonialism, 1539–1689”. *New Literary History* 27, no. 4 (1996): 743–759.

Watt, William C. *Muhammad at Medina*. Oxford: Oxford University Press, 1977.
Wilkin, Robert N. "Cicero: Oracle of Natural Law". *The Classical Journal* 44, no. 8 (1949): 452–456.
Wilson, George G. "Grotius: Law of War and Peace". *American Journal of International Law* 35, no. 2 (1941): 205–226.
Woods, Nicola. *Describing Discourse: A Practical Guide to Discourse Analysis*. London: Hodder Headline Group, 2006.
Wright, Quincy. *A Study of War*. Chicago: The University of Chicago Press, 1942.
Zawati, Hilmi M. *Is Jihad a Just War? War, Peace and Human Rights under Islamic and Public International Law*. Lewiston: Edwin Mellen, 2001.
Zuckert, Michael. "The Fullness of Being: Thomas Aquinas and the Modern Critique of Natural Law". *The Review of Politics* 69, no. 1 (2007): 28–47.

3 Pre-emption, law, and state practice

So far, the focus of the study has been understanding the evolution of the discourse on the use of force in self-defence. Now discussions shift to an explanation of the current state of law and practice, exclusively relevant to the doctrine of pre-emption. In this context, positive international law shall be the principal foci of understanding and analysis. Concerning the methodological underpinnings of this inquiry, however, the discussion on pre-emption shall also involve, albeit on the margins, the study of the norms of self-defence and self-preservation in the natural law and Islamic law traditions. As explained in the previous chapter, positivism does not categorically permit the use of force to pre-empt an armed attack as a *right*. Instead, it treats such a military manoeuvre as an *exception*. Such a doctrinal inquiry, moreover, depends upon the customary law principles to better assess the legal claims and reasoning of a given case of pre-emptive self-defence. The treaty law, in unison with the customary laws, thus, essentially forms the law regulating the use of force in instances of pre-emptive self-defence among states.

Such a law cannot only be "created by certain special law-making authorities in a certain prescribed procedure. Custom, too, is a settled procedure for creating positive law".[1] This fact is nowhere as evident as it is inside the legal construct of self-defence. To formulate such a law, it is argued that the special law-making bodies 'consciously' create the treaty law, whereas customary international law can come into existence in most of the instances 'unconsciously'. As underscored by Josef Kunz, however, again "it is positive international law which prescribes the procedure by which customary international law can be created".[2] The procedure laid down through positive international law contributes to elevating the customary principles to the level of the law proper. To analyse the doctrine of pre-emption, the following discussion shall, therefore, thoroughly engage both the treaty law and customary international law relevant to the use of force among states.

1 Josef L. Kunz, "Roberto Ago's Theory of 'Spontaneous' International Law", *American Journal of International Law* 52, no. 1 (1952): 88.

2 Ibid.

Discourses in positive international law

As explained above, positive international law avails itself as the principal compass guiding and informing the discourse on the doctrine of pre-emption. Undoubtedly, Islamic and natural law discourses did provide the basis for the formulation of such a doctrinal understanding; yet the development and appreciation of this doctrine within positivism offer a better standard to assess the legality of any measure of the use of force in pre-emption. Given its centrality and effectiveness as a primary element of explanation, the discussion now turns to customary international law.

Customary international law

Unlike the treaty law, customs that states practise frequently among themselves form customary international law.[3] Customs, in this context, are pathways that link the "abstract legal concept to the particular factual situation".[4] Because of its centrality as well as importance as a binding norm, a "custom is a law-creating fact".[5] To achieve the status of law, however, these customs should "reflect binding legal obligations".[6] Signalling out this fact, and fixing the role of the obligatory state practice, moreover, the International Court of Justice (ICJ) in its judgment in the *North Sea Continental Shelf* observed that

> [N]ot only must the acts concerned amount to a settled practice, they must also, be such, or be carried out in such a way, as to be evidence of a belief that this practice is rendered obligatory by the existence of the rule of law requiring it.[7]

3 Murphy, *The Philosophy of Positive Law*, 19. Also, for a detailed history of the formation and evolution of customary international law, see Christiana Ochoa, "The Individual and Customary International Law Formation", *Virginia Journal of International Law* 48, no. 1 (2007): 119–186; and Hugh Thirlway, *The Sources of International Law* (Oxford: Oxford University Press, 2014), 56–91.

4 Quoted in Olivier Corten, "The Controversies over the Customary Prohibition on the Use of Force: A Methodological Debate", *European Journal of International Law* 16, no. 5 (2005): 806. Moreover, James Murphy underscores that customary law "refers to that subset of customs deliberately chosen for special enforcement. In this sense, customary law reflects not just the habitual and spontaneous order of custom but also the deliberately stipulated order of law". Murphy, "Habit and Convention at the Foundation of Custom", in *The Nature of Customary Law*, ed. Amanda Perreau-Saussine and James B. Murphy (Cambridge: Cambridge University Press, 2007), 76–77.

5 Kelsen, *General Theory of Law and State*, 126–127.

6 Rüdolf Bernhardt, "Customary International Law", in *Encyclopaedia of Public International Law*, ed. Bernhardt, Vol. 7, 62; and Jack L. Goldsmith and Eric A. Posner, "A Theory of Customary International Law", *John M. Olin Law & Economics Working Paper no.* 63 (The University of Chicago): 5.

7 *North Sea Continental Shelf Cases*, Judgement, ICJ Reports, 1969, 44 at para. 77. The UN Charter, resolutions, statute of ICJ, the decisions of ICJ and ICTY, cited in this study, are accessed through their respective websites.

It raises another question as to what kind of acts and which specific state organ must embody the state practice. It is maintained, in this context, that the activities, and sometimes 'silence and inactivity', of those organs of a state which are part of international conduct, and their 'activities and pronouncements' vis-à-vis international bodies, entail the state practice.[8]

The customary law is also called general or common law. Such a law originates out of the "habitual practice of states" and is "valid for all states belonging to the international community".[9] Customs, it is submitted, do not form any separate body of norms in positivist discourse. Instead, they are the distinct body of norms that find expressions through the 'tacit consent' among states. They are, moreover, distinct from those very norms which form the treaty law.[10] For a custom to attain the status of a binding norm, it should have the consent of a state. In the absence of consent, the very norm cannot apply to a particular state.[11] In this regard, some legal scholars, however, differ to this *consent formula* for ascertaining the validity of a norm, which takes birth as a result of the mandatory state practice. For the elevation of a norm to the level of a valid legal principle, they point out that "international law demands a general practice, not a unanimous one".[12]

Article 38 of the ICJ Statute stipulates that customary law is "international custom as evidence of a general practice accepted as law".[13] Likewise, those who situate customary laws inside the positivist discourse submit that for a customary principle to be a valid norm it should fulfil two requirements: consistent practice and *opinio juris*. A norm becomes valid when it is practised frequently among states "without interruption of continuity".[14] However, there is no binding of any

8 Hersch Lauterpacht, *The Development of International Law by the International Court* (Cambridge: Cambridge University Press, 1996), 360. For a detailed description of the certain activities accounting for the state practice, see Michael Akehurst, "Custom as a Source of International Law", in *Sources of International Law*, ed. Martti Koskenniemi (Aldershot: Ashgate Publishing Company, 2000), 251–260. For further details, also see Igor I. Lukashuk, "Customary Norms in Contemporary International Law", in *Theory of International Law at the Threshold of the 21st Century*, ed. Jerzy Makarczyk (The Hague: Kluwer Law International, 1996), 499.

9 Hans Kelsen, *Principles of International Law* (New York: Reinehart & Company Inc., 1952), 19; and Marek St. Korowicz, *Introduction to International Law* (The Hague: Martinus Nijhoff, 1959), 3.

10 Humphrey Waldock, *General Course of Public International Law* (The Hague: Martinus Nijhoff Publishers, 1962), 49.

11 Lukashuk, "Customary Norms in Contemporary International Law", 489. Also, for a detailed analysis of the vitality of 'state consent' in customary laws and international arbitration, see Anthony A. D'Amato, "The Concept of Special Custom in International Law", *American Journal of International Law* 63, no. 2 (1969): 211–223.

12 Josef L. Kunz, "The Nature of Customary International Law", *American Journal of International Law* 47, no. 4 (1953): 666; and Lauterpacht, *The Development of International Law by the International Court*, 360.

13 The Statute of ICJ.

14 Kunz, "The Nature of Customary International Law", 666; Lukashuk, "Customary Norms in Contemporary International Law", 497; Mark E. Villiger, *Customary International Law and Treaties*

certain time duration. Regarding the second condition, it is argued that in practising a particular norm, the states should be conscious of its legally *binding* nature. Without such conviction, a principle may become 'morally or conventionally binding' but not an obligatory norm of customary law. On the other hand, dissent on the part of a handful of states can effectively block the entry of a particular norm into the sphere of law.[15]

As for a particular act of state practice to become the norm of customary law, there is no definite time limit,[16] whereof "the time necessary to generate custom depends on concrete circumstances and may vary from case to case".[17] In this context, a norm can become part of the customary law even without any persistent 'preceding practice'.[18] To this effect, the entry of humans into space and formulation of space laws is an instructive case. In present times, therefore, given the fact of rapid changes, the burden of evidence rests primarily on fulfilling the requirement of *opinio juris.*[19] That is why "what had previously been perceived as evidence of practice, now to an increasing degree is becoming evidence of *opinio juris*".[20] This shift helped establish the legal character of a given norm. It also formed the 'psychological' component of customary law.[21] This factor "distinguishes [an] act done voluntarily or out of comity from one that a nation follows because required to do so by law".[22] To conclude, one can safely assume that the

(Dordrecht: Martinus Nijhoff Publishers, 1985), 3–39; Brian D. Lepard, *Customary International Law: A New Theory with Practical Applications* (Cambridge: Cambridge University Press, 2010), 20–25; and Shaw, *International Law*, 72–76. Meanwhile, Andrew Guzman and Timothy Meyer note that the state practice is an 'objective requirement', while *opinio juris* denotes the 'subjective belief' of the state. Guzman and Meyer, "Customary International Law in the 21st Century", in *Progress in International Law*, ed. Russell A. Miller and Rebbeca M. Bratspies (Leiden: Martin Nijhoff Publishers, 2008), 199.

15 Kunz, "The Nature of Customary International Law", 667. In order to understand the complexity involved in fulfilling this criteria, see Guzman and Meyer, "Customary International Law in the 21st Century", 199–202; Grigory I. Tunkin, "Remarks on the Juridical Nature of Customary Norms of International Law", *California Law Review* 49, no. 3 (1961): 424–425; Anthea E. Roberts, "Traditional and Modern Approaches to Customary International Law: A Reconciliation", *American Journal of International Law* 95, no. 4 (2001): 757–758; and Roozbeh B. Baker, "Customary International Law in the 21st Century: Old Challenges and New Debates", *European Journal of International Law* 21, no. 1 (2010): 173–204.

16 Tunkin, "Remarks on the Juridical Nature of Customary Norms of International Law", 419–420. Meanwhile for a norm to be applicable under customary international law, it must meet the precondition of sustained practice for some time. For further details, see Lepard, *Customary International Law: A New Theory with Practical Applications*, 6.

17 Lukashuk, "Customary Norms in Contemporary International Law", 503.

18 Akehurst, "Custom as a Source of International Law", 265–266; and Tasioulas, "Customary International Law and the Quest for Global Justice", 324–327.

19 For different approaches regarding this precondition, see Akehurst, "Custom as a Source of International Law", 281–292.

20 Lukashuk, "Customary Norms in Contemporary International Law", 505.

21 Anthony D'Amato, "Trashing Customary International Law", *American Journal of International Law* 81, no. 1 (1987): 102.

22 Goldsmith and Posner, "A Theory of Customary International Law", 5.

customary law is a fact of the state practice, which is borne out of the *legally conscious conduct* of states. With this theoretical understanding in the backdrop, the discussion now shifts to the exploration and explanation of the customary law on the use of force in pre-emption.

The Caroline *criteria*

The unsuccessful Canadian rebellion against the British in 1837 forced the fleeing Canadian rebels to cross into the US. Initially, they found safe havens in areas marking the common border between the two states. Later on, with the active assistance of US nationals, these rebels launched cross-border attacks against the British security forces. These cross-border violent skirmishes gradually became a routine. At the height of this rebellion around 1,000 men, mostly of American origin, encamped themselves on Navy Island inside the Canadian territory. The US government remained strictly neutral vis-à-vis the on-going insurrection in Canada. Yet because of the lack of state control in these bordering areas and despite the fact of repeated British requests, the US failed to curb the cross-border movement of rebels. It implies that the US government was *unable or unwilling* to curb these cross-border movements of violent elements.[23]

To prevent as well as deter the rebels from crossing into Canada and launching attacks against its security forces, Britain launched a military operation against the steam vessel, *Caroline*, involved in transporting men and ammunition across the border. As part of this military action, the British security forces attacked the steam vessel on the night of December 29, 1837, at a time when the vessel was safely docked inside US waters. The armed measure resulted in the destruction of the vessel, loss of life, and a few detentions.[24] A heated war of words ensued after this between the US and Britain. In his letter to the US government, Henry Fox, the British Minister based in Washington, justified this armed measure as follows: (i) the vessel was used for piracy, and thence, was struck under piracy laws; (ii) the domestic laws of US were not effectively implemented at the time of this episode in the given area; (iii) the British security forces reacted to avail their right of *self-defence* and *self-preservation*.[25]

In response, Daniel Webster, the US Secretary of State, wrote and refuted the first claim that the activities of rebels could be equated to pirates and dealt under piracy laws.[26] Secretary Webster also contested other justifications. He argued that the lack or absence of enforcement of domestic laws in a certain area could

23 James L. Brierly, *The Law of Nations: An Introduction to the International Law of Peace* (Oxford: The Clarendon Press, 1928), 158 (emphasis added); and Bin Cheng, *General Principles of Law as Applied by International Courts and Tribunals* (London: Stevens & Sons Ltd., 1953), 85–86.

24 Robert Y. Jennings, "The Caroline and McLeod Cases", *American Journal of International Law* 32, no. 1 (1938): 82–84. For further details and relevant state practice, see Charles G. Fenwick, *International Law*. 2nd ed. (New York: D. Appleton-Century Company, 1934), 167–168.

25 Ibid., 85.

26 Ibid., 85–86.

not be, in itself, an excuse for foreign military intervention in that particular area. It can be, however, in conjunction with the invocation of the right of self-defence and self-preservation, a legitimate reason for any military intervention, he underlined.[27] In subsequent correspondence, Fox, in a letter to the US Secretary of State, ultimately conceded that self-defence can be the basis of the use of force.[28] In this context, however, Britain had to convince the US with coherent legal arguments. The issue thus remained unsettled but not forgotten for the time being.

Later, Webster, finding the earlier British justification unconvincing, again wrote to his British counterpart. He questioned the necessity of self-defence. Secretary Webster underlined that

> [I]t is admitted that a just right of self-defence attaches always to nations—. But the extent of this right is to be judged by the circumstances of each particular case; and when its alleged exercise has led to the commission of hostile acts within the territory of a power at peace, nothing less than a clear and absolute necessity can afford ground for justification.[29]

Furthermore, Secretary Webster took it upon himself to lay down the theoretical legal reasoning for invoking the right of self-defence in pre-emption. Subsequently, this criterion became the cornerstone of customary law. According to Webster's formula, resort to arms in (pre-emptive) self-defence can be lawful provided that:

> [N]ecessity of self-defence [is] instant, overwhelming, leaving no choice of means, and no moment for deliberation. It will be for it to show, also, that the local authorities of Canada, even supposing the necessity of the moment authorized them to enter the territories of [t]he United States at all, did nothing unreasonable or excessive; since the act, justified by the necessity of self-defence, must be limited by that necessity, and kept clearly within it.[30]

Britain conceded her failure in reasonably justifying the practical necessity against the theoretical necessity, laid down by Secretary Webster. After the British government extended an apology for the violation of US territory, as well as for the loss of life, the issue was resolved.[31] In this context, it is important to note that to lay down the legal formula for availing the right of self-defence against an impending security threat, Webster set down two salient principles: *necessity* and *proportionality*. Within the doctrinal discourse of pre-emption these principles complement each other. Violation of one principle can make an episode of use of

27 Ibid., 86.

28 *British and Foreign States Papers*, Vol. 29 (1857), 195.

29 Jennings, "The Caroline and McLeod Cases", 86.

30 Ibid., 89.

31 Ibid., 91; and Robert Phillimore, *Commentaries upon International Law*, Vol. 1 (Philadelphia: T& J. W. Johnson, 1854-1861), 190.

force unlawful. It is important to note here that during the entire event surrounding the *Caroline*, there was no mention of pre-emptive self-defence. Nonetheless, the case and the criteria underline that debate is indeed over the prosecution of the pre-emptive self-defence.[32] In this regard, likewise, the crossing of an international border is a decisive element, which grants the use of force the status of pre-emption. The involvement of violent non-state actors is also telling here, which effectively underscores that any cross-border armed measure in their pursuance can give rise to the debate and discussion of pre-emption.

Necessity of self-defence

The necessity of self-defence forms the first principle of the *Caroline* criteria of pre-emptive self-defence. The term 'necessity', in this context, implies an overarching standard. For explanation, it depends upon different conceptions. Among these, self-preservation is the paramount one. Islamic, natural, and positive legal theorists emphasise the norm of self-preservation to justify the use of force in the face of an imminent threat.[33] Positivists, however, deploy self-preservation to complement the principle of self-protection, a part of domestic laws of individual self-defence,[34] wherein self-preservation embodies procedural parameters of the psychological mapping of a security threat. And therefore, "self-preservation is not a legal right but an instinct, and no doubt when this instinct comes into conflict with legal duty either in a state or an individual; it often happens that the instinct prevails over the duty".[35] Hence it forms the cognitive component of the doctrinal discourse on pre-emption, whereas defence represents its physical aspect.[36]

Within the positivist discourse, the norm of self-preservation was later on transposed into the category of general principles of law. This shift took place due to the changing social and political realities after 1648. Subsequently, certain principles, through state consent, achieved the status of legal rules.[37] To understand this transposition, it is important to know the difference between rules and principles. Rules are not general principles. Instead, they are part of the law prac-

32 Szabo, *Anticipatory Action in Self-Defence*, 74–75; and Jackson N. Maogoto, "New Frontiers, Old Problems: The War on Terror and the Notion of Anticipating the Enemy", *Netherland International Law Review* 51, no. 1 (2004): 5 and 18.

33 For details, please see the chapter above.

34 Vattel, *The Law of Nations*, Book II, 288. Also, see Bowett, *Self-Defence in International Law*, 7. Moreover, Charles C. Hyde also underlines that an "act of self-defence is that form of self-protection which is directed against an aggressor or contemplated aggressor". Hyde, *International Law Chiefly as Interpreted and Applied by the United States*, Vol. 3 (Boston: Little, Brown and Company, 1945), 237.

35 Brierly, *The Law of Nations: An Introduction to the International Law of Peace*, 160.

36 Murray C. Alder, *The Inherent Right of Self-Defence in International Law* (Dordrecht: Springer, 2013), 36.

37 David Kennedy, "Images of Religion in International Legal Theory", in *Religion and International Law*, ed. Mark W. Janis and Carolyn M. Evans (The Hague: Kluwer Law International, 1999), 148–149.

tised by the 'civilised societies' as a 'social phenomenon'.[38] The emphasis on civilised, in this context, was meant to divorce the primitive or tribal social practices from legal effects. With the emergence of the nation-state, however, such a limit was set aside, as it was assumed that any state which is part of the international community is civilised.[39] In explaining the norm of self-preservation, moreover, Cheng observes that the safety of people enacted through the popular maxim *Salus populi suprema lex* (security of the people reigns supreme) has, effectively, emerged as a general principle of international law. States, therefore, have the right to protect themselves against external threats, and "under very exceptional circumstances" may choose to "disregard a minor right of another state or its nationals in order to preserve its own existence".[40]

Despite its significance, positivists do not fully subscribe to the centrality of the norm of self-preservation. Instead, they state that the *so-called* right of self-preservation can only be invoked in conjunction with the necessity of self-defence. And in the absence of any such instance, a state cannot lawfully resort to arms in self-defence under the mere pretext of self-preservation.[41] Nonetheless, one can assume that to invoke the right of self-defence, the legal arguments employed to justify the necessity of such an instance hinges on the principle of self-preservation.[42] Asserting this point, Ian Brownlie underlines that self-preservation is

> a form of, a doctrine of necessity. There would seem analytically to be no distinction between the two and the discussions in works of international law certainly treat them as identical except as in so far necessity is a wider legal category and may, for example, appear in the context of the laws of war.[43]

Adherence to the principle of necessity, therefore, is a precondition to repelling an impending armed attack.[44]

The Court invoked the principle of necessity during the *Nicaragua* case. It noted that the US pre-emptive military strikes against Nicaragua to punish the

38 Cheng, *General Principles of Law as Applied by International Courts and Tribunals*, 24.

39 Ibid., 25.

40 Ibid., 31.

41 Oppenheim, *International Law: A Treatise*, Vol. 1, 173. Herein, the author also lays down the hypothetical sequence of events that can justify the use of pre-emptive force and invoke the principle of self-preservation. While Uwe Steinhoff maintains that "self-defence is a narrower concept than self-preservation". In order to make sense of the concept, the author underlines that it will be unjustifiable for a heart patient to kill a patient lying next door so that the former can get his heart transplantation. Steinhoff, *On the Ethics of War and Terrorism* (New York: Oxford University Press, 2007), 83.

42 Judith Gardam, *Necessity, Proportionality and the Use of Force by States* (Cambridge: Cambridge University Press, 2004), 5–6.

43 Ian Brownlie, *International law and the Use of Force by States* (Oxford: Oxford University Press, 1963), 42.

44 Christine Gray, *International Law and the Use of Force*. 2nd ed. (Oxford: Oxford University Press, 2004), 121.

latter for its role in arming the opposition groups in El Salvador did not fulfil the legal criteria of the necessity of self-defence. The US government failed to prove the requirement of the *imminence* of a security threat here.[45] Subsequently, the Court remained consistent in invoking the principle of necessity while adjudicating numerous other cases related to the use of force in self-defence.[46] For example, in the advisory opinion on the *Israeli Wall*, the Court observed that the principle of 'the state of necessity' enshrined by customary international law cannot be applicable in each case of self-defence. The said principle has 'exceptional basis' and, therefore, can only be applied in a narrowly defined instance, the Court asserted. The state cannot be the sole judge of its lawfulness.[47] In these contexts, one may assume that states do have different past experiences and existent constraints of the capability to determine the nature of the necessity of self-defence. Any such calculus, however, should involve irrefutable evidence of hostile intentions and movements of the adversary.

With the launch of the 'war on terror', however, the legal debate over self-defence shifted to the standards and normative requirements of the nineteenth century. This is because of the nature of the security environment marked and driven by the asymmetric means of warfare: terrorism and weapons of mass destruction. To respond, states reimagined security doctrines to adjust the right of self-defence.[48] In the process, debates about the legal nature of the use of force in self-defence brought the customary practice in instances of pre-emptive self-defence to the fore.[49] An attempt to respond to the reality of the evolving security threats embodies the principal objective to bring back the normative customary practice to assess the principle of necessity. It helps to connect and assess the state

45 *Case Concerning Military and Paramilitary Activities in and against Nicaragua*, Judgement, ICJ Report, 1986, 14 at para. 237.

46 For details, see *Case Concerning Oil Platforms* (Islamic Republic of Iran vs. United States of America), Judgement, ICJ Reports, 2003, 161 at paras. 51 and 76; *Case Concerning Armed Activities on the Territory of Congo* (Democratic Republic of Congo vs. Uganda), Judgement, ICJ Reports, 2005, 116 at paras. 147 and 304; and *Legality of the Threat or Use of Nuclear Weapons*, Advisory Opinion, ICJ Reports, 1996, 226 at para. 41.

47 *Legal Consequences of a Wall in the Occupied Palestinian Territory*, Advisory Opinion, ICJ Reports, 2004, 136, para. 140. Meanwhile, Israel maintained that its actions are aligned with Article 51 of the UN Charter, and are also in conformity with the UN Security Council Resolutions 1368 and 1373. Both of these resolutions were passed in the immediate aftermath of September 11, 2001. For details, see ibid., para. 138 and 139.

48 "The National Security Strategy of the United States", 31; Moore, "Chirac: Nuclear Response to Terrorism is Possible", A22; Singh, "Every Country has Right to Preemption".

49 Chatham House International Law Programme, "Principles of International Law on the Use of Force in Self-Defence", *Royal Institute of International Affairs* (2005): 35–37; Sanjay Gupta, "The Doctrine of Pre-Emptive Strike: Application and Implications during the Administration of President George W. Bush", *International Political Science Review* 29, no. 2 (2008): 183; Michael Byres, "Terrorism, the Use of Force and International Law after 11 September", *International and Comparative Law Quarterly*, 51, no. 1 (2002): 406; and William C. Bradford, "The Duty to Defend Them: A Natural Law Justification for the Bush Doctrine of Preventive War", *Notre Dame Law Review* 79, no. 4 (2004): 1365–1492.

practice with the established legal norms. It is incumbent upon states, therefore, to be cognisant of the weapons possessed by the adversary, the actual movements of the military, the capability of the self-defending state, and the prevailing political environment between the two states before embarking on a course of lawful execution of the right of self-defence.[50] Careful consideration of these factors contributes to fulfilling the narrowly permitted and strictly limited pre-emptive self-defence. To conclude, it is maintained that for the principle of necessity to be relevant, it must be interpreted in a given context of security threat, wherein self-preservation cannot be the sole justification. Instead, in accord with the necessity of self-defence, it can play an important role to better explain the legal recourse to pre-empt terrorism.

Proportionality

Out of the *Carline* criteria, proportionality emerges as the second important legal principle.[51] To explain the principle, Secretary Webster underlined that it was incumbent upon the self-defending state to show that the action taken to defend her is "limited by that necessity, and kept clearly within it".[52] It implies that an armed measure against an impending security threat ought to match the danger.[53] In this context, however, it is important to note that the customary presence of this principle did not start and end with this specific instance. For centuries, it formed an important component of different narratives and frameworks of justice in war. Likewise, it remained the cornerstone of justice of war inside the Islamic law.[54] This principle, however, gained uncommon significance within the discourse on pre-emption. This was because of the strictly set limits and limited scope of the lawful execution of the right of self-defence, whereof a slight measure of disproportionate use of force reduces the violence to preventive, and, of course, illegal.[55]

50 Murray C. Alder, *The Inherent Right of Self-Defence in International Law* (Dordrecht: Springer, 2013), 40.

51 For a detailed historical account of this concept, see Judith G. Gardam, "Proportionality and Force in International Law", *American Journal of International Law* 87, no. 3 (1993): 391–413.

52 Jennings, "The Caroline and McLeod Cases", 89.

53 Inside legal jurisprudence, this customary law principle was later on, effectively, invoked in 1928 during an arbitrational case over the use of excessive force between Germany and Portugal. For details, see Karl J. Partsch, "Naulilaa Arbitration", in *Encyclopaedia of Public International Law*, ed. Bernhardt, Vol. 3, 524–525. Meanwhile, Thomas Franck traces back the origin of the proportionality principle to the 'just war' tradition. He underlines that the doctrine maintained that the response should be proportional to the 'wrong perpetrated' and it should also meet the condition of "minimum force necessary to achieve the redress". Franck, "On Proportionality of Countermeasures in International Law", *American Journal of International Law* 102, no. 4 (2008): 719.

54 Khadduri, *War and Peace in the Law of Islam*, 102–108.

55 Explaining the fact of the intricacy of the juristic application of this principle inside *jus ad bellum*, Judith Gardam maintains that the term "is often misunderstood and misapplied". This fact is the result of an elaborative missing link between *jus ad bellum* and *jus in bello*. For further details, see Gardam, *Necessity, Proportionality and the Use of Force by States*, 20–27.

In terms of their mutual relationship, customary norms of necessity and proportionality are hierarchical. Necessity assesses the recourse to violence, while proportionality is applicable in the conduct of hostilities. Nonetheless, the unlawfulness of one can undermine the legality of the other.[56] Hence, it is important to ensure that the counter armed measure is proportionate in 'nature and degree' to the injury.[57] And under no circumstances, it should exceed the security threat it seeks to quell. For instance, to repel an on-going attack, it is prohibited to use force beyond the point where the attack has ended.[58]

The Court in the *Nicaragua* case noted that the US failed to uphold the customary principle of proportionality while launching a pre-emptive military attack. For instance, attacks against the Nicaraguan ports and oil installations as well as mines around sea-based assets amounted to the disproportionate use of force, the Court established.[59] Likewise, the Court, in its judgment on the *Case Concerning Oil Platforms* (Iran vs. the United States), once more, affirmed the principle of proportionality. The launch of 'Operation Praying Mantis' against both the civilian and the military targets in Iran, and the consequent losses, undermine the principle of proportionality, the Court noted.[60] Furthermore, emphasising the importance of proportionality, the Court in its judgment on the *Case Concerning Armed Activities on the Territory of Congo* (Congo vs. Uganda) upheld that the storming and overtaking of civilian infrastructure and territory deep inside the Congolese state can, in no way, be a proportionate response against cross-border attacks.[61] In these contexts, it is observed that the Court never relents in establishing the vitality and centrality of this principle in assessing the *post-facto* situation. Besides, it also emerges that the Court does not buy into the argument that downgrading the capability of the host state is an essential part of proportional armed countermeasures. It insists that for neutralising a cross-border security threat, the counter force should be limited to the threat.

Caroline *criteria and the current security environment*

The post–September 11 security environment puts to test the limits on the use of pre-emptive force. The terrorist strike against the symbols of US strength shook the confidence of numerous powerful states in the traditional legal architecture to safeguard against such attacks. Back in 2002, the US National Security Strategy

56 Sean D. Murphy, "Self-Defence and the Israeli Wall Advisory Opinion: An Ipse Dixit from the ICJ?" *American Journal of International Law* 99, no. 1 (2005): 71.

57 Rosalyn Higgins, *The Development of International Law Through the Political Organs of the United Nations* (Oxford: Oxford University Press, 1963), 201.

58 James A. Green, *The International Court of Justice and Self-Defence in International Law* (Oxford: Hart Publishing, 2009), 90.

59 *Case Concerning Military and Paramilitary Activities in and against Nicaragua*, Judgement, 96 at para. 237.

60 *Case Concerning Oil Platforms*, 161 at para. 77.

61 *Case Concerning Armed Activities on the Territory of Congo*, 116 at para. 147.

noted this change in the context when it emphasised that the combination of terrorism with weapons of mass destruction has become a paramount challenge for the security of the state.[62] Indeed, the requirements of necessity and proportionality became even more difficult to fulfil in circumstances where terrorists declared the destruction of adversaries. This, thus, puts the limits of temporality and geography to test. The violent exchanges become an unending cycle.

The criterion of necessity, which sets more coherent limits on force employment among states, suffers the dilemma of incoherence in instances of terrorism. As terrorists do not operate from within any certain territory, one cannot trace their hostile movements accurately. At times, they operate from within the civilians and launch surprise attacks, preferably against civilian targets. Also, because they do not wear any specific uniforms, their movement towards the target cannot be tracked. The *Caroline* criterion of necessity thus becomes problematic. Indeed, questions shall arise out of any measure of pre-emptive force employment causing disproportionate loss of life to save the prospective loss of civilian lives in a terrorist attack.

Likewise, the principle of proportionality also faces the dilemma of 'inherent uncertainty' in instances of counter-terror military operations aiming to strike down a *moving target*. Terrorists continue to adapt to new realities, and their mission to inflict harm has become a never-ending campaign. In such circumstances, a total annihilation may be the objective of counter-terror military campaigns. Yet, given that successful terrorist attacks are limited in number, one may raise the question of whether the past attempts by terrorists to inflict harm can be squared off to assess their future scale of violence. Or is it *just* to kill every member of a terrorist organisation before they potentially launch any terrorist violence?[63] Military operations against terrorists may also pose a humanitarian dilemma because the force employment against terrorists can also result in civilian killings. The legal assessment of the criteria of proportionality in the 'war on terror' thus becomes even more complex.

Any relaxation in the limits on the necessity and proportionality of armed measures risks propelling the use of force in the domain of preventive self-defence. So, when the US National Security Strategies of 2002 and 2010 took the intention and capability of terrorists as a yardstick to decide the military operation against them, they have the potential to inflate the boundaries of pre-emption. Furthermore, a closer reading of the US strategy suggests that when put into practice, the requirement of imminence would be ineffective. Instead, it would be the *gravity* of a security threat that would guide threat perception and its assessment to initiate a pre-emptive armed measure against terrorists.[64] It is submitted, however, that the replacement of imminence with gravity will not help to stabilise the discourse. Rather, more fragmentation shall be the outcome. This is because the subjectivity

62 For further details, see "The National Security Strategy of the United States".

63 Lietzau, "Old Laws, New Wars: Jus ad Bellum in the Age of Terrorism", 436–437.

64 Ibid., 439.

of comprehension can impinge upon any objective threat assessment, as there are chances that, out of the dictates of fear and past experiences, a state may interpret the gravity of an impending attack differently in comparison to a state which was never a target of such an attack.

The treaty law

Treaties can be bilateral as well as multilateral. A legal norm set down through a bilateral treaty can also be of universal recognition. However, a norm should be incorporated and endorsed by a multilateral treaty to attain the status of international law. Among them, those very treaties "which a large number of states have concluded for the purpose either of declaring their understanding of what the law is on a particular subject, or of laying down a new general rule for future conduct, or of creating some international institution" can be termed as the law-making treaties.[65] In this context, unlike customary law, a legal norm enacted through a treaty is 'particular international law'. It applies to those states which are signatories to a particular treaty.[66] Treaty law is also a distinct body of law due to its equal treatment of the parties. This is because the notion of sovereign equality remains central to the positivistic discourse marked and protected by treaties.[67] To ensure the political sovereignty and territorial integrity of states, Article 2(4) of the UN Charter provides that the states should avoid 'the threat or use of force' in their bilateral relations.[68] The entry of this norm into the UN Charter must be ascertained in the context of the history of persistent inter-state violence, as well as an attempt to invest legal authority in this collective security instrument. Moreover, the UN Charter was framed to respond to the socio-political realities of the actual world: the inherent function of any convention of legal nature. In its interpretations, therefore, as being a "convention of a constitutional nature—political considerations must be *permanently* taken into account".[69] For realising these objectives, the framers invested "very extensive powers" into the institution of the Security Council.[70]

It is also noteworthy that the treaty obligations relating to the use of force in self-defence are not much developed as compared to the rules of the actual conduct of war. This speaks of the trajectory of the positivistic discourse under the dictates of sovereignty and equality of states,[71] whereof states remain reluctant to

65 Brierly, *The Law of Nations: An Introduction to the International Law of Peace*, 46.
66 Kelsen, *Principles of International Law*, 19.
67 Michael Byers, *Custom, Power and the Power of Rules: International Relations and Customary International Law* (Cambridge: Cambridge University Press, 2003), 36.
68 The UN Charter.
69 Corten, "The Controversies Over the Customary Prohibition on the Use of Force: A Methodological Debate", 806–807. (emphasis added)
70 Franck, *Recourse to Force*, 174.
71 Philip C. Jessup, *A Modern Law of Nations: An Introduction* (New York: The Macmillan Company, 1948), 157.

entrust pressing matters and decisions of their survival to a distant authority. This state behaviour is a consistent marker in the history of nation-states. In effect, the issue of interpretation of the UN Charter "is rather as if the law were to leave to the two drivers in a motor vehicle collision the sole responsibility for apportioning liability helped only by the unruly crowd gathered around them at the scene of the accident".[72] To address this dilemma, the treaty law thus takes into account the customary legal principles of necessity and proportionality.

'Armed attack'

The Charter framework is a principal instrument that sets out conditions under which a state can resort to the use of force in self-defence. It sanctions the use of force in two exceptional circumstances: the first one is under Article 51 and the other one is in an instance of express volition granted by the Security Council. Precisely, Article 51 underlines that a state can avail the right to take up arms "if an armed attack occurs" against her.[73] This phrase embodies a *restrictive* and *qualified* sanction for the use of force. In this context, the condition sets the evidentiary limit of an 'armed attack'. Also, such an armed attack should be underway. As the lexical analysis of this phrase suggests, the use of 'present tense' in the syntax is intentional. Indeed, it aims to cover different phases of an actual armed attack.[74] In essence, it does not treat the notion of an armed attack as a past transaction. Instead, it *essentially* takes into account the coming and continuing features of harm.

The sequel of an armed attack, therefore, may involve actions of a hostile military with aggressive intentions along the border as well as physical crossing into the territory of other states. In this backdrop, however, the condition for the initiation of countermeasure needs to be judged under the given circumstances, which may vary from case to case. Ultimately, the burden of proof lies with "the alleged victim-State—of proving the existence of an armed attack if it wishes to justify any use of force in self-defence".[75] Meanwhile, stressing the importance of 'armed attack' in Article 51, legal scholars maintain that an expansive interpretation to accommodate the use of force in the absence of an armed

72 Thomas M. Franck, "Who Killed Article 2(4)? Or: Changing Norms Governing the Use of Force by States", *American Journal of International Law* 64, no. 4 (1970): 817.

73 Münch and Buske, eds., *International Law: The Essential Treaties and Other Relevant Documents*, 11.

74 Neff, *War and the Law of Nations*, 327. While on the contrary, Hellen Duffy, citing the opinion of the US delegation at San Francisco Conference, illustrates that the provision of 'if armed attack occurs' in Article 51 was in no way meant to include the act of preparation of an armed attack. Instead, the phrase denotes the right to response in an instance where 'an armed attack has occurred. Duffy, *The 'War on Terror' and the Framework of International Law* (Cambridge: Cambridge University Press, 2005), 155.

75 Bruno Simma, ed., *The Charter of the United Nations: A Commentary*, Vol. II, 3rd ed. (Oxford: Oxford University Press, 2012), 1407.

attack is "counter-textual, counter-factual and counter-logical".[76] Irrefutable evidence, therefore, is the *essence* of qualifying for the right of self-defence under the Charter framework.

'Armed attack' and the interpretive practices

In an attempt to explain the meaning of 'armed attack' in Article 51, the Court, in its judgment on the *Nicaragua* case, maintains that not only the actions of 'armed bands' against the victim state but also the aid of such groups with arms and other 'enabling means' amounts to an actual armed attack. In this context, the Court, however, underlines that the right of self-defence resides with the victim state.[77] By contrast, Judge Schwebel observed that Article 51 also permits the use of force in instances other than an 'armed attack'. The condition of an 'armed attack' is one of them, he emphasised.[78] In this decision relating to the right of self-defence, the Court attempted to locate the *threshold* of the armed attack.[79] The Court, meanwhile, failed to address the question surrounding those attacks that do not qualify as armed attacks.[80] An obvious question arises here as to what legal measures a state may avail to thwart an attack that does not fulfil the requirement of an armed attack under the Charter framework.[81] It is assumed that the right of self-defence

76 Dinstein, *War, Aggression and the Self-Defence*. 4th ed., 183–186. In its attempt to elaborate on the concept of *armed attack*, the author lays down different hypothetical scenarios, under which an armed attack begins. He concludes that the gist of the matter "is not who fired the first shot but who embarked on an apparently irreversible course of action, thereby crossing the legal Rubicon", ibid., 191. On the Contrary, Derek Bowett did not agree with those who encourage the restrictive interpretation of Article 51. He claims that any interpretation that does not take into account the traditional international law requirement of the imminence of an armed attack in applying the legal right of self-defence runs the risk of being too restrictive to serve the purpose of the Article. Bowett, *Self-Defence in International Law*, 188–189. Also, see Stanimir A. Alexrandov, *Self-Defence against the Use of Force in International Law* (The Hague: Kluwer Law International, 1996), 100.

77 *Case Concerning Military and Paramilitary Activities in and against Nicaragua*, para. 195. Stephen Neff also explains that although not expressly mentioned, the Article 2 (4) bans the use of aggressive measures, short of war (forcible reprisals), and terms it unlawful under the Charter. For further details, see Neff, *War and the Law of Nations*, 318–319.

78 Dissenting Opinion Schwebel, *Case Concerning Military and Paramilitary Activities in and against Nicaragua*, 347–348.

79 Franck, *Recourse to Force*, 63.

80 John L. Hargrove, "The Nicaragua Judgment and the Future of the Law of Force and Self-Defence", *American Journal of International Law* 81, no. 1 (1981): 139. Moreover, James Green asserts that the Court, through the adjudication of *Nicaragua* case, has made the already problematic issue more uncertain and incoherent. Green, *The International Court of Justice and Self-Defence in International Law*, p. 112.

81 ICJ Judge Simma in his separate opinion in *Oil Platforms* Case embarks on settling this nagging question. He observes:

> [O]n the use of force/self-defence aspect of the present case, there are two levels to be distinguished: there is, first, the level of 'armed attack' in the substantial, massive sense of amounting to 'une aggression arm`ee, to quote the French authentic text of Article 51. Against such

under the Charter, in its literal sense, does not comprehend any instance of lawful invocation of this right, except in an instance of 'armed attack'.[82]

The Court remained faithful to the interpretation of the 'armed attack'. As in its judgment in the *Case Concerning Armed Activities on the Territory of Congo*, it ruled that since Uganda failed to prove the attribution of the armed activities of the irregular forces to Congo, she had no right to invoke the right of self-defence in the absence of any 'armed attack'.[83] One may observe here that the Court further qualifies the 'armed attack' with the attribution to state. Judges Kooijmans and Simma, however, took a different view of the situation. They noted that even though violent non-state attacks were not attributed to the Government of Congo, the Government of Uganda had the right to act in self-defence.[84] Judge Kooijmans further added that if a state loses control over its territory to the militias and irregular armed-groups, and thereafter, if these groups perpetrate any violent attack against the neighbouring state, it will be, in effect, attributable to the host state. Such terrorist actions qualify as the contemporary phenomenon of 'international terrorism', he concluded.[85]

Besides, the dominant legal discourse on the use of force in self-defence underscores that the phrase 'armed attack' denotes a 'grave' act of use of force.[86]

> armed attacks, self-defence in its not infinite, but still considerable, variety would be justified. But we may encounter also a lower level of hostile military action, not reaching the threshold of an 'armed attack' within the meaning of Article 51of the United Nations Charter. Against such hostile acts, a State may of course defend itself, but only within a more limited range and quality of responses (the main difference being that the possibility of collective self-defence does not arise, cf. *Nicaragua*) and bound to necessity, proportionality and immediacy in time in a particularly strict way.

Separate Opinion of Judge Simma, *Case Concerning Oil Platforms*, para. 13.

82 Josef Kunz further observes that the term *attack* has 'strategic' rather than 'legal' connotation. Kunz, "Individual and Collective Self-Defence in Article 51 of the Charter of the United Nations", *American Journal of International Law* 41, no. 4 (1947): 878.

83 *Case Concerning Armed Activities on the Territory of the Congo*, 222–223 at para. 146. Moreover, the International Law Commission in its report on State Responsibility laid down the legal criteria for attributing the actions of a person or group of persons to a state; if "it is established that such person or group of persons was, in fact, acting on behalf of that State". *Yearbook of the International Law Commission*, 1980, 31.

84 Separate Opinion Judge Kooijmans, *Case Concerning Armed Activities on the Territory of the Congo,* para. 32; and Separate Opinion Judge Simma, *Case Concerning Armed Activities on the Territory of the Congo,* para. 12.

85 Separate Opinion Judge Kooijmans, *Case Concerning Armed Activities on the Territory of the Congo,* para. 30.

86 The International Law Commission, during its 30-second session, while formulating reports on State Responsibility, laid down this principle to judge the wrongfulness of an act amounting to the armed attack. For details, see *Yearbook of the International Law Commission*, 1980, 34. Also, see Simma ed., *The Charter of the United Nations: A Commentary*, 1409; James A. Green, "Self-Defence: A State of Mind for States", *Netherland International Law Review* 55, no. 02 (2008): 186; Green, *The International Court of Justice and Self-Defence in International Law,* 116. Moreover, James Green notes that even though the provision of 'grave' use of force is equated with 'armed attack' and thence with treaty law yet one cannot assume that this provision is absent in

The UN General Assembly, in its 'Definition of Aggression', laid down that the Security Council is a competent authority to assess the temporal evidence of the aggression against the fact of 'sufficient gravity'.[87] Hence, there arises a question of what amount of armed acts accounts for gravity. Is it prudent to assume that the victim state would wait for the judgment of the Security Council?[88] In contrast to this, state practice underlines that the sequel or even a small-scale border incident between two states may account for a 'grave' use of force. This, in effect, can trigger the threshold and justify the presence of prior armed attack for the lawful resort to arms in self-defence.[89] For example, the Israeli armed resolve against Hezbollah in 2006 and the Russian invasion of Georgia in 2008 were tailored around the notion of small-scale border incursions labelled as 'grave' use of force amounting to the legal requirement of the threshold of armed attack.[90] Such developments "confounded the bright line drawn by the law", which (the law) requires states to wait until an 'armed attack' occurs.[91] While states, out of self-help, may choose to resort to force in anticipation and end up violating Article 51,[92] to the contrary, those who take an expansive view of Article 51 believe that one cannot interpret it in its literal restrictive sense. As in an era of modern means of delivering lethal weaponry, a state cannot sit idle and wait for an actual armed attack to avail the right of self-defence.[93]

'Armed attack' and terrorism

Terrorist attacks on September 11, 2001, amounted to an explicit instance of 'grave' use of force. They met the threshold of self-defence in the face of an 'armed attack'.[94] And the Security Council resolutions 1368 and 1373 aptly documented it.[95] These resolutions also portrayed the level of the terrorist threat as 'a threat to international peace and security'.[96] In this context, some legal scholars claim that with the enactment of these resolutions, the prior controversies around

---

customary law. Rather, he maintains that the term finds manifestation inside customary law along with the necessity of proportionality. Green, *The International Court of Justice and Self-Defence in International Law,* 131–132.

87 UN General Assembly Resolution 3314 (XXIX), 1974.

88 For a detailed state practice after the formation of the UN and controversy over the quantification and qualification of this term, see Green, *The International Court of Justice and Self-Defence in International Law,* 116–121.

89 Simma, ed., *The Charter of the United Nations: A Commentary,* 1409–1410.

90 For details, see Green, *The International Court of Justice and Self-Defence in International Law,* 125.

91 Franck, *Recourse to Force,* 3 and 50; and Gray, *International Law and the Use of Force.* 2nd ed., 108.

92 Franck, *Recourse to Force,* 3 and 50.

93 Neff, *War and the Law of Nations,* 329.

94 Green, *The International Court of Justice and Self-Defence in International Law,* 45 and 124.

95 UN Security Council Resolutions 1368 and 1373, 2001.

96 Ibid.

the actions of terrorists and conditions of armed attack in Article 51 are settled. Now any instance of large-scale terrorist attack will 'constitute an armed attack'.[97] NATO and the OAS also subscribed to this view when they treated the terrorist attacks as an instance of 'armed attack'.[98] Perhaps one may assume that the large-scale support for resolutions ended up modifying the customary law on the use of force in self-defence.[99] In addition to this, the fact of the submission of a letter by the US Ambassador to the UN elucidating that his country may initiate armed actions against other states as well as terrorist groups also has a bearing on the law of self-defence. Presumably, this practice blurred the boundaries of self-defence and pre-emption.[100] In this context, however, it is submitted that any opinion which entertains the possibility of amendment of customs is an overstatement of facts. As in this particular situation, the Security Council has already taken action and accepted the right of self-defence.

Interestingly, the calls for legal invention relevant to the right of self-defence also resonated in the Court. Judge Kooijmans, in his Separate Opinion on the Construction of the *Israeli Wall*, mentioned that the Resolution 1373 inserted "a new element" in the interpretation of Article 51. Without attributing the terrorist attacks to any state, it ended up invoking the right of self-defence, he points out. This view finds plenty of support among legal scholars.[101] Yet some do not agree with any expansive interpretation of these resolutions. For them, these resolutions cannot be, in any reasonable way, interpreted to justify actions against 'terrorist perpetrators',[102] as the mere presence of terrorists on the territory of a certain state does not automatically allow the attacking of the other state. Any such instance of the use of force, under the guise of self-defence, is 'impressible'.[103] In this context, it is important to point out that the passive role of the Security Council beyond sanctioning the use of force in self-defence contributed to creating the prevalent 'fog of law'. Meanwhile, self-defence armed measures spread out to Pakistan, Libya, and Yemen. Therefore, while the Security Council succeeded in 'legitimating' the use

97 Michael Byres, "Terrorism, the Use of Force and International Law after 11 September", *International & Comparative Law Quarterly* 51, no. 2 (2002): 412.

98 Gray, *International Law and the Use of Force*, 159 and 165; and Natalino Ronzitti, "The Expanding Law of Self-Defence", *Journal of Conflict & Security Law* 11, no. 3 (2006): 348.

99 Byres, "Terrorism, the Use of Force and International Law after 11 September", 409 and 411.

100 Ibid., 411. Moreover, the author observes that this overstretch of the right of self-defence will create challenges of 'evidence and authority' when it comes to the question of implementation. Thus, the application of this right (pre-emptive) will lead to further contestation. For details, see ibid., 413.

101 Steven R. Ratner, "Jus ad Bellum and Jus in Bello after September 11", *American Journal of International Law* 92, no. 2 (2002): 906–907; and Christopher Greenwood, "International Law and the Pre-emptive Use of Force: Afghanistan, Al-Qaida and Iraq", *San Diego International Law Journal* 4, no. 7 (2003): 17.

102 Jordan J. Paust, "Use of Armed Attacks against Terrorists in Afghanistan, Iraq, and beyond", *Cornell International Law Journal* 35, no. 3 (2002): 533–557.

103 Ibid., 540.

of force in self-defence, it failed in 'regulating' it.[104] Indeed, it left the provision of 'armed attack' against terrorism in a state of permanent perplexity. Persistent contestation over the interpretation becomes the obvious consequence.

The inherent right of self-defence

Inside the positivistic discourse, self-defence subsisted merely as a "privilege justifying action otherwise illegal".[105] Indeed, this privilege safeguards 'certain rights' of a state party to a treaty.[106] The idea was imported from the natural law where it denotes 'natural right'. It also happened to be "an anachronistic residue from an era in which, international law was dominated by ecclesiastical doctrines".[107] Legal developments during the seventeenth and eighteenth centuries led to the incorporation of this eternal right into the corpus of international law.[108] In this context, the term 'legitimate defence' found its first expression while formulating the Treaty of Locarno in 1925, whereof the state parties agreed not to resort to war against each other but in case of a 'legitimate defence'.[109] It did get another reference, albeit implicitly, inside the Kellogg-Briand Pact later on. Here the US Secretary of State Kellogg emphasised that the right of self-defence is 'inherent'. And essentially, it is part of any treaty regulating the use of force among states. Every state is free to choose and "decide whether circumstances require the recourse to war in self-defence", he noted.[110]

The framers of the UN Charter in an attempt to address the immediate needs also paid heed to history. They peeped farther into the future before concluding that the phrase 'inherent right of self-defence' is comprehensive enough to encompass the right to initiate a war. For them, the purpose was obvious: to reconcile customary law with the treaty law.[111] Likewise, the Court, in the *Nicaragua* case, elaborated that the term *inherent* in Article 51 refers to the customary law of self-defence.[112] Legal scholars also concluded that the concept of inherent right was indeed borrowed from customary law.[113] Hence, it is a common

104 For a detailed commentary on the role of the Security Council in the post–September 11 period, see Eric P. Myjer and Nigel D. White "The Twin Towers Attack: an Unlimited Right to Self-Defence", *Journal of Conflict and Security Law*, 7, no. 1 (2002): 5–17; and Gray, *International Law and the Use of Force*. 2nd ed., 171–175.

105 Bowett, *Self-Defence in International Law*, 117–119.

106 Ibid.

107 Dinstein, *War, Aggression and the Self-Defence*, 180.

108 Ibid.

109 "Treaty of Locarno, 1925", accessed January 10, 2020, http://avalon.law.yale.edu/20th_century/locarno_001.asp

110 Neff, *War and the Law of Nations*, 304; Dinstein, *War, Aggression and the Self-Defence*. 4th ed., 180; and Bowett, *Self-Defence in International Law*, 133.

111 Bowett, *Self-Defence in International Law*, 184–185.

112 *Case Concerning Military and Paramilitary Activities in and against Nicaragua*, para.176.

113 Gupta, "The Doctrine of Pre-emptive Strike: Application and Implications during the Administration of President George W. Bush", 184. Dinstein also corresponds to this relation of

understanding that 'the modern law of self-defence was born' out of customary law.[114] Noting this fact, Simma Bruno, in his authoritative commentary of the UN Charter, also suggests that the Charter does not affect the customary right of self-defence. Instead, it puts 'particular emphasis' on it and declares its sanction in an event of 'armed attack'.[115]

The endeavour to transpose a customary right into treaty law and subject it to the qualification of an *armed attack* made its interpretation difficult for an era marked by new means and actors of warfare. To address this complexity, legal scholars emphasise that it is vital for the relevance of the right of self-defence that it "has to be an inherently relative concept".[116] It should move with the pace of the development of means of warfare. Yet one ought to take note that "there are limits to the burden which the concept of self-defence can safely, and legally, be called upon to bear".[117] In these contexts, the motive behind the invocation decision of the right of self-defence becomes an important determinative factor of the lawfulness of an armed attack.[118]

Nonetheless, one cannot downplay the fact that any just application of the right of self-defence becomes challenging due to the entry of two variables into the arena of warfare: small-scale wars involving proxy actors, operating out of the intent to surprise the state enemies, and the spread of nuclear weapons. In fact, these factors did not seek much attention from the framers, who were responding to the contemporary phenomena of warfare involving regular security forces among states.[119] Yet different organs of the UN took into account a more pragmatic view of the factual circumstances leading up to the invocation of the right of self-defence rather than sticking to the 'traditional armed attack' provision of Article 51.[120] To make it relevant, therefore, the 'inherent right of self-defence' should be interpreted within the context of its invocation while keeping in view the intentions of framers.

---

the customary law of self-defence with Article 51 of the UN Charter. For details, see Dinstein, *War, Aggression and the Self-Defence*. 4th ed., 181.

114 Byres, "Terrorism, the Use of Force and International Law after 11 September", 406.

115 Simma, ed., *The Charter of the United Nations: A Commentary*, 1404.

116 Arthur Watts, "The Importance of International Law", in *The Role of Law in International Politics*, ed. Michael Byres (Oxford: Oxford University Press, 2000), 11.

117 Ibid.

118 Bowett, *Self-Defence in International Law*, 142–143. The International Military Tribunal at Nuremberg laid down this principle by stating that the Nazi invasion of Norway during the Second World War was purely an act of aggression, devoid of legal necessity. The Nazis captured Norway not to thwart an impending Allied invasion of Norway; rather, the former attacked out of an understanding that the Allied forces may take over Norway in the future course of the war. For details, see International Military Tribunal, Nuremberg, "Judicial decisions involving Questions of International Law: Judgment and Sentences", *American Journal of International Law* 41 (1947): 172 and 205.

119 Franck, "Who Killed Article 2(4)? Or: Changing Norms Governing the Use of Force by States", 811–812.

120 Franck, *Recourse to Force*, 67.

The inherent right and interpretive practices

The Security Council applies the customary principles of necessity and proportionality to assess the use of force in self-defence. For instance, discussing the legality of the Israeli attacks against the Iraqi nuclear reactor in 1981, it deplored the Israeli actions for their failure to qualify the imminence of security threat. It termed them a breach of the Charter provisions regulating the use of force in self-defence.[121] While it did not condemn the Israeli pre-emptive attacks against Egypt and Syria in 1967, perhaps it sanctioned their permissibility implicitly. Israel, on the other hand, termed her armed acts against Syria and Egypt as the lawful invocation of the right of "anticipatory self-defence against an imminent armed attack", permitted under the Charter framework.[122] In this context, due to the fact of time constraint, it is left to the defending state to ascertain the fact that the resort to armed action is necessary. Any such decision, however, demands that the state in question shall consider the fact that its action does not "transform the self-defence into an instrument of conquest and lawlessness" and ends up making it an aggressor.[123]

The interpretive discourse is marked by *restrictionists* and *expansionists*. While being true to the literal interpretation, those who ignore the context of the application of the right of self-defence emphasise that Article 51 does not permit the resort to arms in the face of an imminent threat. For them, in this context, any other interpretation of the right of self-defence would "not suffice under Article 51".[124] They believe that the narrow interpretation of the UN Charter is a far better option in upholding the restrictions on the use of force: the primary objective of the UN Charter.[125] An expansive interpretation of the rules will lead to their

121 Ibid., 105–106.

122 Ibid., 103. Moreover, Thomas Franck underlines that neither UN Security Council nor General Assembly, explicitly, recognised the rule of pre-emptive self-defence. Yet, on factual grounds, this particular case became an almost perfect instance of the legal use of pre-emptive self-defence in the post-Charter era. For details, see Franck, *Recourse to Force*, 104–105; Neff, *War and the Law of Nations*, 329; William V. O'Brien, *The Conduct of Just and Limited War* (New York: Praeger Publishers, 1981), 133; Gray, *International Law and the Use of Force*. 2nd ed., 130; Antony Lamb, *Ethics and the Laws of War: The Moral Justification for Legal Norms* (London: Routledge, 2013), 95. To the contrary, Stanimir Alexandrov negates the stance of those, supporting this particular case as a lawful resort to war in pre-emptive self-defence. Alexandrov, *Self-Defence Against the Use of Force in International Law*, 153–154.

123 Quoted in Franz B. Schick, "The Nuremberg Trial and the International Law of the Future", *American Journal of International Law* 41, no. 4 (1947): 774.

124 Kunz, "Individual and Collective Self-Defence in Article 51 of the Charter of the United Nations", 878.

125 For a study of the detailed restrictive interpretation of Article 51, see Hans Kelsen, *The Law of the United Nations: A Critical Analysis of its Fundamental Problems* (New York: Frederick A. Praeger, 1950), 497; Jessup, *A Modern Law of Nations*, 165–166; Dinstein, *War, Aggression and the Self-Defence*, 178–181; Gideon Boas, *Public International Law: Contemporary Principles and Perspectives* (Cheltenham: Edward Elgar Publishing, 2012), 328; Quincy Wright, "The Cuban Quarantine", *American Journal of International Law* 57, no. 3 (1963): 546 and 560; Murphy, "Terrorism and the Concept of 'Armed Attack' in the Article 51 of the UN Charter", 41 and 44;

arbitrary application. They concede, however, that the final right to decide and interpret UN Charter rules rests with the state.[126] Especially in contexts of counter-terrorism, such a "burden of proof must be particularly high in the case of military action against non-state actors which are about to use conventional weapons in their attributable attack".[127]

On the other hand, those who support the idea of an *expansionist* interpretation[128] of Article 51 believe that in exceptional circumstances involving 'substantial' and 'imminent' security threats, a state may adopt the recourse to self-defence.[129] They argue that while Article 51 permits the use of force once the armed attack has occurred, it also retains the right of self-defence under the acceptable norms of customary international law going beyond the instance of an armed attack.[130] Such an interpretation was also supported by the UN in its report, 'A More Secure World: Our Shared Responsibility', prepared after the September 11 terrorist attacks.[131] It is worth mentioning here that the said report also refused to buy into the broader concept of pre-emption[132] borne out of the US National Security Strategy.[133] Some powerful states, such as Russia, Israel, France, and India, how-

---

Abdul G. Hamid, "The Legality of Anticipatory Self-Defence in the Twenty First Century Legal Order: A Re-Appraisal", *Netherland International Law Review* 54, no. 3 (2007): 441–490.

126 Simma, ed., *The Charter of the United Nations: A Commentary*, 1422; Dinstein, *War, Aggression and the Self-Defence*, 186–188; and the Secretary General, "A More Secured World: Our Shared Responsibility", United Nations, 2004, accessed January 10, 2020, http://www.un.org/en/peacebuilding/pdf/historical/hlp_more_secure_world.pdf

127 Simma, ed., *The Charter of the United Nations: A Commentary*, 1424.

128 For a detailed study of the expansionist interpretation of the right of self-defence under Article 51, see Leo Van den hole, "Anticipatory Self-Defence Under International Law", *American University International Law Review*, 19, no. 1 (2003): 69–106; Corten, "The Controversies Over the Customary Prohibition on the Use of Force: A Methodological Debate", 803–822; Abraham D. Sofaer, "On the Necessity of Pre-emption", *European Journal of International Law* 14, no. 2 (2003): 209–226; and Julius Stone, *Aggression and World Order* (Berkley: California University Press, 1958), 96.

129 Sofaer, "International Security and the Use of Force", 563; Ronzitti, "The Expanding Law of Self-Defence", 346; and Christopher Greenwood, "International Law and the Pre-emptive Use of Force: Afghanistan, Al-Qaida and Iraq", *San Diego International Law Journal* 4, no. 7 (2003): 15.

130 Oscar Schachter, "The Right of States to Use Armed Force", *Michigan Law Review*, 82, no. 5/6 (1984): 1633–1634; and Daniel Bethlehem, "Principles Relevant to a State's Right of Self-Defence against an Imminent or Actual Armed Attack by Non-State Actors", *American Journal of International Law* 106, no. 4 (2012): 773.

131 "A More Secured World: Our Shared Responsibility", 63.

132 Ibid.

133 "The National Security Strategy of the United States of America", 6. Furthermore, it underlines that the mere presence of capability, that is, weapons of mass destructions and other modern weapons, and intentions on the part of the adversary to strike the US and its interests, make her the legitimate target for the use of force, ibid. Moreover, concerning the history of policy of the US government, one finds that during 1980s the then Secretary of State George Schultz announced the 'Shultz Doctrine'. In this doctrine, he emphasised the right of pre-emptive self-defence against terrorists and states supporting and harbouring these terrorists. For further details, also see Maogoto, "New Frontiers, Old Problems: The War on Terror and the Notion of Anticipating the Enemy", 6–7.

ever, backed the US position. Incidentally, these states were also engaged in the fight against terrorists in one way or the other. In their case, it seems plausible to side with the expansive understanding of the self-defence framework. Before 2001, these states employed the right of self-defence to launch attacks inside the territory of other states, allegedly involved in aiding or abetting terrorism. For example, in 1958, the French military invaded Tunisian territory for its alleged role in supporting the Algerian rebels. Israel blamed Jordan in 1968 for helping armed attackers responsible for attacks inside the Israeli territory. In response to this, Israel pounded Jordanian military posts along their mutual borders. Likewise, Portugal invoked the right of self-defence in attacking the terrorist organisations based in Senegal during the 1960s.[134] In these contexts, however, the fact remains that to justify their acts, states do engage the legal procedures and categories of 'inherent right of self-defence' and 'necessity of self-defence'.

Security of nationals abroad

A state can be held liable for injuring the nationals of other states.[135] In case of any failure to protect its nationals, another state may employ the notion of forcible self-help when it is proven that the host state is 'unable or unwilling' to defend.[136] For example, to decide upon the extraterritorial jurisdictional issues in the *Lotus* case, the Permanent Court of International Justice (PCIJ) invoked the "passive personality" principle of law. Though it was not part of the treaty law then, it was useful in fending off non-state security threats.[137] Perhaps such a principle can be deployed to claim the right of states to use force to defend against suffering and injuries of one's citizens in another state.[138] Some legal scholars believe that it is a norm of the customary law to use force in self-defence in such circumstances. Nevertheless, it is a highly contentious issue.[139]

Concerning the state practice, from 1813 to 1927, the US used force on almost 70 occasions to protect its nationals abroad.[140] Other states also followed suit. Thus, there exists persistent state practice to use force for the protection of nationals abroad. The forcible armed interventions in Suez (1956), Lebanon (1958),

134 For further details, see Tom Ruys and Sten Verhoeven, "Attacks by Private Actors and the Right of Self-Defence", *Journal of Conflict & Security Law* 10, no. 3 (2005): 292–296.

135 David J. Gordon, "Use of Force for the Protection of Nationals Abroad: The Entebbe Incident", *Case Western Reserve Journal of International Law* 9, no. 1 (1977): 118.

136 Jessup, *A Modern Law of Nations*, 169.

137 *The Case of the S.S. 'Lotus'*, Judgement, PCIJ, 1927, p. 23. For further details, also see Rosalyn Higgins, "The General International Law of Terrorism", in *Terrorism and International Law*, ed. Rosalyn Higgins and Maurice Flory, 23–24.

138 Bowett, *Self-Defence in International Law*, 87.

139 Klabbers, *International Law*, 195–196. For further details, also see Gordon, "Use of Force for the Protection of Nationals Abroad: The Entebbe Incident", 117–119; and Anthony D'Amato, *International Law and Political Reality: Collected Papers*, Vol. 1 (The Hague: Kluwer Law International Law, 1995), 123–124.

140 Bowett, *Self-Defence in International Law*, 97.

Congo (1960), the Dominican Republic (1965), Entebbe (1976), Iran (1980), Grenada (1983), and Panama (1989) were all proclaimed as instances of the right of self-defence to protect national abroad.[141] Among these, the US interventions in Grenada and Panama invited widespread condemnations in the UN General Assembly for the use of force going far beyond the protection of nationals abroad. In the case of Panama, the armed measures ended up installing a new government. In the case of Grenada, it protected the incumbent government against an allegedly imminent socialist coup. Overall, in these contexts except Entebbe and Iran, the criteria of necessity and proportionality were put to question in most of the cases.[142]

In the case of Entebbe, a relatively legitimate case of the use of force to protect nationals abroad,[143] Israel launched a commando raid to rescue its nationals held hostage at the Entebbe Airport. As a result, Israel succeeded in rescuing her nationals in a strictly proportionate armed response. Before this armed action, the Ugandan government not only failed to discharge its duties to safeguard Israeli nationals on her territory; she was 'unwilling' to act for the safety of Israelis. Hence, Israel took it to herself and resorted to *self-help* to launch a military operation to protect her nationals, who were otherwise in 'imminent' danger of harm.[144] This case speaks of the norm of 'exceptional circumstances' to avail the right of self-defence.[145] Adherence to the proportionality of such a unilateral operation, however, does not conform to the principles of non-intervention and non-use of force outlined in Article 2(4). Yet some legal scholars maintain that a small dose of force, situated within the dictates of collateral damage[146] and aiming at the protection of nationals, does not impinge upon the sanctity of Article 2(4). No amount of compelling reasoning can be a substitute for the absence of a permanent norm in the positivist legal discourse regulating the use of force to protect nationals abroad. It is imperative thus to assess the merits of each case separately to form any conclusions.

To conclude, one may assume that a certain interpretation of the law and the right of self-defence is an elusive reality. Such elusiveness becomes further obstinate at a time when the Court and the Security Council stand apart in interpreting the laws. Yet a longer view of the discourse suggests that this disagreement is not unusual. After all, the law is all about the interpretation and argumentation of given legal content in an evolving context. Among laws, the legal rules related

141 Gray, *International Law and the Use of Force*, 126–129; and Franck, *Recourse to Force*, 76–96.

142 Gray, *International Law and the Use of Force*, 127–128.

143 Ruys, *'Armed Attacks' and Article 51 of the UN Charter: Evolutions in Customary Law and Practice*, 272.

144 Gordon, "Use of Force for the Protection of Nationals Abroad: The Entebbe Incident", 127–128. Also, see Simon Chesterman, *Just War or Just Peace?: Humanitarian Intervention and International Law* (Oxford: Oxford University Press, 2001), 75.

145 Francis A. Boyle, "International Law in Time of Crisis: From the Entebbe Case to the Hostages Convention", *Northwestern University Law Review* 75, no. 5 (1980): 783; and Alexandrov, *Self-Defence against the Use of Force in International Law*, 203.

146 Franck, *Recourse to Force*, 85.

to the use of force are the most tumultuous one. Perhaps this is because this very body of law seeks to balance out the instinct of existence and survival of states. Pre-emption which directly appeals to the instinct of survival evades a clear legal rule. Hence, states also avoid using pre-emption to denote force employment in the absence of an armed attack.[147] The primary reason is the satisfaction of necessity and proportionality criteria, which is far more difficult to prove in the case of pre-emptive self-defence than the self-defence.

Discourses in Islamic and natural laws

At times when the positivist discourse around pre-emption struggles to be coherent, the Islamic and natural law discourses reside deeper into the abyss of fragmentation. This is primarily due to their relative notional futility and doctrinal backwardness in comprehending and regulating the use of force. Likewise, the Islamic and natural law of nations remain stuck in the past and engage with the legal terrain of war more from a (religious) ideological and political perspective rather than from the standpoint of qualitative security threat perception. For instance, the Islamic law of nations treats the non-Islamic world as the 'potential enemy' and, hence, deals with the latter as such.[148] The question of the imminence of a security threat, a foundational norm in the positive legal discourse, does not have much significance in Islamic law. Though in the beginning, the message of revelations was defensive, with the rise in military prowess, however, it morphed into an offensive one.[149] God commands,

> And slay them wherever ye find them, and drive them out of the places whence they drove you out, for persecution is worse than slaughter. And Fight not with them at the Inviolable Place of Worship until they first attack you there, but if they attack you (there) then slay them. Such is the reward of disbelievers.[150]

Here the permission for war is *obvious* and *offensive* in nature and scope without any ostensible regard for temporal and spatial limits. Given the chronological order of revelations, this verse follows verse 2:190 in Qur'an, and therefore the fighting is permitted even in instances of pre-emption.[151] Such jurists believe that this permission is meant to avert the persecution of Muslim brethren in far off lands and to spread the message of Islam.[152] This command may also be interpreted as a legal justification for the security of nationals abroad.

147 Gray, *International Law and the Use of Force*, 130–132.
148 Peters, *Jihad in Medieval and Modern Islam*, 4. For further details, also see Leamann, ed., *The Qur'an: An Encyclopaedia*, 679–682.
149 Shah, "The Use of Force under Islamic Law", 346.
150 (Q. 2:191).
151 Firestone, *Jihad: The Origin of Holy War in Islam*, 55.
152 Leamann, ed., *The Qur'an: An Encyclopaedia*, 690.

In natural law, the question of pre-emption is treated within the scope of an aggressive and offensive war. In essence, it is a military expedition undertook to neutralise a security threat already set on the recourse to cause harm. Natural law, though, treats it as an evil; yet it is "a right and necessary" evil.[153] Its necessity stems out of the reason "to ward off acts of injustice and to hold enemies in check. Nor would it be possible, without these wars, for states to be maintained in peace".[154] Likewise, resorting to the use of pre-emptive force aims to "lawfully prevent an Insult which seems to threaten" a state even though the threat is not yet upon it.[155] Natural law also permits the use of force to attack an enemy who has already accumulated an excessive amount of power and expressed a motive to inflict injury.[156] In this context, one may assume that given the positivist legal reasoning, such a justification falls under the domain of an offensive war. That is why, in an attempt to divorce the history of excessive violence in the seventeenth and eighteenth centuries, positive international law restricted the use of force in pre-emption to the express intent and irreversible and tangible hostile moves of the enemy to cause harm. In contrast to this, the natural law reasoning appeals more to political justifications.

Furthermore, it is submitted that Grotius, being a *rationalist* as well as a *naturalist*, was comfortable with an expansive meaning of self-defence due to the subjective realities of the contemporary world.[157] This is because offensive wars were a common norm then. Natural law theorists developed rules to create order in an unruly world.[158] Hence, the qualitative change in the legal justifications was gradual, as the later-day theorists did not subscribe to the idea of offensive wars. Yet, when one analyses the legal reasoning supporting the continuation of a defensive war to the point where the adversary promises not to repeat past mistakes, this sort of disproportionate use of force amounts to pre-emptive self-defence.[159] In sum, one may safely assume that like Islamic law, the natural law also provides an obvious approval of pre-emption.

Summary

This chapter traced and situated the doctrine of pre-emption within the discourse(s) of positive international law. The explanations surrounding customary and treaty laws on the doctrinal contours were part of this chapter. To contextualise such

153 Scott, ed., *Selections from Three Works of Francisco Suarez*, 803.
154 Ibid., 804. For further details, also see Herfried Münkler, *The New Wars*, trans. by Patrick Camiller (Cambridge: Polity Press, 2005), 63.
155 Grotius, *The Rights of War and Peace*, Book II, 416–417.
156 Ibid., 1102.
157 Szabo, *Anticipatory Action in Self-Defense: Essence and Limits under International Law*, 51.
158 For further details, also see Benjamin Straumann, "Ancient Caesarian Lawyers in a State of Nature: Roman Tradition and Natural Rights in Hugo Grotius's De iurepraedae", *Political Theory* 34, no. 3 (2006): 331.
159 Pufendorf, *On the Duty of Man and Citizen According to Natural Law*, Book II, 168.

justificatory interpretive practices, the relevant state practice and its understanding within international institutions were also discussed. It underscored that though the doctrine of pre-emption has a different discourse, it cannot be separated from the laws of self-defence. It also highlighted the complexity as well as the existent fragmentation in understanding and interpreting the relevant laws vis-à-vis pre-emption within different legal discourses and state practices. Especially, it uncovered how the discourse has become so evasive when treating terrorist threats as security threats after the September 11 terrorist attacks.

Bibliography

Akehurst, Michael. "Custom as a Source of International Law". In *Sources of International Law*. Edited by Martti Koskenniemi, 251–260. Aldershot: Ashgate Publishing Company, 2000.

Alder, Marry C. *The Inherent Right of Self-Defence in International Law*. Dordrech: Springer, 2013.

Alexrandov, Stanimir A. *Self-Defence Against the Use of Force in International Law*. The Hague: Kluwer Law International, 1996.

Baker, Roozbeh B. "Customary International Law in the 21st Century: Old Challenges and New Debates". *European Journal of International Law* 21, no. 1 (2010): 173–204.

Bernhardt, Rüdolf. "Customary International Law". In *Encyclopaedia of Public International Law*. Vol. 7. Edited by Rüdolf Bernhardt, 61–66. Amsterdam: Elsevier Science Publishers, 1984: 61–66.

Bethlehem, Daniel. "Principles Relevant to the Scope of a State's Right of Self-Defence Against an Imminent or Actual Armed Attack by Non-State Actors". *American Journal of International Law* 106, no. 4 (2012): 770–777.

Boas, Gideon. *Public International Law: Contemporary Principles and Perspectives*. Cheltenham: Edward Elgar Publishing, 2012.

Boyle, Francis A. "International Law in Time of Crisis: From the Entebbe Case to the Hostages Convention". *Northwestern University Law Review* 75, no. 5 (1980): 769–856.

Bradford, William C. "The Duty to Defend Them: A Natural Law Justification for the Bush Doctrine of Preventive War". *Notre Dame Law Review* 79, no. 4 (2004): 1365–1492.

Brierly, James L. *The Law of Nations: An Introduction to the International Law of Peace*. Oxford: The Clarendon Press, 1928.

British and Foreign States Papers. Vol. 29, 1857.

Brownlie, Ian. *International Law and the Use of Force by States*. Oxford: Oxford University Press, 1963.

Byres, Michael. "Terrorism, the Use of Force and International Law after 11 September". *International & Comparative Law Quarterly* 51, no. 2 (2002): 401–414.

Byres, Michael. *Custom, Power and the Power of Rules: International Relations and Customary International Law*. Cambridge: Cambridge University Press, 2003.

Case Concerning Armed Activities on the Territory of Congo (Democratic Republic of Congo vs. Uganda), Judgement, ICJ Reports, 2005.

Case Concerning Military and Paramilitary Activities in and Against Nicaragua, Judgement, ICJ Report, 1986.

Case Concerning Oil Platforms (Islamic Republic of Iran vs. United States of America), Judgement, ICJ Reports, 2003.

Chatham House International Law Programme. "Principles of International Law on the Use of Force in Self-Defence". Working Paper 05/01. Royal Institute of International Affairs. 2005.

Cheng, Bin. *General Principles of Law as Applied by International Courts and Tribunals*. London: Stevens & Sons Ltd., 1953.

Chesterman, Simon. *Just War or Just Peace?: Humanitarian Intervention and International Law*. Oxford: Oxford University Press, 2001.

Corten, Olivier. "The Controversies Over the Customary Prohibition on the Use of Force: A Methodological Debate". *European Journal of International Law* 16, no. 5 (2005): 803–822.

D'Amato, Anthony A. "The Concept of Special Custom in International Law". *American Journal of International Law* 63, no. 2 (1969): 211–223.

D'Amato, Anthony A. "Trashing Customary International Law". *American Journal of International Law* 81, no. 1 (1987): 101–105.

D'Amato, Anthony. *International Law and Political Reality: Collected Papers*. Vol 1. The Hague: Kluwer Law International Law, 1995.

Dinstein, Yoram. *War, Aggression and Self-Defence*. 4th ed. Cambridge: Cambridge University Press, 2005.

Dissenting Opinion Schwebel. *Case Concerning Military and Paramilitary Activities in and Against Nicaragua*. ICJ, 1986.

Duffy, Hellen. *The 'War on Terror' and the Framework of International Law*. Cambridge: Cambridge University Press, 2005.

Fenwick, Charles G. *International Law*. 2nd ed. New York: D. Appleton-Century Company, 1934.

Firestone, Reuven. *Jihad: The Origin of Holy War in Islam*. Oxford: Oxford University Press, 1999.

Franck, Thomas M. "Who Killed Article 2(4)? Or: Changing Norms Governing the Use of Force by States". *American Journal of International Law* 64, no. 4 (1970): 809–837.

Franck, Thomas M. *Recourse to Force: State Action Against Threats and Armed Attacks*. Cambridge: Cambridge University Press, 2004.

Franck, Thomas M. "On Proportionality of Countermeasures in International Law". *American Journal of International Law* 102, no. 4 (2008): 715–767.

Gardam, Judith G. "Proportionality and Force in International Law". *American Journal of International Law* 87, no. 3 (1993): 391–413.

Gardam, Judith G. *Necessity, Proportionality and the Use of Force by States*. Cambridge: Cambridge University Press, 2004.

Goldsmith, Jack L. and Eric A. Posner. "A Theory of Customary International Law". John M. Olin Law & Economics Working Paper, no. 63. University of Chicago Law School, 1998, 1–82.

Gordon, David Jo. "Use of Force for the Protection of Nationals Abroad: The Entebbe Incident". *Case Western Reserve Journal of International Law* 9, no. 1 (1977): 117–134.

Gray, Christine. *International Law and the Use of Force*. 2nd ed. Oxford: Oxford University Press, 2004.

Green, James A. "Self-Defence: A State of Mind for States". *Netherland International Law Review* 55, no. 2 (2008): 181–206.

Green, James A. *The International Court of Justice and Self-Defence in International Law*. Oxford: Hart Publishing, 2009.

Greenwood, Christopher. "International Law and the Pre-emptive Use of Force: Afghanistan, Al-Qaida and the Iraq". *San Diego International Law Journal* 4, no. 7 (2003): 7–38.

Grotius, Hugo. *The Rights of War and Peace*. Book II. Edited by Richard Tuck. Indianapolis: Liberty Fund Inc., 2005.

Gupta, Sanjay. "The Doctrine of Pre-emptive Strike: Application and Implications during the Administration of President George W. Bush". *International Political Science Review* 29, no. 2 (2008): 181–196.

Guzman, Andrew and Timothy Meyer. "Customary International Law in the 21st Century". In *Progress in International Law*. Edited by Russell A. Miller and Rebbeca M. Bratspies, 197–218. Leiden: Martin Nijhoff Publishers, 2008.

Hamid, Abdul G. "The Legality of Anticipatory Self-Defence in the Twenty First Century Legal Order: A Re-Appraisal". *Netherland International Law Review* 54, no. 3 (2007): 441–490.

Hargrove, John L. "The Nicaragua Judgment and the Future of the Law of Force and Self-Defence". *American Journal of International Law* 81, no. 1 (1981): 135–143.

Higgins, Rosalyn. *The Development of International Law Through the Political Organs of the United Nations*. Oxford: Oxford University Press, 1963.

Higgins, Rosalyn. "The General International Law of Terrorism". In *Terrorism and International Law*. Edited by Rosalyn Higgins and Maurice Flory, 13–29. London: Routledge, 2003.

Hyde, Charles C. *International Law Chiefly as Interpreted and Applied by the United States*. Vol. 3. Boston: Little, Brown and Company, 1945.

Jennings, Robert Y. "The Caroline and McLeod Cases". *American Journal of International Law* 32, no. 1 (1938): 82–99.

Jessup, Philip C. *A Modern Law of Nations: An Introduction*. New York: The Macmillan Company, 1948.

International Military Tribunal,Nuremberg. "Judicial Decisions Involving Questions of International Law: Judgment and Sentences". *American Journal of International Law* 41, no. 1 (1947): 172–333.

Kelsen, Hans. *General Theory of Law and State*. Translated by Anders Wedberg. Cambridge: Harvard University Press, 1945.

Kelsen, Hans. *The Law of the United Nations: A Critical Analysis of its Fundamental Problems*. New York: Frederick A. Praeger, 1950.

Kelsen, Hans. *Principles of International Law*. New York: Reinehart & Company Inc., 1952.

Kennedy, David. "Images of Religion in International Legal Theory". In *Religion and International Law*. Edited by Mark W. Janis and Carolyn M. Evans, 145–153. The Hague: Kluwer Law International, 1999.

Khadduri, Majid. *War and Peace in the Law of Islam*. Baltimore: The Johns Hopkins Press, 1955.

Klabbers, Jan. *International Law*. Cambridge: Cambridge University Press, 2013.

Korowicz, Marek S. *Introduction to International Law*. The Hague: Martinus Nijhoff, 1959.

Kunz, Josef L. "Individual and Collective Self-Defence in Article 51 of the Charter of the United Nations". *American Journal of International Law* 41, no. 4 (1947): 872–879.

Kunz, Josef L. "Roberto Ago's Theory of 'Spontaneous' International Law". *American Journal of International Law* 52, no. 1 (1952): 85–90.

Kunz, Josef L. "The Nature of Customary International Law". *American Journal of International Law* 47, no. 4 (1953): 651–667.

Lamb, Antony. *Ethics and the Laws of War: The Moral Justification for Legal Norms*. London: Routledge, 2013.

Lauterpacht, Hersch. *The Development of International Law by the International Court*. Cambridge: Cambridge University Press, 1996.

Leamann, Oliver, ed. *The Qur'an: An Encyclopaedia*. London: Routledge, 2006.

Legal Consequences of a Wall in the Occupied Palestinian Territory, Advisory Opinion, ICJ Reports, 2004.

Legality of the Threat or Use of Nuclear Weapons, Advisory Opinion, ICJ Reports, 1996.

Lepard, Brian D. *Customary International Law: A New Theory with Practical Applications*. Cambridge: Cambridge University Press, 2010.

Lietzau, William K. "Old Laws, New Wars: Jus ad Bellum in an Age of Terrorism". *Max Planck United Nations Yearbook* 8 (2004): 384–455.

Lukashuk, Igor I. "Customary Norms in Contemporary International Law". In *Theory of International Law at the Threshold of the 21st Century*. Edited by Jerzy Makarczyk, 487–508. The Hague: Kluwer Law International, 1996.

Maogoto, Jackson N. "New Frontiers, Old Problems: The War on Terror and the Notion of Anticipating the Enemy". *Netherland International Law Review* 51, no. 1 (2004): 1–41.

Moore, Molly. "Chirac: Nuclear Response to Terrorism is Possible". *The Washington Post*, January 20, 2006.

Münkler, Herfried. *The New Wars*. Translated by Patrick Camiller. Cambridge: Polity Press, 2005.

Murphy, James Bernard. *The Philosophy of Positive Law*. New Haven: Yale University Press, 2005.

Murphy, James Bernard. "Habit and Convention at the Foundation of Custom". In *The Nature of Customary Law*. Edited by Amanda Perreau-Saussine and James B. Murphy, 106–155. Cambridge: Cambridge University Press, 2007.

Murphy, Sean D. "Terrorism and the Concept of 'Armed Attack' in the Article 51 of the UN Charter". *Harvard International Law Journal* 43, no. 1 (2002): 41–52.

Murphy, Sean D. "Self-Defence and the Israeli Wall Advisory Opinion: An Ipse Dixit from the ICJ"? *American Journal of International Law* 99, no. 1 (2005): 62–76.

Myjer, Eric and James White. "The Twin Towers Attack: An Unlimited Right to Self-Defence". *Journal of Conflict & Security Law* 7, no. 1 (2002): 5–17.

Neff, Stephen C. *War and the Law of Nations*. Cambridge: Cambridge University Press, 2005.

North Sea Continental Shelf Cases, Judgements, ICJ Reports, 1969.

O'Brien, William V. *The Conduct of Just and Limited War*. New York: Praeger Publishers, 1981.

Ochoa, Christiana. "The Individual and Customary International Law Formation". *Virginia Journal of International Law* 48, no. 1 (2007): 119–186.

Oppenheim, Francis L. *International Law: A Treatise*. Vol. 1. 2nd ed. London: Longman, Greens and Co., 1912.

Partsch, Karl J. "Naulilaa Arbitration". In *Encyclopaedia of Public International Law*. Vol. 3. Edited by Rüdolf Bernhardt, 373–375. Amsterdam: Elsevier Science, 1997.

Paust, Jordan J. "Self-Defense Targetings of Non-state Actors and Permissibility of U.S. Use of Drones in Pakistan". *Journal of Transnational Law & Policy*19, no. 2 (2010): 237–289.

Peters, Rudolph. *Jihad in Mediavel and Modern Islam: The Chapter on Jihad from Averroes Legal Handbook "Bidayat al-Mujtahid" and the Treatise "Koran and Fighting" by the Late Shaykh of Azhar Mahmud Shaltut*. Leiden: E.J. Brill, 1977.

Phillimore, Robert. *Commentaries upon International Law*. Vol. 1. Philadelphia: T& J. W. Johnson, 1854–1861.
President George W. Bush. *The National Security Strategy of the United States*. Washington: The White House, 2002.
Pufendorf, Samuel. *On the Duty of Man and Citizen According to Natural Law*. Book II. Translated by Michael Silverthorne. Edited by James Tully. Cambridge: Cambridge University Press, 1991.
Ratner, Steven R. "Jus ad Bellum and Jus in Bello after September 11". *American Journal of International Law* 92, no. 2 (2002): 905–921.
Roberts, Anthea E. "Traditional and Modern Approaches to Customary International Law: A Reconciliation". *American Journal of International Law* 95, no. 4 (2001): 757–791.
Ronzitti, Natalino. "The Expanding Law of Self-Defence". *Journal of Conflict & Security Law* 11, no. 3 (2006): 343–359.
Ruys, Tom and Sten Verhoeven. "Attacks by Private Actors and the Right of Self-Defence". *Journal of Conflict & Security Law* 10, no. 3 (2005): 289–320.
Ruys, Tom. *'Armed Attacks' and Article 51 of the UN Charter: Evolutions in Customary Law and Practice*. Cambridge: Cambridge University Press, 2010.
Schachter, Oscar. "The Right of States to Use Armed Force". *Michigan Law Review* 82, no. 5/6 (1984): 1620–1646.
Schick, Franz B. "The Nuremberg Trial and the International Law of the Future" *American Journal of International Law* 41, no. 4 (1947): 770–796.
Scott, James B., ed. *Selections from Three Works of Francisco Suarez*. Translated by Gwladys L. Williams, Ammi Brown, and John Waldron. Oxford: The Clarendon Press, 1944.
Separate Opinion Judge Kooijmans. *Case Concerning Armed Activities on the Territory of the Congo*. ICJ Reports, 2005.
Separate Opinion of Judge Simma. *Case Concerning Oil Platforms*. ICJ Reports, 2004.
Separate Opinion Judge Simma. *Case Concerning Armed Activities on the Territory of the Congo*. ICJ Reports, 2005.
Shah, Niaz A. "The Use of Force under Islamic Law". *European Journal of International Law* 24, no. 1 (2013): 343–365.
Shaw, Malcolm N. *International Law*. 6th ed. Cambridge: Cambridge University Press, 2008.
Simma, Bruno, ed. *The Charter of the United Nations: A Commentary*. Vol. II. 3rd ed. Oxford: Oxford University Press, 2012.
Singh, Jaswant. "Every Country has Right to Preemption". *Press Trust of India*, September 30, 2002.
Sofaer, Abraham D. "On the Necessity of Pre-emption". *European Journal of International Law* 14, no. 2 (2003): 209–226.
Sofaer, Abraham D. "International Security and the Use of Force". In *Progress in International Law*. Edited by Russell A. Miller and Rebbeca M. Bratspies, 541–570. Leidenn: Martin Nijhoff Publishers, 2008.
Steinhoff, Uwe. *On the Ethics of War and Terrorism*. New York: Oxford University Press, 2007.
Stone, Julius. *Aggression and World Order*. Berkley: California University Press, 1958.
Straumann, Benjamin. "Ancient Caesarian Lawyers in a State of Nature: Roman Tradition and Natural Rights in Hugo Grotius's De iure praedae". *Political Theory* 34, no. 3 (2006): 328–350.

Szabo, Kinga T. *Anticipatory Action in Self-Defence: Essence and Limits under International Law*. The Hague: T.M.C Asser Press, 2011.

Tasioulas, John. "Customary International law and the Quest for Global Justice". In *The Nature of Customary Law: Legal, Historical and Philosophical Perspectives*. Edited by Perreau-Saussine and James B. Murphy, 307–325. Cambridge: Cambridge University Press, 2007.

The Case of the S.S. "Lotus", Judgment, PCIJ, 1927.

The Secretary General. "A More Secured World: Our Shared Responsibility". *The United Nations*, 2004.

The Statute of the International Court of Justice. San Francisco. 1945.

Thirlway, Hugh. *The Sources of International Law*. Oxford: Oxford University Press, 2014.

Tunkin, Grigory I. "Remarks on the Juridical Nature of Customary Norms of International Law". *California Law Review* 49, no. 3 (1961): 419–430.

UN General Assembly Resolution 3314 (XXIX), 1974.

UN Security Council Resolutions 1368 and 1373.

Van den hole, Leo. "Anticipatory Self-Defence under International Law". *American University International Law Review* 19, no. 1 (2003): 69–106.

Vattel, Emer de. *The Law of Nations*. Book II. Edited by Bela Kapossy and Richard Whatmore. Indianapolis: Liberty Fund, Inc., 2008.

Villiger, Mark E. *Customary International Law and Treaties*. Dordrecht: Martinus Nijhoff Publishers, 1985.

von Münch, Ingo and Andreas Buske, eds. *International Law: The Essential Treaties and Other Relevant Documents*. Berlin: Walter de Gruyter, 1985.

Waldock, Humphrey. *General Course of Public International Law*. The Hague: Martinus Nijhoff Publishers, 1962.

Watts, Arthur. "The Importance of International Law". In *The Role of Law in International Politics*. Edited by Michael Byres, 5–16. Oxford: Oxford University Press, 2000.

Wright, Quincy. "The Cuban Quarantine". *American Journal of International Law* 57, no. 3 (1963): 546–565.

Yearbook of the International Law Commission. The International Law Commission,1980.

4 Recourse to war and the 'war on terror'

By deploying related laws and state practice, thus far, the discussions explored and explained the discourse of pre-emptive self-defence. The current chapter discusses the conceptions of harm and state responsibility, both of which serve the purpose of signposts in any recourse to the right of self-defence. With these discussions in the backdrop, the second section focuses on the specific case of the 'war on terror'. It analyses its constitutive elements as well as operational dynamics. It is hoped that it would help in understanding the legal notions of harm and state responsibility. The principal focus shall be the analysis of legal and normative discourses related to the recourse to the use of force among states.

War is a permanent feature of the human condition. No amount of qualitative change displaced it from the realm of human conduct. Concerning laws of war, international law never sought to institute war. Instead, it introduced rules and norms to regulate the circumstances of war and limit the carnage.[1] Such an attempt found different expressions in different legal discourses. In general, it marks the transition from self-preservation to self-defence. With the insertion of self-defence, the word 'war' disappeared from the treaty law. It was meant to discourage the states from creating a 'state of war' in any instance of the use of force in self-defence.[2] Also, it sought to reduce the related state practice to one that is temporary in scope and limited in scale.[3] The use of restrictive terminology also speaks of the principal objective of the UN Charter: "to save the succeeding generations from the scourge of war".[4] It is, moreover, an uncommon piece of treaty legislation on the account that it establishes a narrowly defined right of

1 John Westlake, *International Law*. Vol. 2, 2nd ed. (Cambridge: The University Press, 1910), 3.

2 Louis Henkin, "War and Terrorism: Law or Metaphor", *Santa Clara Law Review* 45 (2004–2005): 817–827. For details of different meanings and geography of war, see Dinstein, *War, Aggression and Self-Defence*, 3–20.

3 For details, see Joseph B. Kelly, "A Legal Analysis of the Changes in War", *Military Law Review* 13 (1962): 115–116; Christopher Greenwood, "The Concept of War in Modern International Law", *International & Comparative Law Quarterly* 36 (1987): 283; Nathaniel Berman, "Privileging Combat? Contemporary Conflict and the Legal Construction of War", *Columbia Journal Transnational Law* 43, no. 1 (2004): 5; Gamal M. Badr, "The Exculpatory Effect of Self-Defence in State Responsibility", *Georgia Journal of International & Comparative Law* 10, no. 1 (1980): 4–5; and Neff, *War and the Law of Nations*, 286.

4 The Preamble of the UN Charter.

self-defence as a legitimate redress for any harm. This redress in a 'narrow sense' permits a response to "the attack but going no further than that".[5] Indeed, it allows the use of force to ward off aggression but discourages a situation of a protracted war.[6] An expansive understanding of war was thus replaced by the restricted conception of self-defence.

A general discourse on war

This part discusses the *harmful act* and its *legal effect*. In this context, an act means the relinquishing of responsibility in controlling one's territory and citizens from causing harm. Such a failure causes an injury, which may invite foreign military intervention. In its legal treatment, 'war' is synonymous with an armed indulgence, involving 'intense', 'protracted', and organised violence.[7] A 'state of war' commences with a declaration to indulge in active hostilities, setting aside a 'state of peace' and replacing it with the legal fact of war, which would otherwise be illegal.[8] Acts constituting a war include the invasion of the territory of the belligerent and attack on the public forces of a state within its territory or outside of its territorial jurisdiction.[9] In this backdrop, once the fact of war is established, then only the laws governing the actual conduct of hostilities can ascertain the legality or illegality of actions between the two belligerents.[10] Over time, war became a "legal procedure for the redress of wrongs".[11] This shift in the scope of war was evident especially in the realm of laws in war during the second half of the nineteenth century. Civil wars waged against colonial rule marked this era.[12] It is assumed, however, that

> law's role in relation to war is not one of opposition but [one] of construction—the facilitation of war through the establishment of a separate legal

5 Neff, *War and the Law of Nations*, 319.

6 Ibid.

7 Ingrid Detter, *The Law of War*. 2nd ed. (Cambridge: Cambridge University Press, 2000), 3–17; Mary O'Connell, "When Is a War not a War? The Myth of the Global War on Terror", *Journal of International & Comparative Law* 12 (2006): 539; Daniel Brunstetter and Megan Braun, "From *Jus Ad Bellum* to *Jus Ad Vim*: Recalibrating Our Understanding of the Moral Use of Force", *Ethics & International Affairs* 27, no. 1 (2013): 92.

8 Quincy Wright, "Changes in the Conception of War", *American Journal of International Law* 18, no. 4 (1924): 757. To the contrary, Susan Breau and Marie Aronsson underscore that the formal declaration of war is not necessary to take the legal regime effect. Breau and Aronsson, "Drone Attacks, International Law and the Recording of Civilian Casualties of Armed Conflict", *Suffolk Transnational Law Review* 35, no. 2 (2012): 264.

9 Ibid., 756.

10 Ibid., 756–757.

11 Wright, "Changes in the Conception of War", 757; and Greenwood, "The Concept of War in Modern International Law", 284.

12 A more robust International Humanitarian Law was realised during these times. It saw the bifurcation of the Law of International Armed Conflict and the Law of non-International Armed Conflict. These new categories helped regulating the inter-state as well as intra-state conflicts.

> sphere immunizing some organized violence from normal legal sanction and, inevitably, privileging certain forms of violence at the expense of others.[13]

In customary law, a state has two legal remedies to redress the harm caused by another state: reprisal or war. It is maintained that

> [R]eprisals are a limited; war is an unlimited, violation of interests of the State against which they are directed. But reprisals, as well as war consist in forcible deprivation of life, liberty, or property of human beings belonging to the State against which these sanctions are directed.[14]

In this context, reprisals may involve "the sequestration of property" as well as other temporary forcible measures, such as bombardment.[15] It is important to mention, however, that though reprisals do not themselves constitute a war, they may lead to wars.[16] During the inter-war period, the Covenant of the League of Nations and the Kellogg-Briand Pact failed to grasp and decide upon the scope and legality of reprisals.[17] Although the UN Charter does not touch upon the issue of reprisals, it underlines that the measure of 'armed attack' is the only delict unlocking a forcible armed retaliation.[18] On the contrary, in natural law discourse measures short of physical force like economic and political interference into the domestic affairs, as well as the sphere of influence may also cause harm—punishable through armed retaliation. In these circumstances, Islamic law also permits the recourse to the use of arms under the dictates of self-preservation of Muslims.

Moreover, war is a "contest between two or more states through their armed forces".[19] It implies that an instance of 'enforcement action' by only one state does not constitute war. Sometimes, the bilateral element may not be a binding fact for a state of war and its legal effects to prevail. For example, during the Anglo-German and the Italian blockade of Venezuela in 1902, the US government questioned the limits and scope of the Pacific blockade as a unilateral forcible measure as it affected the rights of neutral states under the circumstances.[20] The condition

13 Berman, "Privileging Combat? Contemporary Conflict and the Legal Construction of War", 1.

14 Kelsen, *General Theory of Law and State*, 356; Fenwick, *International Law*, 434–435; Kelsen, *Principles of International Law*, 23–25; and Helmut Rumpf, "Is a Definition of War Necessary?" *Boston University Law Review* 18 (1938): 691–692.

15 Neff, *War and the Law of Nations*, 301.

16 Wright, "Changes in the Conception of War", 759.

17 For details, see Neff, *War and the Law of Nations*, 298–300.

18 Ibid., 318.

19 Kelsen, *Principles of International Law*, 27. Moreover, the 'essence of war' also underscores that it is an armed conflict between two groups and they do not share any 'political bond' between them. For details, see John S. Baker, Jr., "A War, Yes; Against Terror, No", *Michigan State Journal of International Law* 19, no. 1 (2010): 125.

20 Fenwick, *International Law*, 208–209. For further details of the relevant state practice, see Rumpf, "Is a Definition of War Necessary?" 688–689.

of war thus unlocks the regime of "obligations and rights of belligerents and neutrals", adherence to which makes the war a legal means to seek redress.[21]

In this context, adherence to the principle of the declaration of war and ascertainment of the fact of a state of war is not an easy task. Sometimes, states deliberately choose not to declare war in order to deny certain rights to the opposing or neutral state. For instance, during the inter-war period, Paraguay chose to declare war on Bolivia at a later stage. At the same time, it refused to concede that her prior warlike acts cast any legal impact on, that is, on the rights and obligations of, the adversary. On the other hand, Paraguay maintained that it was responding to Bolivian aggression and, therefore, the sanctions regime of the League of Nations did not apply. Bolivia, in this context, blamed the Paraguayan government for following the Machiavellian script of treachery by declaring war at a later stage so that the laws of neutrality would take effect and the landlocked Bolivia would be denied the opportunity of 'arms shipments' through the neutral states. To the sheer disappointment of Bolivia, the League decided the case in favour of the Paraguayan government.[22] Thus, the formal declaration of war does make a difference.[23]

A state of war, once initiated, can only be terminated through the enactment of a peace treaty or a formal declaration of the cessation of hostilities.[24] It implies that war is a finite fact of violence. It ought to be a continuous violent exercise to distinguish the 'state of war' from the 'state of peace'.[25] Indeed, an enemy has a 'temporal character', which expires with the termination of the exceptional legal space where a sovereign operates to prosecute her right of self-defence. For example, in the Second World War, Germany and Japan were enemies of the Allied Powers. This status slapped against Germany and Japan terminated with the end of active hostilities. Thereafter, an era of normal relations proceeded among the once declared enemies.[26] It is emphasised in this context, however, that adherence

21 Kelsen, *Principles of International Law*, 26. Likewise, Grotius also maintains that war is not a mere instance of the use of force between two entities; rather, it is a state of affairs involving plenty of authorities and actors. For details, see Grotius, *The Rights of War and Peace*, Book I, 1625.

22 Neff, *War and the Law of Nations*, 302–303. For further details on the legal impact of the declaration of war and of the mere existence of the state of war, see Philip C. Jessup, "Intermediacy", *Nordisk Tidsskrift International Ret* 23 (1953): 16–26.

23 Carl Schmitt, *Writings on War*, trans. Timothy Nunan (Cambridge: Polity Press, 2011), 31; Kelsen, *Principles of International Law*, 32; Frederic Megret, "War? Legal Semantics and the Move to Violence", *European Journal of International Law* 13, no. 2 (2002): 363; Berman, "Privileging Combat? Contemporary Conflict and the Legal Construction of War", 9.

24 Kelsen, *Principles of International Law*, 26–27. Also, see Werner Meng, "War", in *Encyclopaedia of Public International Law*, ed. Bernhardt, Vol. 4, 283–289; and Wright, "Changes in the Conception of War", 760.

25 Hew Strachan and Sybille Scheipers, eds., *The Changing Character of War* (Oxford: Oxford University Press, 2011), 10–11.

26 Paul W. Kahn, "Imagining Warfare", *European Journal of International Law* 24, no. 1 (2013): 210.

to this norm becomes even more crucial in the case of recourse to arms to pre-empt an emerging security threat.

Further on, the nature of actors is also important to determine and establish the legality of the war. The laws of war are premised "on the assumption that each party to an armed conflict has the right to participate" in violence.[27] Combatants, therefore, must consist of the armed forces of states to avail the privilege to kill.[28] So while war in self-defence is a right, it has also evolved into a complex enterprise—weighed down by the numerous obligations. Any advancements in warfighting technology as well as the nature and character of combatants ought to follow the basic legal norms.

State responsibility and the attribution of wrongful armed acts

Effective governing of territory and peoples grants legitimacy to a state in the international system. Only thence the sanctity of mutual borders shall prevail among states. In this context, state responsibility forms a foundational constitutive element of the law.[29] It enshrines the duties of a state towards other states. International legal order, therefore, manifests as an accumulative effect of the adequate performance of such obligations by states. Any negligence paves the way for redress.[30] To invoke state responsibility, however, the attribution of a particular delict to the state is a precondition.[31] A state must ensure that her nationals don't harm another state and her nationals. Harmful actions of nationals of a state can be attributed to a state in instances where nationals commit international crimes against another state with the permission or approval of the former.[32] A state is not only responsible for the actions of its legitimate organs, the conduct of which accounts for 'act of state'. Instead, it is liable for the acts of its nationals within its territory if and when such actions cause "moral and material damage".[33]

Understandably, in the case of the acts of state organs, the issue of imputation seems simple. The issue becomes complex, however, when the damage is caused by the nationals, not under the 'effective control' of the state. The Court pronounces that a state can only be held accountable for the acts of those nationals who are under her 'effective control'.[34] The International Law Commission also

27 Christopher Greenwood, "War, Terrorism, and International Law", *Current Legal Problems* 56 (2004): 528.

28 Ibid.

29 Ian Brownlie, "State Responsibility and the International Court of Justice", in *Issues of State Responsibility before International Judicial Institutions*, ed. Malgosia Fitzmaurice and Dan Sarooshi (Oxford: Hart Publishing, 2004), 12.

30 "Draft Articles on the Responsibility of States for Internationally Wrongful Acts", *Yearbook of International Law Commission*, 1980, Article, 42.

31 Ibid., Article, 2.

32 Vattel, *The Law of Nations*, Book III, 469.

33 Kelsen, *General Theory of Law and State*, 359.

34 *Case Concerning Military and Paramilitary Activities in and against Nicaragua*, 64–65 at para. 115. Herein, the Court maintained that the mere fact of providing weapons and training to the

maintains that a state can only be held responsible for those acts committed under her 'direction or control'.[35] So any wrongful action can be attributed to a state if an organ of the state was controlling the operation or was its 'integral part'.[36] In the absence of any direct link and control over the action, a state cannot be held liable for the harm, even though, in this context, armed attacks are originating from its territory. In this situation, nevertheless, the state would be responsible for her failure to stop terrorists from committing harm and not for the injury.[37] However, if a state is found guilty of collaboration, then she carries the blame for the authorship of harmful acts. She can, in this context, "even become the direct target of forcible action in self-defence".[38] The Commission, however, elucidates that due to the fact of control over a portion of territory and declaration of the formation of a new state, the acts of an insurrectional group may not be attributed to the state.[39] Some legal scholars, however, maintain that a cross-border insurrection by a terrorist group operating in bordering areas can, in fact, invoke state responsibility since the victim state may read the presence of terrorists as an instance of the failure of the host state's agents to safeguard her interest. Thus, the victim state could attribute the act of violating mutual territorial borders to the host state. Weaker states fall victim to this violation more often.[40]

State responsibility and adjudicative practices

It is important to note that there lies a deep chasm between state responsibility for harmful acts in general and state responsibility for acts, which may invite the use of force. For example, the Court in the *Nicaragua* case was categorical that the provision of arms, logistical support, and guidance by the US to the non-state armed group (Contras) amounts to a violation of the obligations of non-use of force and non-interference in the domestic affairs of other states.[41] The Court,

---

extra-state entities by a state does not implicate the state for the harmful acts. For further details, see Ibid., pp. 62–63 at para. 109–112.

35 "Draft Articles on the Responsibility of States for Internationally Wrongful Acts", *Yearbook of International Law Commission*, 1980, Article, 8. For further details, see Crawford, *Brownlie's Principles of Public International Law*, 542–547.

36 Luigi Condorelli, "The Imputability to States of Acts of International Terrorism", *Israel Yearbook on Human Rights* 19 (1989): 233.

37 Tal Becker, *Terrorism and the State: Rethinking the Rules of State Responsibility* (Oregon: Hart Publishing, 2006), 3.

38 Ibid., 3; and Rosalyn Higgins, "Issues of State Responsibility before the International Court of Justice", in *Issues of State Responsibility before International Judicial Institutions*, ed. in Malgosia Fitzmaurice and Dan Sarooshi (Oxford: Hart Publishing, 2004), 1–2.

39 "Draft Articles on the Responsibility of States for Internationally Wrongful Acts", *Yearbook of International Law Commission*, 1980, Articles 9 and 10. For further details, also see Rüdiger Wolfrum, "International Wrongful Acts", in *Encyclopaedia of Public International Law*, ed. Bernhardt, Vol. 10, 271–276.

40 Becker, *Terrorism and the State: Rethinking the Rules of State Responsibility*, 77.

41 *Case Concerning Military and Paramilitary Activities in and against Nicaragua*, 118–119 at paras. 227–228.

however, stopped short of invoking any direct US responsibility for the armed actions of Contras.[42] In the *Oil Platform* case, likewise, the Court laid down that in the absence of any clear link between the state and wrongful armed acts attributed to it, the right of self-defence cannot be invoked. It conceded though that the US ships and flagged vessels suffered losses in international waters. Without establishing evidentiarily that Iran was involved in these attacks, the US government has no right to use force in self-defence against Iran.[43] Further on, to uphold this principle the Court ruled in the *Armed Activities* case that Uganda cannot lawfully invoke the right of self-defence against Congo, at a time when Uganda failed to prove that the armed actions of rebels are attributable to the Congolese government.[44] Here we see that the Court was persistent that without the attribution of harm, there cannot be any claim of forcible counter-armed measures against a state.

In addition to the attribution, state responsibility is also assessed through the criteria of the magnitude of the use of force or the 'gravity of attack'. As the Court laid down in the *Nicaragua* case that a state can be held liable for support to a harmful act only if the link between the state and the violent non-state group (terrorist) is strong and the gravity of violence amounts to an 'armed attack'.[45] Likewise, in the *Oil Platforms* case, the Court asserted that a state cannot claim the right of self-defence in the absence of gravity of the attack.[46] The Commission also subscribes to this principle and notes that only a grave violation of obligation constitutes an armed response. Without establishing the gravity, the wrongfulness of an act cannot be fixed.[47] It is noted that judgements and lines of arguments of the Commission and the Court remain consistent—rather, they supplement each other.[48]

To establish the broader contours of state responsibility, in the *Corfu Channel* case, the Court illustrated the mere fact of control over territory does not make a state liable for the armed actions of miscreants. However, the Court suggested that a state must ensure that its territory, with its knowledge, is not used in violating the rights of other states.[49] In this context, although the Court did not hold

42 Ibid., 61–65 at paras. 109–116.

43 *Case Concerning Oil Platforms*, 33, paras. 61–62.

44 *Case Concerning Armed Activities on the Territory of Congo*, at paras. 146–147.

45 *Case Concerning Military and Paramilitary Activities in and against Nicaragua*, 110 at paras. 210–211. For a detailed analysis of this case and relevant discussions, see Byres, "Terrorism, the Use of Force and International Law after 11 September", 408; and I.M. Lobo De Souza, "Revisiting the Right of Self-Defence against Non-State Armed Entities", *The Canadian Yearbook of International Law* 53 (2015): 9–10.

46 *Case Concerning Oil Platforms*, 33 at para. 62.

47 "Draft Articles on the Responsibility of States for Internationally Wrongful Acts", Article 21.

48 For a detailed analysis, see Christian J. Tams, "Law-making in Complex Processes: The World Court and the Modern Law of State Responsibility", in *Sovereignty, Statehood and State Responsibility: Essays in Honour of James Crawford*, ed. Christine Chinkin and Freya Baetens (Cambridge: Cambridge University Press, 2015), 297–306.

49 *The Corfu Channel Case*, 18 and 22.

Albania directly responsible for the damages caused to the British Naval Ships by sea mines, it did invoke the principle of 'shared responsibility' to hold Albania accountable for the damages.[50] In this backdrop, it is submitted that the mere presence of terrorists does not authorise a state to use force in self-defence against the host state.[51] Such acts of nationals, however, become a liability, which gets state endorsement *post facto*. For example, after the US embassy took over, statements of the Iranian authorities endorsing the acts of the hostage-takers effectively led to holding the state liable for the actions of her nationals.[52]

International Criminal Tribunal for the former Yugoslavia (ICTY), however, in this backdrop of consistent interpretations of state responsibility, chose to take a different view. During the *Tadic* case before the Appeals Chamber, the prosecution argued for linking the individual criminality to the state. The prosecution proposed that a test of 'effective control' is too narrow to apply. It must be replaced with the 'demonstrable link' criterion of IHL.[53] The Appeals Chamber did buy into this argument and took exception to the decision of the Trials Chamber, and also differed with the conception of state responsibility set inside the *Nicaragua* case. The Appeals Chamber stressed upon the fact that every case has a distinct factual background. It is legally imprudent, therefore, to invoke one decision repeatedly for deciding all the cases of state responsibility. It ruled that under the circumstances of the current case, it is the opinion of the Chamber that 'overall control' test is more appropriate to fix state responsibility.[54] Though this was a remarkable jurisprudential shift, it did not go too far in the practices of courts, as the Court took exception to the calls for application of lax criterion to decide upon state responsibility. In its judgment on the *Case Concerning Application of the Convention on the Prevention and Punishment of the Crime of Genocide* (Bosnia and Herzegovina vs. Serbia and Montenegro), the Court asserted that any relaxation in the test of 'effective control' does not conform to the customary law. It is "unsuitable, for it stretches too far, almost to [a] breaking point, the connection which must exist between the conduct of a state's organs and its international responsibility", the Court further added.[55] Thus, it is maintained that though all

50 Andre Gattini, "Breach of International Obligations", in *Principles of Shared Responsibility in International Law: An Appraisal of the State of the Art*, ed. Andre Nollkaemper and Ilias Plakokefalos (Cambridge: Cambridge University Press, 2014), 39.

51 Megret, "War? Legal Semantics and the Move to Violence", 383–384.

52 *United States Diplomatic and Consular Staff in Tehran* (United States of America vs. Iran), ICJ Reports, 1980, 3 at paras. 31–34. For further details of this case, see Becker, *Terrorism and the State: Rethinking the Rules of State Responsibility*, 73–74.

53 *State Prosecutor vs. Dusko Tadic*, case IT-94-1-A, Appeals Trial Judgment, ICTY, 1999, 31–32, paras. 70–72.

54 Ibid., 47–51 at paras. 115–123.

55 *Case Concerning Application of the Convention on the Prevention and Punishment of the Crime of Genocide* (Bosnia and Herzegovina vs. Serbia and Montenegro), Judgement, ICJ Reports, 2007, 171 at para. 406. Meanwhile, there are international law scholars who oppose such an entrenched approach on the part of ICJ. For details, see Cassese, *International Law*, 247–250; Antonio Cassese, "The Nicaragua and Tadic Tests Revisited in Light of the ICJ Judgment on Genocide in Bos-

these cases are based on different factual circumstances, they speak to the centrality of certain basic principles to the determination of state responsibility.

Nevertheless, a state cannot be fully absolved of the actions of non-state violent elements on its territory. It is true, however, that there can be different layers of causation linking the state and non-state violent elements. And not every case of forfeiting of state responsibility gives rise to the use of force in self-defence. However, finding a balance between the obligations and rights of states poses a serious challenge. Such a challenge becomes even more serious in situations involving the use of force between non-state violent actors and states. In this context, the issue of ascertaining the lawfulness of an armed action demands legal scrutiny on two different and mutually exclusive planes: First, the question of fixing the state responsibility for the delict, and, secondly, to assess the gravity of the prior armed act, and its relevance to the 'armed attack' provision of the UN Charter framework.

Likewise, to assess the fact of attributability also poses a challenge in an environment where the violent non-state actors are operating globally through their amorphous structures and shadowy networks of persons belonging to different states. To exhibit violence, they pass through various states and seek assistance from their members spread across numerous states. In this backdrop, it is argued that since the state claims and also "is the recognized organ of international discourse, it must bear that measure of international responsibility which corresponds to its real control, regardless of the names chosen for it".[56] In addition, since any state shall abhor the idea of its representation by the violent non-state actors, they must ensure 'effective control' over its territorial jurisdiction and the people living within it. Moreover, given the fact that state responsibility is an effect of attribution,[57] the fulfilment of this precondition for launching a pre-emptive attack against the adversary poses a complex challenge, as the time constraint can exact a heavy price for the one waiting too long to meet the legal formalities of state responsibility for a harmful act.

State complicity for internationally wrongful acts

Fixing the role of a state in the wrongful acts of its nationals is a complex task.[58] As explained above, the Court always took a conservative view and applied tough standards to attribute violent acts to the state. However, the UN Security Council

nia", *European Journal of International Law* 18, no. 4 (2007): 649–668; and Nicholas Tsagourias, "Self-Defence against Non-State Actors: The Interaction between Self-defence as a Primary Rule and Self-Defence as Secondary Rule", *Leiden Journal of International Law* 29, no. 3 (2016): 805–808.

56 Wolfgang Friedman, "The Growth of State Control over the Individual and its Effect upon the Rules of International State Responsibility", *British Yearbook of International Law* 19 (1938): 118 and 144.

57 David Kennedy, *Of War and Law* (Princeton: Princeton University Press, 2006), 153.

58 Miles Jackson, *Complicity in International Law* (Oxford: Oxford University Press, 2015), 125.

took exception to this prevalent understanding after the September 11 terrorist attacks and set down standards for states to meet their obligations to fight terrorism.[59] The Commission also revisited the provisions of state responsibility after 2001. It elaborated that a state can be *indirectly* responsible for internationally wrongful acts in circumstances relating to the aiding or abetting of wrongful acts.[60] Besides, there is an emerging state practice of finding the state complicit in its failure to stop violent actors from using its territory, whereof the Bush administration was more vocal than anyone else when it suggested that the US should give the same treatment to supporters as to terrorists.[61] To follow through its change of mind, the US launched the 'war on terror' across multiple states. Israel also followed this policy by killing Palestinian policemen at a West Bank security check post for their failure to stop Palestinian assailants who killed Israeli citizens.[62] Can this state practice create a coherent customary law norm of state complicity for violent acts of its nationals operating within its territory?

State complicity is a derivative rule of state responsibility. When studied in conjunction with the rule of neutrality of states, such a derivative character becomes clearer. For example, Article 2(5) of the UN Charter prohibits states from assisting a state against which the world body has already initiated a "preventive or enforcement action".[63] In this context, it becomes easier to fix state complicity for any violation of obligations. Complexity, however, arises in the case of a nexus between violent non-state elements and states.[64] For example, it is easy to hold a state responsible for forfeiting her obligations in instances of direct support and control of violent non-state actors. Whereas in the absence of any direct relationship, a state may still be complicit in wrongful acts because of her failure to prevent such acts and causing injury.[65] Such a normative understanding is evident in the context of the contemporary state practice of counter-terrorism. With or without the evidence of state support, states like the US, France, Britain, Russian, and Israel mount frequent counter-attacks to curb violent non-state activities on the territory of other states.

Furthermore, with no direct normative relation between state complicity and positive international law, the consonant context of domestic criminal law may lend a framework to explain and understand this norm. In criminal law, a person

59 For details, see UN Security Council Resolution 1373 (2001) and UN General Assembly Resolution 2625 (XXV), 1970.

60 "Draft Articles on Responsibility of State for Internationally Wrongful Acts, with Commentaries", *Yearbook of International Law Commission*, 2001, 65–67. For further details, also see Jackson, *Complicity in International Law*, 147–150.

61 The United Nations General Assembly, "Statement of the President George W. Bush", 56th Session, New York, November 10, 2001.

62 Jane Bennet, "Israel steps up Counter Strikes; 22 Palestinians slain", *The New York Times*, February 21, 2002.

63 For details, see Article 2 (5) of the UN Charter.

64 Tal Becker, *Terrorism and the State: Rethinking the Rules of State Responsibility* (Oxford: Hart Publishing, 2006), 19.

65 Ibid., 3.

with the authority to stop and curb wrongful acts is held responsible for any negligence. Similarly, a state by dent of its legal personality can be held responsible for any failure or consent to the commissioning of any wrongful terrorist act against other states.[66] Even any toleration of terrorists in one's territorial jurisdiction who subsequently perpetrate violence against another state may give rise to indirect belligerence.[67] Many instances of the use of force between Israel and Lebanon during the 1960s and 1980s are cases in point here, whereof even without any clear link between the Palestine Liberation Organization (PLO) and the Lebanese government, Israel launched military operations in Lebanon to kill and capture those PLO members allegedly involved in harming security interests of Israel.[68]

In these contexts, when state responsibility receives a more categorical appreciation inside the positivistic discourse, the status of state complicity to determine the *fact* of injury is somewhat unsettled. This is because of the fact that subsidiary principles informing the coherent criterion for the application of the state complicity framework for addressing any delict are missing. Nonetheless, one may note that the emerging treaty and customary obligations to curb terrorism compel states to meet higher standards of control over the territory. It is more evident in the post–September 11 times when victim states have dearly realised the costs of inaction against terrorist threats. In these circumstances, the attributed causal and demonstrable link between a security threat and the territory of a state unlocks the remedial recourse.

The frame of the 'war on terror'

State violence in self-defence is a measure to repel an impending attack or avenge an injury. The armed forces and critical infrastructure of the enemy state are targets of such violence. In contrast to this, terrorist violence, in its theoretical conception and character, is mostly directed against civilians. The killing of a maximum number of civilians determines its success. A loss of no substantial number of civilian lives denotes the failure of a terror attack.[69] For terrorists, the intended killing of civilians, moreover, is a *means* to achieve certain *ends*, especially striking fear among civilians.[70] Targeting and killing of civilians in terrorist violence pose a serious challenge to state security. Religiously induced terrorist violence,

66 Ibid., 174–176. Meanwhile, Bernhard Graefrath maintains that complicity denotes a separate and distinct category of wrongful acts. He suggests that while drawing analogies between criminal law and international law, one should not mix them together. Graefrath, "Complicity in the Law of International Responsibility", *Revue Belge De Droit International* 2 (1996): 371–372.

67 Kelsen, *Principles of International Law*, 62–63 (emphasis added) Also, see MacDougal and Feliciano, *Law and Minimum World Public Order*, 192; and Rosalyn Higgins, "Legal Limits to the Use of Force by Sovereign States: United Nations Practice", *British Yearbook of International Law* 37 (1961): 278.

68 For details of the relevant state practice, see Becker, *Terrorism and the State: Rethinking the Rules of State Responsibility*, 191–208.

69 Steinhoff, *On the Ethics of War and Terrorism*, 37.

70 Ibid., 38.

however, renders the violence even deadlier. Indeed, "it is the zeal which nurtures the propensity for apocalypse",[71] as Al-Qaeda terrorism "makes the identification of [the] opponent and any realistic assessment of the danger impossible. This intangibility is what lends terrorism a new quality".[72]

Furthermore, terrorists, unlike state actors, do not abide by the principle of concluding a violent campaign within a certain time frame. They prefer to launch violent attacks again and again.[73] In addition, they do not seek any direct military confrontations. They launch sporadic attacks against soft targets, inviting excessive military responses over an extended period of time.[74] Terrorists, moreover, not only threaten the security of states; they also pose a danger to the safety of one's nationals abroad. Any conflict with the terrorists, therefore, is assumed to undermine the temporal and geographical dimensions of violent conflict, which, in turn, makes it difficult to curb terrorism within a given timeframe. In this situation, it is possible that while living in times of democracy and the rule of law, we may also 'live in an age of terror' for longer periods of time.[75]

The conflict between Al-Qaeda and the US embodies the traditional traits of terrorist violence. Since the late 1990s, Al-Qaeda carried out sporadic attacks against the US interests and nationals abroad. This violent exchange peaked on September 11, 2001, when it targeted both military and civilian installations with uncommon ease. These attacks killed "five times of as many Americans as the total number of people killed during the last three decades of terrorism activities" combined.[76] The gravity, as well as the scale, of the damage was not, in any meaningful way, less than the destruction of any single blow in an inter-state conflict. The loss of lives was more than the Japanese attack on Pearl Harbour. Indeed, this savagery of violence left the US horrified. In its initial shock response, the US government denounced the efficacy of international law as a regulatory framework. She labelled contemporary times as an era of no rules.[77] Thus ensued a regime of legal, political, and security counter-measures popularly known as the 'war on terror'.

Constitutive elements

In its response, the UN Security Council invoked the right to use force under Article 51 against terrorists.[78] Labelling the attack as an instance of 'armed attack',

71 Ian Ward, "God, Terror and Law", *Oxford Journal of Legal Studies* 28, no. 4 (2008): 783.

72 Borradari, *Philosophy in a Time of Terror: Dialogues with Jürgen Habermas and Jacques Derrida*, 29.

73 Ibid., 120.

74 Wouter G. Werner, "The Changing Face of Enmity: Carl Schmitt's International Theory and the Evolution of the Legal Concept of War", *International Theory* 2, no. 3 (2010): 363.

75 Ward, "God, Terror and Law", 784.

76 Talbott and Chanda, eds., *The Age of Terror: America and the World after September 11*, x.

77 For details, see Ian Ward, *Law, Text, Terror* (Cambridge: Cambridge University Press, 2009), 10–11; Jack Goldsmith, *The Terror Presidency: Law and Judgement Inside the Bush Administration* (New York: W.W. Norton & Company, 2007), 74–75; and Harold H. Koh, "The Spirit of the Laws", *Harvard Journal of International Law* 43, no. 1 (2002): 23.

78 Berman, "Privileging Combat? Contemporary Conflict and the Legal Construction of War", 32.

the UN Security Council did not *directly* blame any state for the attack.[79] Instead, the responsibility was fixed on Al-Qaeda and its affiliated groups. The right to self-defence under the said Article involves two dimensions: first, to ascertain *against whom* the force will be applied and, second, to decide *whether* the above-mentioned condition of 'armed attack' was met.[80] To contextualise the permission to use force in self-defence, the UN Security Council in a separate Resolution 1378 blamed the Taliban regime in Afghanistan for harbouring Al-Qaeda, and for remaining tolerant towards its terrorist activities.[81] Likewise, the UN Security Council had earlier passed resolutions 1267 (1999) and 1333 (2000) demanding the closure of Al-Qaeda terrorist training camps in Afghanistan and the handing over of the Al-Qaeda leadership to a relevant international body. To frame these charges, the UN Security Council nowhere addressed the question of 'effective control' of the Taliban regime over Al-Qaeda. It relied on the criteria of tangible material and ideological links between the two entities.

In these contexts, however, it is important to note that the UN Security Council *apparently* attributed the responsibility for terrorist attacks against the US to Afghanistan, but not beyond that.[82] Harold Koh, who later joined the Obama administration in 2002, proposed that the US must seek UN Security Council approval for the use of force against terrorist targets located outside Afghanistan.[83] Yet it is also noteworthy that these resolutions invoked Chapter VII of the UN Security Council mandate while characterising the threat of terrorism as an international security threat. However, one ought to take note that the UN Security Council resolutions do not embrace an *element of automation* for applying wilfully in case of any security threat or failure of a state to meet its obligations under these resolutions. Moreover, these resolutions can also not be read along the domestic constitutive *doctrines* and *principles* of national security to address international security threats.[84]

79 Eric A. Heinze, "The Evolution of the International Law in the Light of the 'Global War on Terror'", *Review of International Studies* 37, no. 3 (2011): 1080.

80 Heinze, "The Evolution of the International Law in the Light of the 'Global War on Terror'", 1080 (emphasis added).

81 UN Security Council Resolution 1378. Also, see Sonja Cenic, "State Responsibility and Self-Defence in International Law Post 9/11: Has the Scope of Article 51 of the United Nations Charter been Widened as a Result of the US Response to 9/11?" *Australian International Law Journal* 14 (2007): 202.

82 Remarks by Marry E. O'Connell, "Rise of the Drones II: Unmanned Systems and the Future of War", hearing before the Subcommittee on National Security and Foreign Affairs, Committee on Oversight and Government Reforms, House of Representatives, 111th Congress, 2nd Session, Serial No. 111–120 (April 28, 2010), 50, accessed January 10, 2020, http://www.fdsys.gov; Franck, *Recourse to Force*, 66; and Rosa Brooks, "Drones and the International Rule of Law", *Ethics & International Affairs* 28, no. 1 (2014): 91. In the similar vein, in a letter to the President of the Council on October 7, 2001, permanent representative of the US maintained that the attacks on his country were made possible by the permission of Taliban regime in Afghanistan to Al-Qaeda to operate in its territory. For details, see *Letter from the Permanent UN Representative of the United States to the President of the UN Security Council*, October 7, 2001, UN Doc. S/2001/946.

83 Koh, "The Spirit of the Laws", 25.

84 Benedetto Conforti, *The Law and Practice of the United Nations*. 3rd ed. (Leiden: Martinus Nijhoff Publishers, 2005), 12–13. Meanwhile, Michael Doyle underlines that the resolutions of the UN

Besides the reference to the right of self-defence in these resolutions is a crucial move. Normally, the UN Security Council refrains from invoking this right.[85] Such an interpretation of Article 51 set a novel practice.[86] Subsequently, it found resonance on numerous occasions. In November 2015, the French government to respond to the Islamic State terrorist attacks invoked the right of self-defence. This invocation got the endorsement of the European states under the 'mutual defence' provision of the Treaty of the European Union.[87] After terrorist attacks in Brussels in 2016, Belgium also invoked her right to self-defence against terrorists under Article 51. Concerning this emerging state practice to invoke the right of self-defence against terrorism, one may also keep in view the interpretive practices of the Court. Indeed, legal interpretations of the Court carry weight as it is a legal instrument making *post facto* legal judgments in a given instance of the use of force among states. And thus, it is *the* competent body to set legal precedents.

Yet some legal scholars maintain that a close reading of resolutions 1368 and 1373 suggests that they did not *specifically* invoke the right of self-defence. Instead, these resolutions mention such an invocation in the preamble in rather 'abstract terms'. Besides, there is no mention of 'all necessary measures', which is a permanent feature of the resolutions authorising the use of force in self-defence.[88] So the language, circumstances, and the UN Charter provisions under which the Resolution 1373 was adopted cannot be interpreted to intercept future terrorist attacks.[89] As with the enactment of these resolutions, the UN Security Council did not seek to "dispose of the issue once for all, and the picture that emerges is more that of a Council stumbling in the dark".[90] Furthermore, the issue of the fixing of 'state responsibility' beyond Afghanistan remains unsettled.[91] It is submitted therefore that the legal mandate of the 'war on terror' embodies an *implicit geographical* element.

Security Council when passed under Chapter VII entails binding norms, and therefore, such resolutions needed to be heeded. For details, see Doyle, *Striking First*, 62–63.

85 Gray, *International Law and the Use of Force*, 165.

86 Stahn, "Terrorist Acts as 'Armed Attack': The Right to Self-Defence, Article 51 (1/2) of the UN Charter, and International Terrorism", 51.

87 De Souza, "Revisiting the Right of Self-Defence against Non-State Armed Entities", 21.

88 Megret, "War? Legal Semantics and the Move to Violence", 374; Amos, O. Enabulale, "Use of Force by International/Regional Non-State Actors: No Armed Attack, No Self-Defence", *European Journal of Law Reform* 12, no. 3–4 (2010): 217–218; and Rob Mclaughlin, "The Legal Regime Applicable to Use of Lethal Force When Operating under a United Nations Security Council Chapter VII Mandate Authorising 'All Necessary Means'", *Journal of Conflict & Security Law* 12, no. 3 (2008): 389–417.

89 Byres, "Terrorism, the Use of Force and International Law after 11 September", 402.

90 Megret, "War? Legal Semantics and the Move to Violence", 375; and Henkin, "War and Terrorism: Law or Metaphor", 824–825.

91 Alex Conte, "The War on Terror: Self-Defence or Aggression?" in *The Challenge of Conflict: International Law Responds*, ed. Ustinia Dolgopol and Judith Gardam (Leiden: Martin Nijhoff Publishers, 2006), 410–411.

One can safely conclude that the right of self-defence gets different interpretative treatments in the Court and the UN Security Council. Perhaps it is because of the mandate and orientation of the two institutions, whereof the Council "is an executive organ, not a legislature",[92] while the Court is not a legislature. The Court has been reluctant to set the tangible threshold for the 'armed attack' under Article 51. The Security Council failed to assess the *post facto* use of force against the set norms. Hence, given the cautiousness of the one and boldness of the other, the 'war on terror' continues unsettling the law of war among states.[93]

Operational dynamics

'Temporal paradox' was also an outcome of the 'war on terror'. As the US is not only waging war against a perpetrated attack rather but also willing to disrupt an enemy who may intend to threaten security in future.[94] The battlespace is simultaneously local and global, impinging upon the *linear* characteristic of the war.[95] For the US, the disregard for the battlespace helped to achieve the military objectives, as, under such circumstances, the US can avail 'the privilege to kill' globally.[96] As a result, "destabilization of the legal construction of war as a separate sphere" by both adversaries "have not (only) sought to conflate the distinction between war and not-war; but rather, to deploy the two rubrics' categories and practices for strategic effect".[97] Conversely, it is undermining the "international law's few long-standing and self-explanatory prohibitions".[98] Among these, territorial sovereignty is the paramount one.

Conventionally, the use of force against states in exercising the right of self-defence is permissible. The UN Security Council, after the September 11 attacks, invoked the right of self-defence against a non-state entity and social phenomena. It did not mention the names of the guilty states. In effect, it created an exception by sanctioning the use of force against a social phenomenon: terrorism. The choice of the term 'war' by the US to denote a campaign against terrorism underlines that she is intended to take armed action against states harbouring terrorists.[99] Apparently, through this choice, the US ended up relaxing the principle of 'state responsibility',[100] as concerning the state responsibility framework,

92 Derek Bowett, "The Impact of Security Council Decisions on Dispute Settlement Procedures", *European Journal of International Law* 5, no. 1 (1994): 93.

93 Koh, "The Spirit of the Laws", 23.

94 Megret, "War? Legal Semantics and the Move to Violence", 376–377.

95 Kennedy, *Of War and Law*, 112–113; and Berman, "Privileging Combat? Contemporary Conflict and the Legal Construction of War", 33.

96 Kennedy, *Of War and Law*, 121.

97 Berman, "Privileging Combat? Contemporary Conflict and the Legal Construction of War", 37.

98 Megret, "War? Legal Semantics and the Move to Violence", 377; and Kennedy, *Of War and Law*, 123.

99 Megret, "War? Legal Semantics and the Move to Violence", 380.

100 For a detailed discussion, see Derek Jinks, "State Responsibility for the Acts of Private Armed Groups", *Chicago Journal of International Law* 4, no. 1 (2003): 83–95; Rene Värk, "State

the usage of the phrase 'war on terror' helps to shift the burden of responsibility to the targeted state. Since this war is in response to an act of terrorism, it will be against those responsible for this act, directly or indirectly. Conversely, the era marked by state-led armed action against terrorism ushered in a "regime of non-state responsibility", which led to "the expansion of the right of self-defence under international law".[101] However, the right of state sovereignty and obligation of state responsibility for injury set down limits. War, as a lawful delict of state sovereignty, is permitted once state responsibility for prior 'armed attack' is established.

As a trend, states may rely less on the customary legal principle of the necessity of self-defence and rather readily invoke Article 51 to justify the use of force against terrorists.[102] The mere presence of terrorists in her territory may leave a state liable. Also, earlier the idea of a *qualified* enemy was central to the conception of war. Whereas concerning the 'war on terror', where the war is not between armed forces, the idea of the enemy becomes problematic.[103] Furthermore, technological advancement (drone warfare) also contributed to reducing an enemy to a discreet entity. Due to their absence from the battlefield, drone operators become faceless. Thus, new methods and actors challenge the established norms and values of the war.[104]

One may construe, thus, that the contemporary age is not that much a product of terror. Instead, it is the result of political 'misspeak',[105] and even of the political loud speak with legal ramifications. In this context, divisions between politics and law have become tenuous. Terrorism, as well as counter-terrorism, is endangering the fundamental principles of the rule of law.[106] Perhaps the former US President Bush was prescient as he announced soon after the September 11 attacks that we

Responsibility for Private Armed Groups in the Context of Terrorism", *Juridicia International* XI (2006): 184–193; Cenic, "State Responsibility and Self-Defence in International Law Post 9/11: Has the Scope of Article 51 of the United Nations Charter been Widened as a Result of the US Response to 9/11?" 202. Moreover, the NATO even went a step further in invoking the right of collective self-defence under Article 5 of the Treaty of Washington in the aftermath of the September 11 attacks. It only took the instance of 'directed from abroad' as a legitimate cause of applying the force in self-defence. "Statement of the North Atlantic Council", September 12, 2001.

101 Eric A. Heinze, "The Evolution of the International Law in the Light of the 'global War on Terror'", *Review of International Studies* 37, no. 3 (2011): 1079–1080.

102 Stahn, "Terrorist Acts as 'Armed Attack': The Right to Self-Defence, Article 51 (1/2) of the UN Charter, and International Terrorism", 37.

103 Kahn, "Imagining Warfare", 207.

104 Ibid., 224. It is submitted, however, that CIA drone operators are non-combatants and cannot under the customary international law participate directly in hostilities. Civilian participation in armed activities are prohibited by two 1977 protocols to the 1949 Geneva Conventions. Although the US is not a party to the 1977 Geneva Protocols, the participation of civilians in combat violates customary laws of armed conflict. For details of the origin and development of this principle, see Giladi, "Francis Lieber on Public War", 447–477.

105 David Hare, *Stuff Happens* (London: Faber & Faber, 2004), 32 and 117.

106 Ward, *Law, Text, Terror*, 10.

live in a world of no rules.[107] It may not be that much surprising when looked through the prism of ideological fissures.[108] After all, the act of labelling a military campaign an ideological struggle is itself a political hedge against its legal merits. Concerning the discourse, it enables a reverse transition: from self-defence to self-preservation. Nonetheless, some anomalies had to be *inherent* in this sort of military campaign. Terrorists exploit security vacuums. Before they strike, only the intelligence agencies and political decision-makers may have prior knowledge of their planning and operational readiness. Inversely, state citizens encounter this violent reality once it has struck. This irony is part of the war of our times. Besides breaking open the legal holes, it is unsettling the legal categories of this violent enterprise.

Summary

This chapter discussed the legal discourse concerning the duties of states. It also explored the dynamics of the 'war on terror'. As this study situates and explains the terrorist threat within the framework of state security threat, it was important to know about the nature of harms, the committing of which may lead to the initiation of the use of force. Hence, legal norms and practices of state responsibility and liability formed the first part of this chapter. With this knowledge in the backdrop, the second part charted the legal course built and actions undertaken by the US government and international institutions to eliminate the terrorist threats from within the territorial jurisdiction of other states. It is assumed that before moving to a certain case study, these discussions shall be useful in understanding the background of the launch of drone attacks.

Bibliography

Article 2 (5) of the UN Charter.

Badr, Gamal M. "The Exculpatory Effect of Self-Defence in State Responsibility". *Georgia Journal of International & Comparative Law* 10, no. 1 (1980): 1–28.

Baker Jr., John S. "A War, Yes; Against Terror, No". *Michigan State Journal of International Law* 19, no. 1 (2010): 119–128.

Becker, Tal. *Terrorism and the State: Rethinking the Rules of State Responsibility*. Oxford: Hart Publishing, 2006.

Berman, Nathaniel. "Privileging Combat? Contemporary Conflict and the Legal Construction of War". *Columbia Journal of Transnational Law* 43, no. 1 (2004): 1–71.

Borradari, Giovanna. *Philosophy in a Time of Terror: Dialogues with Jürgen Habermas and Jacques Derrida*. Chicago: The University of Chicago Press, 2003.

107 For further details, see Hurrell, "'There Are No Rules' (George W. Bush): International Order after September 11", 185; and Dominic McGoldrick, *From '9-11' to the 'Iraq War 2003': International Law in an Age of Complexity* (Oxford: Hart Publishing, 2004), 87.

108 For details, see Ward, *Law, Text, Terror;* Ward, "God, Terror and the Law"; Hare, *Stuff Happens;* Borradari, *Philosophy in a Time of Terror: Dialogues with Jürgen Habermas and Jacques Derrida.*

Bowett, Derek. "The Impact of Security Council Decisions on Dispute Settlement Procedures". *European Journal of International Law* 5, no. 1 (1994): 89–101.

Breau, Susan and Marie Aronsson. "Drone Attacks, International Law and the Recording of Civilian Causalities of Armed Conflict". *Suffolk Transnational Law Review* 35, no. 2 (2012): 259–285.

Brooks, Rosa. "Drones and the International Rule of Law". *Ethics & International Affairs* 28, no.1 (2014): 83–103.

Brownlie, Ian. "State Responsibility and the International Court of Justice". In *Issues of State Responsibility before International Judicial Institutions*. Edited by Malgosia Fitzmaurice and Dan Sarooshi, 11–18. Oxford: Hart Publishing, 2004.

Brunstetter, Daniel and Megan Braun. "From *Jus Ad Bellum* to *Jus Ad Vim*: Recalibrating Our Understanding of the Moral Use of Force". *Ethics & International Affairs* 27, no. 1 (2013): 87–106.

Byres, Michael. "Terrorism, the Use of Force and International Law after 11 September". *International & Comparative Law Quarterly* 51, no. 2 (April 2002): 401–414.

Carsten, Stahn. "Terrorist Acts as 'Armed Attack': The Right to Self-Defence, Article 51 (1/2) of the UN Charter, and International Terrorism". *Fletcher Forum of World Affairs* 27, no. 2 (2003): 35–54.

Case Concerning Application of the Convention on the Prevention and Punishment of the Crime of Genocide (Bosnia and Herzegovina vs. Serbia and Montenegro), Judgement, ICJ Reports, 2007.

Case Concerning Armed Activities on the Territory of Congo (Democratic Republic of Congo vs. Uganda), Judgement, ICJ Reports, 2005.

Case Concerning Military and Paramilitary Activities in and Against Nicaragua (Nicaragua vs. United States of America), Judgement, ICJ Reports, 1986.

Case Concerning Oil Platforms (Islamic Republic of Iran vs. United States of America), Judgement, ICJ Reports, 2003.

Cassese, Antonio. *International Law*. 2nd ed. Oxford: Oxford University Press, 2005.

Cassese, Antonio. "The Nicaragua and Tadic Tests Revisited in Light of the ICJ Judgment on Genocide in Bosnia". *European Journal of International Law* 18, no. 4 (2007): 649–668.

Cenic, Sonja. "State Responsibility and Self-Defence in International Law Post 9/11: Has the Scope of Article 51 of the United Nations Charter Been Widened as a Result of the US Response to 9/11"? *Australian International Law Journal* 14 (2007): 201–216.

Condorelli, Luigi. "The Imputability to States of Acts of International Terrorism". *Israel Yearbook on Human Rights* 19 (1989): 233–246.

Conforti, Benedetto. *The Law and Practice of the United Nations*. 3rd revised ed. Leiden: Martinus Nijhoff Publishers, 2005.

Conte, Alex "The War on Terror: Self-Defence or Aggression"? In *The Challenge of Conflict: International Law Responds*. Edited by Ustinia Dolgopol and Judith Gardam, 393–412. Leiden: Martin Nijhoff Publishers, 2006.

Corfu Channel Case (United Kingdom and Northern Ireland vs. People's Republic of Albania), Judgement, ICJ Reports, 1949.

De Souza, I.M. Lobo. "Revisiting the Right of Self-Defence Against Non-State Armed Entities"? *The Canadian Yearbook of International Law* 53 (2015): 1–42.

Detter, Ingrid. *The Law of War*. 2nd ed. Cambridge: Cambridge University Press, 2000.

Dinstein, Yoram. *War, Aggression and Self-Defence*. 4th ed. Cambridge: Cambridge University Press, 2005.

Doyle, Michael W. *Striking First: Pre-emption and Prevention in International Conflict*. Princeton: Princeton University Press, 2008.

"Draft Articles on the Responsibility of States for Internationally Wrongful Acts." *Yearbook of International Law Commission*, 1980.

"Draft Articles on Responsibility of State for Internationally Wrongful Acts, with Commentaries"? *Yearbook of International Law Commission*. Vol. II, 2001.

Enabulale, Amos O. "Use of Force by International/Regional Non-State Actors: No Armed Attack, No Self-Defence"? *European Journal of Law Reform* 12, no. 3–4 (2010): 209–217.

Fenwick, Charles G. *International Law*. 2nd ed. New York: D. Appleton-Century Company, 1934.

Franck, Thomas. *Recourse to Force: State Action Against Threats and Armed Attacks*. Cambridge: Cambridge University Press, 2004.

Friedman, Wolfgang. "The Growth of State Control Over the Individual and its Effect upon the Rules of International State Responsibility". *British Yearbook of International Law* 19 (1938): 118–150.

Gattini, Andre. "Breach of International Obligations". In *Principles of Shared Responsibility in International Law: An Appraisal of the State of the Art*. Edited by Andre Nollkaemper and Ilias Plakokefalos, 25–59. Cambridge: Cambridge University Press, 2014.

Giladi, Rotem. "Francis Lieber and Public War". *Goettingen Journal of International Law* 4, no. 2 (2012): 447–477.

Goldsmith, Jack. *The Terror Presidency: Law and Judgement Inside the Bush Administration*. New York: W.W. Norton & Company, 2007.

Graefrath, Bernhard. "Complicity in the Law of International Responsibility". *Revue Belge De Droit International* 2 (1996): 371–380.

Gray, Christine. *International Law and the Use of Force*. 2nd ed. Oxford: Oxford University Press, 2004.

Greenwood, Christopher. "The Concept of War in Modern International Law". *International & Comparative Law Quarterly* 36 (1987): 279–309.

Greenwood, Christopher. "War, Terrorism, and International Law". *Current Legal Problems* 56 (2004): 505–530.

Grotius, Hugo. *The Rights of War and Peace*. Book I. Edited by Richard Tuck. Indianapolis: Liberty Fund Inc., 2005.

Hare, David. *Stuff Happens*. London: Faber & Faber, 2004.

Heinze, Eric A. "The Evolution of the International Law in the Light of the 'global War on Terror'". *Review of International Studies* 37, no. 3 (2011): 1069–1094.

Henkin, Louis. "War and Terrorism: Law or Metaphor". *Santa Clara Law Review* 45 (2004–2005): 817–827.

Higgins, Rosalyn. "Legal Limits to the Use of Force by Sovereign States: United Nations Practice". *British Yearbook of International Law* 37 (1961): 269–319.

Higgins, Rosalyn. "Issues of State Responsibility before the International Court of Justice". In *Issues of State Responsibility before International Judicial Institutions*. Edited by Malgosia Fitzmaurice and Dan Sarooshi, 1–10. Oxford: Hart Publishing, 2004.

Hurrell, Andrew. "There are no Rules' (George W. Bush): International Order after September 11". *International Relations* 16, no. 2 (2002): 185–204.

Jackson, Miles. *Complicity in International Law*. Oxford: Oxford University Press, 2015.

Jane, Bennet, "Israel Steps up Counter Strikes; 22 Palestinians Slain". *The New York Times*, February 21, 2002.

Jessup, Philip C. "Intermediacy". *Nordisk Tidsskrift Int'l. Ret.* 23 (1953): 16–26.
Jinks, Derek. "State Responsibility for the Acts of Private Armed Groups". *Chicago Journal of International Law* 4, no. 1 (2003): 83–95.
Kahn, Paul W. "Imagining Warfare". *European Journal of International Law* 24, no. 1 (2013): 199–226.
Kelly, Major Joseph B. "A Legal Analysis of the Changes in War". *Military Law Review* 13 (1961): 89–120.
Kelsen, Hans. *General Theory of Law and State*. Translated by Anders Wedberg. Cambridge: Harvard University Press, 1945.
Kelsen, Hans. *Principles of International Law*. New York: Reinehart & Company Inc., 1952.
Kennedy, David. *Of War and Law*. Princeton: Princeton University Press, 2006.
Koh, Harold H. "The Spirit of the Laws". *Harvard Journal of International Law* 43, no. 1 (2002): 23–39.
Letter from the Permanent UN Representative of the United States to the President of the UN Security Council, October 7, 2001, UN Doc. S/2001/946.
Mary, O'Connell. "Rise of the Drones II: Unmanned Systems and the Future of War". *Hearing before the Subcommittee on National Security and Foreign Affairs, Committee on Oversight and Government Reforms, House of Representatives, 111th Congress, 2nd Session*, Serial No. 111-120, April 28, 2010.
McGoldrick, Dominic. *From '9–11' to the 'Iraq War 2003': International Law in an Age of Complexity*. Oxford: Hart Publishing, 2004.
Mclaughlin, Rob. "The Legal Regime Applicable to Use of Lethal Force When Operating under a United Nations Security Council Chapter VII Mandate Authorising 'All Necessary Means'". *Journal of Conflict & Security Law* 12, no. 3 (2008): 389–417.
Megret, Frederic. "War? Legal Semantics and the Move to Violence". *European Journal of International Law* 13, no. 2 (2002): 361–399.
Meng, Werner. "The Caroline". In *Encyclopaedia of Public International Law*. Vol. 3. Edited by Rüdolf Bernhardt, 81–82. Amsterdam: Elsevier Science Publishers, 1984.
Neff, Stephen C. *War and the Law of Nations*. Cambridge: Cambridge University Press, 2005.
O'Connell, Mary E. "When is a War not a War? The Myth of the Global War on Terror". *International & Comparative Law* 12 (2006): 535–539.
Preamble of the UN Charter.
Rumpf, Helmut. "Is a Definition of War Necessary"? *Boston University Law Review* 18 (1938): 686–714.
Schmitt, Carl. *Writings on War*. Translated by Timothy Nunan. Cambridge: Polity Press, 2011.
State Prosecutor vs. Dusko Tadic, Case IT-94-1-A, Appeals Trial Judgment, ICTY, 1999.
"Statement of the President George W. Bush." The United Nations General Assembly, 56th Session, New York, 2001.
Steinhoff, Uwe. *On the Ethics of War and Terrorism*. New York: Oxford University Press, 2007.
Strachan, Hew and Sybille Scheipers, eds. *The Changing Character of War*. Oxford: Oxford University Press, 2011.
Talbott, Strobe and Nayan Chanda, eds. *The Age of Terror: America and the World after September 11*. New York: Basic Books, 2001.
Tams, Christian J. "Law-making in Complex Processes: The World Court and the Modern Law of State Responsibility". In *Sovereignty, Statehood and State Responsibility:*

Essays in Honour of James Crawford. Edited by Christine Chinkin and Freya Baetens, 297–306. Cambridge: Cambridge University Press, 2015.

Tsagourias, Nicholas. "Self-Defence Against Non-State Actors: The Interaction between Self-defence as a Primary Rule and Self-Defence as Secondary Rule". *Leiden Journal of International Law* 29, no. 3 (2016): 801–825.

United States Diplomatic and Consular Staff in Tehran (United States of America vs. Iran), ICJ Reports, 1980.

Värk, Rene. "State Responsibility for Private Armed Groups in the Context of Terrorism". *Juridicia International* xi (2006): 184–193.

Ward, Ian. *Law, Text, Terror*. Cambridge: Cambridge University Press, 2009.

Werner, Wouter G. "The Changing Face of Enmity: Carl Schmitt's International Theory and the Evolution of the Legal Concept of War". *International Theory* 2, no. 3 (2010): 351–380.

Westlake, John. *International Law*. 2nd ed. Vol. 2. Cambridge: The University Press, 1910.

Wolfrum, Rüdiger. "International Wrongful Acts". In *Encyclopaedia of Public International Law*, Vol. 10. Edited by Rüdolf Bernhardt, 271–276. Amsterdam: Elsevier Science Publishers, 1984.

Wright, Quincy. "Changes in the Conception of War". *American Journal of International Law* 18, no. 4 (1924): 755–767.

5 Pre-emption and the US drone attacks in Pakistan

Within the context of pre-emption, this chapter explains and analyses the US drone attacks in Pakistan. On the margins of these discussions, the case of Yemen is also featured. Concerning the centrality of the positivist discourse, the 'inherent right of self-defence', which is also taken as an appropriate legal framework to defend against an impending security threat, shall remain the main focus. It is pertinent to mention here that though the positivist legal discourse shall be the main fulcrum upon which the entire debate pivots, the natural and Islamic laws of nations shall also be deployed to supplement the discussion. It is essential to highlight the existent primacy of the positivist discourse. In addition to this, it helps to ascertain why both the natural and the Islamic legal discourses are inadequate as explanatory tools to understand the debate on pre-emption and combat drones against terrorism.

Pre-empting terrorism

The history of the use of force underscores that, as a matter of legal practice, states avoid *directly* invoking pre-emptive self-defence to defend against a security threat; instead, they prefer the frame of legal arguments under the 'inherent right of self-defence' to justify such exceptional military actions.[1] This reluctance becomes even more profound in counter-terror operations. Perhaps the reluctance to invoke the right of self-defence is also because how the Court treats such instances, as the Court, in adjudicating such cases, often takes a careful view of the factual circumstances and judges them against the standards of 'armed attack', 'effective control', and the 'gravity of the use of force'.

Within the parameters of military security and threat perception, the pre-emptive use of force against terrorism centres on the understanding that a terrorist not only intends to harm but is also determined to do so. It is, therefore, necessary to employ violent force to eliminate the threat. Characteristically, such types of violence poses a serious challenge to the law since labelling the enemy as terrorists is itself an act of transforming the status of the enemy to a level where pre-emption

1 Doyle, *Striking First*, 17; and Murphy, "The Doctrine of Pre-emptive Self-Defence", 710.

would be a necessity. This peculiar dilemma flows out of the complexity in judging the impending hostile acts. Unlike states, terrorists have an *inherent* propensity to operate clandestinely which, in turn, compounds the effectiveness of deterrence to compel terrorists not to adopt violent recourse.[2] Besides, a state that has already experienced a terrorist attack would operate out of a heightened threshold of security threat perception. It would prefer to kill (the terrorists) first before they (attempt to) strike again. Such an interplay of the terrorist threat and pre-emptive self-defence compounds the sphere of the related laws to regulate the use of force.[3] On top of all this, it is the entry of combat drones to kill terrorists which further complicates the understanding of the legal discourse on the use of force. In attempts to explore and explain the matter, the subsequent part of this chapter dwells upon the legal arguments given by the US to justify its drone strikes, carried out primarily in Pakistan and Yemen, in the name of pre-emptive self-defence.

Elements of the US legal argumentation

The US categorically pronounced that it would not wait too long to address the terrorist threat. It further continued to express the determination that, when and where necessary, it would act 'pre-emptively' to protect its people and territory.[4] In similitude, before the invasion of Iraq in 2003, it asserted once more that "terrorists and terror states do not reveal these threats in fair notice, in formal declarations—and responding to such enemies only after they have struck first is not self-defence, it is suicide".[5] Clearly, these shifts seek to recalibrate the response to confront those security threats which are credible and non-traditional.[6] After all, the existence of terrorism as a security threat is itself beyond the comprehension of legal norms—conceived and based on the centrality of state actors.

Furthermore, underlining the policy to take the war closer to terrorists, former President Barack Obama stressed that "we act against terrorists who pose a

2 Martha Crenshaw, "Will Threats Deter Nuclear Terrorism?" in *Deterring Terrorism: Theory and Practice*, ed. Andreas Wenger and Alex Wilner (Stanford, CA: Stanford University Press, 2012), 143. For further details, also see Gregory D. Miller, "Terrorist Decision-Making and the Deterrence", *Studies in Conflict & Terrorism* 36, no. 2 (2013): 132–151; and Matthew Kroenig and Barry Pavel, "How to Deter Terrorism", *The Washington Quarterly* 35, no. 2 (2012): 21–36.

3 Neta C. Crawford, "Just War Theory and the U.S. Counterterror War", *Perspectives on Politics* 1, no. 1 (2003): 15; and William C. Marra and Sonia K. McNeil, "Understanding 'The Loop': Regulating the Next Generation of War Machines", *Harvard Journal of Law & Public Policy* 36, no. 3 (2013): 1178.

4 "The National Security Strategy of the United States", 6.

5 Remarks by the President in Address to the Nation, "President Says Saddam Must Leave Within 48 Hours", *The White House*, Washington, March 17, 2003, accessed January 10, 2020, http://georgewbush-whitehouse.archives.gov/news/releases/2003/03/20030317-7.html

6 Gabriella Blum and Phillip Heymann, "Law and Policy of Target Killing", *Harvard National Security Journal* 1 (2010): 147; and Mahmoud C. Bassiouni, "Legal Control of International Terrorism: A Policy-Oriented Assessment", *Harvard International Law Journal* 43 (2002): 85–86.

continuing and *imminent* threat to the American people, and when there are no other governments capable of effectively addressing the threat".[7] To provide the legal cover for such policy prescriptions, former Attorney General Eric Holder, Jr., emphasised that "it is entirely lawful—under both United States law and applicable law of war principles—to target specific senior operational leaders of (A)l Qaeda and associated forces".[8] Specifically concerning the pre-emption of terrorism, the criteria for 'imminent threat' involves "considerations of the relevant window of opportunity to act, the possible harm that missing the window would cause to civilians, and the likelihood of heading off future disastrous" strikes against the US, noted the Attorney General.[9] An armed measure, however, should seek to balance against "the long-standing principles of the law of war; such as necessity, distinction, proportionality, and humanity", he conceded.[10]

Given this focus to lay down and meet the legal standards of pre-emption, the operational details, which ultimately create the balance between procedures and established legal principles of 'necessity and proportionality', remain vague.[11] This is evident from the fact that the US government did not share much information about the criteria to designate an individual terrorist and then about the targeting of this designated terrorist when he resides and operates from within the civilians. Some legal scholars, however, argue that perhaps the "unprecedented mobility and adaptability [of terrorists] were not considered when formulating key facets of international law".[12] And, therefore, it is difficult to explain the procedures related to the principles of necessity and proportionality.[13] Yet one cannot ignore the fact that the framers of the UN Charter infused the element of legal elasticity to sustain the pressure of future security threats. For instance, the inclusion of the phrase 'inherent right of self-defence' in Article 51 bears testimony to this fact.[14] And thus, paying close attention to the circumstances that set this inheritance (Caroline criteria) can help appreciate the procedures. Concerning

7 Remarks by the US President at the National Defence University, Washington, May 23, 2013, accessed January 30, 2020, https://www.whitehouse.gov/the-press-office/2013/05/23/remarks-president-national-defense-university (emphasis added)

8 Attorney General Eric Holder Speech at Northwestern University School of Law, March 5, 2012, accessed January 20, 2019, http://www.justice.gov/opa/speech/attorney-general-eric-holder-speaks-northwestern-university-school-law

9 Ibid.

10 Ibid.

11 Brooks, "Drones and the International Rule of Law", 90.

12 For details of this emerging understanding of the international security and legal norms, see Franck, *Recourse to Force: State Actions against Threats and Armed Attacks*, 4; and Ariel Colonomos, "Preventive war a l' Americaine: In the Fog of Norms", in *War, Torture and Terrorism: Rethinking the Rules of International Security*, ed. Anthony F. Lang, Jr. and Amanda R. Beattie (New York: Routledge, 2008), 90–93.

13 Franck, *Recourse to Force: State Actions against Threats and Armed Attacks*, 4.

14 "A More Secure World", 62–63 at paras. 183–190; Bowett, *Self-Defence in International Law*, 187; Myres S. MacDougal, "The Soviet-Cuban Quarantine and Self-Defense", *American Journal of International law* 57 (1963): 597–604; and Ruys, *'Armed Attack' and the Article 51 of the UN Charter*, 55–59.

pre-emption, it is worth mentioning that while pondering over the *cause* of a pre-emptive armed measure, it is hard to ignore the *effect* of such an armed measure.

Understanding the viewpoint of host states

At best, the legal position of the Pakistani government regarding the US drones strikes remains vague. In 2004, the then President of Pakistan, Pervez Musharraf, controverted the media reports of consenting to the US drone strikes in Pakistan. But later he, however, conceded that his government approved a few drone attacks against high-value terrorist targets, and this consent was subsequently withdrawn. In any case, Pakistan never approved the extensive use of combat drones.[15] Condemning the extensive use of drones, the Pakistani Parliament unanimously passed a resolution which declared that the US drone strikes violate state sovereignty and political integrity and asked the US government to stop them.[16] The Pakistani Parliament also suggested the government to pursue the legal course of action by raising the issue at the UN Security Council.

Such demands, however, did not yield any result, and the US continued to strike terrorists in Pakistan. Perhaps a clandestine agreement between the two states forced Pakistan to avoid any serious legal manoeuvre, for an American journalist claimed that in his meeting with the CIA Chief in 2009, Pakistani President Zardari *approvingly* told the CIA Chief to continue targeting the senior Al-Qaeda leaders.[17] Later on, Pakistan raised the issue of the US drone strikes at the Human Rights Council. The Pakistani Ambassador along with Ben Emmerson, the UN Special Rapporteur on Human Rights and Counter-Terrorism, apprised the Human Rights Council members that the US drone strikes violate the fundamental rights and principles of humanitarian law.[18] As a result, the Human Rights Council (in a resolution) called upon the states to uphold human rights in counter-terror operations.[19] It is important to mention here that neither the Pakistani government nor the UN Special Rapporteur raised questions about the merits of the case under the law of self-defence.

On the other hand, Yemen remained somewhat reticent. The Yemeni government needed foreign legitimacy to rule the country, and hence, it could not afford to offend the US government. It not only consented to the drone attacks but, most

15 For a detailed treatment of this controversy, see Christine S. Rinehart, *Drones and the Targeted Killing in the Middle East and Africa: An Appraisal of American Counterterrorism Policies* (New York: Lexington Books, 2016), 46–47.

16 For further details, see Christine C. Fair and Ali Hamza, "From Elite Consumption to Popular Opinion: Framing of the US Drone Program in Pakistani Newspapers", *Small Wars & Insurgencies* 27, no. 4 (2016): 579–580.

17 Bob Woodward, *Obama's Wars* (London: Simon & Schuchter, 2010), 26.

18 Ben Emmerson, "Report of the Special Rapporteur on the Promotion and Protection of Human Rights and Fundamental Freedoms while Countering Terrorism", UN Document A/68/389, 2013.

19 It is important to mention here that Ben Emmerson visited Pakistan personally in March 2013 to inquire into and investigate the civilian losses of lives out of the CIA drone strikes inside Pakistani tribal areas. He made a large number of case studies, part of his report, submitted to the UN.

of the time also cooperated with the US military and the CIA.[20] The Yemeni Foreign Minister, while discussing the role of his government, said that this was a "necessary evil" and "very limited affair", which was, of course, happening with their coordination.[21] The Yemeni government, however, wanted the US to keep the drone attacks secret.[22] Among other power centres, no one either dared to speak or perhaps felt no need to do so. After the killing of senior Al-Qaeda leader Al-Awlaki in 2011, however, the Parliament of Yemen ended the silence and condemned the use of drone attacks on Yemeni territory.[23] Similarly, in August 2013, the National Dialogue Congress passed a resolution proposing to criminalise the US drone attacks.[24]

It is interesting to note that both Pakistan and Yemen often deployed political argumentation to oppose the US drone attacks. They did not refer to any specific legal norm or principle in their opposition. Moreover, while these states want the US to uphold territorial sovereignty, there is no mention of the presence of terrorists inviting armed intervention.

Pre-emption and positive international law

International law is a code of rights and duties, and the fulfilment of duties leads to securing of rights. Any failure to fulfil the duties may cause an injury to the other state. Given the phenomenon of globalised terrorism, this scenario becomes probable as the injured state can invoke its legal right to seek redress to the injury. The following discussion encompasses this interplay and interconnection of state responsibility and state right vis-à-vis the doctrine of pre-emptive self-defence.

Necessity of self-defence

To ward off an impending security threat, an armed measure of self-defence must comply with the necessity of self-defence and the proportionality of the counter armed measures.[25] To ascertain the legal justifications, the necessity for such a measure is further assessed against various qualifying standards. In this context, the first part is devoted to assessing the justifications (against the relevant legal

20 Walter Pincus, "Missile Strike Carried out with Yemeni Cooperation", *Washington Post*, November 6, 2002, A10.

21 Maha El Dahan and Mohammad Ghobari, "Yemeni Parliament in Non-Binding Vote against Drone Attacks;" *Reuters*, December 15, 2013, accessed January 10, 2020, https://www.reuters.com/article/us-yemen-drones/yemeni-parliament-in-non-binding-vote-against-drone-attacks-idUSBRE9BE0EN20131215

22 David Kretzmer, "US Extra-Territorial Actions Against Individuals: Bin Laden, Al Awlaki and Abu Khattalah", in *The Use of Force in International Law: A Case-Based Approach*, ed. Tom Ruys, Olivier Corten, and Alexandra Hofer (Oxford: Oxford University Press, 2018), 769.

23 Ibid.

24 For further details, also see Ann Rogers and John Hill, *Unmanned: Drone Warfare and Global Security* (New York: Pluto Press, 2014), 89.

25 For detailed analysis of these two requirements, see the second chapter above.

standards) put forward by the US administration for launching drone strikes in Pakistan and Yemen. As explained earlier, it is important to point out that the US based and justified its drone attacks against terrorists under the right of self-defence enshrined in Article 51 of the UN Charter.

'Unwilling or unable'

On the recourse to pre-emptive self-defence, 'unwilling or unable' serves as the first requirement to justify an armed intervention in the territory of another state. The idea, as we know it today, came up during the *Caroline* case. Subsequently, it became a standard procedure to claim the right of self-defence against states as well as non-state armed actors.[26] It seems a simple yardstick to measure the ability and willingness of a state to curb and curtail non-state armed activities on its territory. In essence, it speaks of the issues of capacity and political will of a state to govern its territory to avail the right of territorial sovereignty. Indeed, states have disparity in national power, and they approach their respective strategic security interests and threats differently. Thus, an intervening state should consider multiple factors before concluding about the success or failure in meeting this formula. These factors include seeking the cooperation of host state in neutralising a security threat, apprising it about the seriousness of a security threat, considering the capacity of the host state, and assessing the gravity and urgency of a security threat.[27] Despite these normative frameworks, questions may arise over any objective fulfilment of this formula. It becomes even more probable in the context of the evolving terrorist security threat.

After thc September 11 terrorist attacks, the US declared to launch armed interventions against other states to kill or capture Al-Qaeda leaders if and when the host state failed to eliminate the threat of terrorism.[28] Given the terrorist activities in its territorial jurisdiction, Pakistan initiated counter-terror measures. It carried out legislation to ban terrorist organisations which directly or indirectly supported Al-Qaeda and launched targeted security operations to *kill* or *capture* Al-Qaeda leaders. According to government estimates, Pakistan apprehended around 689 Al-Qaeda leaders. Among these, more than 369 were handed over to the US government. They subsequently landed in Afghanistan and Guantanamo

26 Elizabeth Wilmshurst, "The Chatham House Principles of International Law on the Use of Force in Self-Defence", *International & Comparative Law Quarterly* 55, no. 4 (2006): 969.

27 Ashley S. Deeks, "'Unwilling or Unable': Toward a Normative Framework for Extraterritorial Self-Defence", *Virginia Journal of International Law* 52, no. 3 (2012): 519–532. For further details of this conception under contemporary circumstances of international terrorism, see Olivier Corten, "The 'Unwilling or Unable' Test: Has it Been, and Could it be, Accepted?" *Leiden Journal of International Law* 29, no. 3 (2016): 777–799.

28 "The National Security Strategy of the US", 2002; Dan Balz, "Obama Says He Would Take Fight to Pakistan", *The Washington Post*, August 2, 2007, A1; and Harold H. Koh, "The Obama Administration and International Law", *Speech at Annual Meeting of the American Society of International Law*, Washington, DC, March 25, 2010, accessed January 10, 2020, http://www.state.gov/s/l/releases/remarks/139119.htm

Bay jails.[29] Among these, the masterminds of the September 11 terrorist attacks, Khalid Sheikh Muhammad, Ramzi Bin al Shibh, Sayyd Amin, Abu Zubeida, and Abu Badr, are prominent ones.[30] Given these counter-terror efforts, Pakistan claims to have been doing more than any other state to disrupt and destroy the Al-Qaeda network on its soil.[31]

Yet the alleged presence of Al-Qaeda leaders in Pakistan continued raising various questions over the *ability* of Pakistan to kill or capture them. The primary reason was the fact that Pakistan only apprehended those Al-Qaeda leaders who resided in the settled areas. Even in this context, the killing of the Al-Qaeda Chief, Osama bin Laden, in a city near the capital of Pakistan contributed towards the suspicions of the *complicity* of the state as well as its *inability* to arrest Al-Qaeda leaders.[32] Besides, terrorists remained at large along the region of Pakistan bordering Afghanistan since the presence of Pakistani security forces in this region was thin initially. This was construed as an enabling factor for the Al-Qaeda terrorists to cross into Pakistan and reside there.

In the case of Yemen, the country served as the prime destination for Al-Qaeda to establish its base and target US interests and security forces.[33] In 1992, Al-Qaeda attacked hotels in Aden frequented by the US military personnel while fighting in Somalia. In January 2000, Al-Qaeda allegedly planned attacks against the US military ships in Aden. Eventually, it succeeded in launching attacks against the USS *Cole* in October, killing numerous sailors and causing serious damage to the ship.[34] Following this, the US government demanded the arrest of the Al-Qaeda leaders in Yemen. The central government faced severe resistance from the Islamists to initiate arrests or even cooperate with the US government. In addition to this, tribal leaders sympathetic to Al-Qaeda controlled large parts of state territory, impinging upon the ability of the state to impose its juridical writ. For instance, in December 2001, the Yemeni soldiers attempted to capture three Al-Qaeda terrorists and aborted the mission after facing serious armed resistance from the tribesmen.[35] Likewise, the local tribesmen frustrated attempts to arrest al Harethi, the prime suspect in the USS *Cole* terrorist attack. He remained protected there for almost two years. Also, in an attempt to capture him, the Yemeni security forces faced

29 Pervez Musharraf, *In the Line of Fire: A Memoir* (London: Simon & Schuster UK Ltd., 2006), 237.

30 Ibid., 220, 237, and 238; and Sabir Shah, "Top Al-Qaeda Leaders Captured or Killed on Pakistani Soil", *The News*, May 3, 2011.

31 Musharraf, *In the Line of Fire*, 223. Also, see Peter L. Bergen and Daniel Rothenberg, ed. *Drone Wars: Transforming Conflict, Law, and Policy* (New York: Cambridge University Press, 2015), 92.

32 Rober Baer, "Finding Bin Laden Raises Questions about Pakistan's Complicity", *Time*, New York, May 2, 2011, accessed January 10, 2020, http://content.time.com/time/world/article/0,8599,2069012,00.html

33 For a detailed overview of Al-Qaeda operations in Yemen, see Gregory D. Johnsen, *The Last Refuge: Yemen, al-Qaeda and America's War in Arabia* (New York: W.W. Norton & and Company, 2013).

34 Aaron Mannes, *Profile in Terror: The Guide to Middle East Terrorist Organizations* (Lnaham: Rowman & Littlefield Publishers, Inc., 2004), 49–50.

35 Ibid., 50.

serious resistance from the tribesmen, leaving 19 security forces personnel dead.[36] Moreover, in 2006, 23 Al-Qaeda members escaped from a prison in the Yemeni capital Sanaa, which was run by the political security agency under the control of the Yemeni President.[37] Allegedly, jailers helped the Al-Qaeda members to flee. The loss of security forces and the mounting pressure from the Islamist opposition gradually forced the then President Saleh to relinquish cooperation with the US government to hunt down Al-Qaeda. These practices underline the scale of political and military challenges to the central government in establishing its writ.

In these contexts, the application of the 'unwilling or unable' formula to justify the right of self-defence in Pakistan raises some difficult questions. Such a formula can, however, be applied to the case of Yemen, as in the case of Yemen, Al-Qaeda and its affiliated groups controlled the territory and ran parallel systems and the writ of central government was too weak to control its territorial jurisdictions.[38] On the contrary, there is no evidence that Al-Qaeda and its affiliated groups have substantive control over any part of the state territory in Pakistan. Yet a question remains about the willingness and ability of Pakistan in tackling the issue of terrorism within its territorial bounds.[39] These questions, which are explained below, continue to persist despite Pakistan's claims of apprehending 650 Al-Qaeda members and its fight against terrorism to the fullest of its ability. This has been acknowledged by US higher officials as well. For instance, former CIA Chief and Assistant to the former President Obama on Homeland Security and Counterterrorism, John O. Brennan, noted that Pakistan did its utmost to degrade the capabilities of Al-Qaeda and downgrade its ability to launch terrorist attacks.[40]

The cross-border terrorist attacks can also be a justification to point out the failure of Pakistan to fight terrorism. This, in turn, can justify attacking terrorists in self-defence. On numerous occasions, the US military commanders in Afghanistan blamed Pakistan for tolerating and abetting the cross-border activities of the terrorists.[41] However, the attribution of these cross-border attacks to the Pakistani

36 Brian G. Williams, *Predators: The CIA's Drone War on al-Qaeda* (Washington, DC: Potomac Books, 2013), 42.

37 Stephen W. Day, *Regionalism and Rebellion in Yemen: A Troubled National Union* (New York: Cambridge University Press, 2012), 222–223.

38 UNSC Rep. of the Sect. General, UN Documents, S/2010/394, July 26, 2010); and Ryan J. Vogel, "Drone Warfare and the Law of Armed Conflict", *Denver Journal of International Law & Policy* 39, no. 1 (2010): 132.

39 Brunstetter and Braun, "From *Jus Ad Bellum* to *Jus Ad Vim*: Recalibrating Our Understanding of the Moral Use of Force", 89.

40 John O. Brennan, "The Ethics and Efficacy of the President's Counterterrorism Strategy", *Woodrow Wilson Center*, Washington, 30 April, 2012, accessed January 10, 2020, https://www.wilsoncenter.org/event/the-efficacy-and-ethics-us-counterterrorism-strategy

41 Statement of Admiral Michael Mullen, US Navy Chairman Joint Chiefs of Staff before the Senate Armed Services Committee on Afghanistan and Iraq, Washington, DC, September 22, 2011. For further details, see Anders Henriksen, "*Jus ad bellum* and American Targeted Use of Force to Fight Terrorism around the World", *Journal of Conflict & Security Law* 19, no. 2 (2014): 241–242.

government and its legitimate organs is missing. Nonetheless, it is important to assess such allegations against the backdrop that Pakistan has a porous border with Afghanistan. Due to its rugged and tortuous hilly terrain, this border is among the most complicated borders to guard. Pakistan has deployed more than 80,000 security forces on the border and constructed around 900 security check posts to control the cross-border movements of the terrorists.[42] Hence, sporadic cross-border attacks that are not apparently attributable to Pakistan do not provide justification to invade the Pakistani territory, at least, not according to the legal precedents set down by the Court.[43] In addition to this, one needs to take note that Pakistan has no intention to harm the US citizens and security forces in Afghanistan or on its own territory.

It is, however, submitted that this factual background and legal analysis may fall short of fully comprehending the issue of threat perception. This is due to the orientation of the respective states towards the issue of terrorist security threat. The US, because of past injury and great strength of arms, wants and expects other states to kill or capture every potential terrorist. The less powerful states, however, find it difficult to track down every terrorist.[44] For them, fears of blowback and political polarisation are real. Hence it seems that the formula of 'unwilling or unable' falls victim to power disparity. Most importantly, it is suggested that in the absence of any prior 'armed attack', the formula of 'unwilling or unable' does not *automatically* justify the use of force in self-defence; instead, together with other requirements of necessity, it informs the legal recourse to pre-empt.[45]

Thus, questions remain about the application and fulfilment of the formula of 'unwilling or unable'. Among these questions, the fundamental one is of locating as well as balancing the fact of the ability of the host states and of the intervening states. Sadly enough, positive international law does not offer a clear answer to this contemporary dilemma. Yet, in practice, more and more states are taking the *unwillingness* or *inability* of host states to contain the threat of terrorism as the sole justification to intervene and neutralise the security threat. Is this emerging state practice giving rise to any new norm of customary international law? For any certain answer, one needs to closely watch the unfolding landscape of pre-emptive violence between states and non-state armed actors.

Direct causation

To explain direct causation, the subsidiary norms of state responsibility shall be the primary focus. In this context, it is submitted that given the terrorist threat

42 Kaushik Roy, *Military Manpower, Armies and Warfare in South Asia* (New York: Routledge, 2013), 139.

43 *Military and Paramilitary Activities in and against Nicaragua*, 93 at para. 195.

44 Kenneth Watkin, *Fighting at the Legal Boundaries: Controlling the Use of Force in Contemporary Conflict* (New York: Oxford University Press, 2016), 50.

45 For details, see Tsagourias, "Self-Defence against Non-State Actors: The Interaction between Self-defence as a Primary Rule and Self-Defence as Secondary Rule", 809–811.

and pre-emption, any argumentation over the norm of direct causation should revolve around two axes: (i) *the causative link of a security threat to the security of a threatened state, its territory, and nationals abroad*; and (ii) *the relationship of such a security threat to the host state and its territory*. As explained earlier, the Court remains insistent that a right of self-defence against non-state armed actors only exists when the link between the host state and non-state armed actors is explicit. Conversely, the customary international law recognises the right of self-defence to avert an attack without the exception of actors or the establishment of the link between them as a pre-requisite. For the necessity of self-defence under the doctrine of pre-emption requires a direct link to the security threat as the *Caroline* criteria explicate the need to show that the link between the security threat and armed counter-measure is *direct*.[46]

In this context, the ensuing discussion explores and explains the link of the September 11 attacks to Pakistan and Yemen. It then discusses the link between the security threat posed by Al-Qaeda for the security of the US interests and nationals and the territories of Pakistan and Yemen. It is maintained that when a victim state chooses to attack the bases as well as persons affiliated to the non-state armed entity and the armed action remains restricted to the eradication of non-state actors, the victim state does not violate any rule under the UN Charter as per the Articles 2 (4) and 51.[47] Undoubtedly, the US suffered an 'armed attack' on the morning of September 11, 2001. The UN Security Council, responding to this attack, passed resolutions invoking the right of self-defence against terrorists. It played the role of the 'proper authority' for legally allowing the use of force in self-defence.[48] These resolutions reaffirmed the earlier Resolution 1269 of 1999, which called upon the states to 'take all necessary measures' to curb terrorism.[49] None of the two post–September 11 resolutions blamed any particular state for the terrorist attacks. Yet these terrorist attacks were conveniently attributed to the Taliban regime in Afghanistan.[50] After this, NATO invoked Article 5 and contributed militarily in attacking the Taliban. In a similar vein, the OAS also adopted a resolution invoking Article 3 of the Inter-American Treaty of Reciprocal Assistance. This resolution emphasised the importance of collective self-defence

46 Myres S. McDougal and Florentino P. Feliciano, *The International Law of War: Transnational Coercion and World Public Order* (Dordrecht: Martinus Nijhoff Publishers, 1994), 231–232.

47 Kimberly Trapp, "Back to Basics: Necessity, Proportionality, and the Right of Self-Defence Against Non-State Terrorists Actors", *International & Comparative Law Quarterly* 56, no. 1 (2007): 141–142; and Wilmshurst, "The Chatham House Principles of International Law on the Use of Force in Self-Defence", 969.

48 Vaughan Lowe, et al. eds., *The United Nations Security Council and War: The Evolution of Thought and Practice since 1945* (New York: Oxford University Press, 2008), 26.

49 For details, see the UN Security Council Resolutions 1269, 1368 and 1373.

50 Jack M. Beard, "America's New War on Terror: The Case for Self-Defence Under International Law", *Harvard Journal of Law & Public Policy* 25 (2001): 578–582; Christian J. Tams and James G. Devaney, "Applying Necessity and Proportionality to Anti-terror Self-Defence", *Israel Law Review* 45, no. 1 (2012): 99; and George W. Bush Address to the Nation, Washington, September 20, 2001, accessed January 22, 2020, http://www.presidentialrhetoric.com/speeches/09.20.01.html

under the given circumstances.[51] Both of these regional organisations, however, did not go along with the US campaign against terrorism in other states. In this context, one may safely conclude that the international community accepted the US right of self-defence in this particular case a right to avenge the past harm linked to Afghanistan.[52]

Some legal scholars argue that the post–September 11 era is instructive in a sense that any failure of the host state to rein in terrorists or tolerating their presence can give way to the right of self-defence. And the violation of the territorial integrity in this context would be permitted.[53] It is because neither the UN Security Council nor NATO had any precise target state in view while invoking the right of self-defence. This is a "normatively significant omission"[54] with a potential of manipulation. Yet one cannot ignore the factual context of these redress measures taken by the UN Security Council. As Al-Qaeda was based in Afghanistan and the country tolerated its presence for many years. After the US military operation, Al-Qaeda leaders moved out of Afghanistan and settled in Pakistan. Just because Pakistan had relations with the Afghan Taliban, it does not make the former responsible for the September 11 attacks as well as the legitimate target of any military action in the execution of the right to self-defence.[55] Any attempt to link Pakistan, Al-Qaeda, and past crime can be an *overstretching* of the criteria of direct causation.

But Ramzi al Shibh, a planner of the September 11 terrorist attacks, is a Yemeni citizen.[56] Yet given the juridical history and practices, the Yemeni nationality of this Al-Qaeda leader does not, in any reasonable way, make the state or the government of Yemen liable for the terrorist attacks against the US. Likewise, there is no evidence that Al-Qaeda operatives residing on the Yemeni territory, at the time of the September 11 terrorist attacks, were involved in the planning or execution of the attacks.

51 Twenty-fourth Meeting of Ministers of Foreign Affairs, "Terrorist Threat to the Americas", OEA/Ser.F/II.24 RC.24/RES.1/01, Washington, September 21, 2001, accessed January 20, 2020, http://www.oas.org/oaspage/crisis/rc.24e.htm

52 Brownlie, *Principles of Public International Law*, 746; Kurt Larson and Zachary Malamud, "The United State, Pakistan, the Law of War and the Legality of Drone Attacks", *The Journal of International Business & Law* 10, no. 1 (2011): 8; Remarks by O'Connell, "Rise of the Drones II: Unmanned Systems and the Future of War", 50; and Brooks, "Drones and the International Rule of Law", 91.

53 Michael N. Schmitt, "Responding to Transnational Terrorism under Jus Ad Bellum: A Normative Framework", in *International Law and Armed Conflict: Exploring the Faultlines, Essays in Honour of Yoram Dinstein*, ed. Michael N. Schmitt and Jelena Pejic (Leiden: Martin Nijhoff Publishers, 2007), 176–177.

54 Schmitt, "Counter-terrorism and the Use of Force in International Law", 9.

55 Murphy, "The International Legality of US Military Cross-Border Operations from Afghanistan into Pakistan", 129–131.

56 Mannes, *Profile in Terror: The Guide to Middle East Terrorist Organizations*, 50. For a detailed understanding of the Al-Qaeda arrival and operations in Yemen, see Gregory D. Johnsen, *The Last Refuge: Yemen, al-Qaeda and America's War in Arabia* (New York: W.W. Norton & Company, 2013).

Furthermore, in line with the UN Security Council resolutions under Chapter VII, Pakistan cooperated with the US to launch attacks against Al-Qaeda and Taliban in Afghanistan. Pakistan shared crucial intelligence and provided logistical support.[57] Before the attack on Afghanistan, Pakistan tried to convince the Taliban regime in Kabul to hand over the Al-Qaeda chief to the US, but to no avail.[58] So the stretch of counter-terror war into Pakistan raises questions as to how a party in a conflict can claim to have the same right of self-defence years later.[59] Also, there can be legitimate questions about the *temporal* limits of a military campaign in self-defence. International law, however, does not inform us about how a conflict should end. Instead it only provides guidance about the measures—fulfilment of which can help conclude a conflict. These include cessation of hostilities and the signing of a peace agreement between the adversaries.

Besides the missing of a direct link between the September 11 attacks and Pakistan and Yemen, there were instances of harm to the US security interests and nationals linked to the territories of the two states. In Pakistan, Al-Qaeda kidnapped and killed a US national and journalist working for the *Wall Street Journal*.[60] Al-Qaeda–affiliated terrorists carried out the London bombing in 2005 and plotted to blow up trans-Atlantic flights in 2006. Similarly, a failed car bomb attack in the Times Square by a US national of Pakistani origin had a *demonstrable* link to the Pakistani territory for training and guidelines.[61] The US Consulate in Peshawar also came under attack in 2010, though no American national was hurt.[62] In the case of Yemen, Al-Qaeda did not look back after a successful USS *Cole* attack. Its presence, control over territory, recruits, and planning of terrorist attacks continued to threaten the US interests in Yemen. The Christmas eve bomb plot, was a hallmark of the *continuous* security threat posed by Al-Qaeda in Yemen.[63]

57 Samina Yasmeen, "Unexpectedly at Center Stage: Pakistan", in *Global Responses to Terrorism: 9/11, Afghanistan and Beyond*, ed. Mark Buckley and Rick Fawn (New York: Routledge, 2003), 192.

58 Pervez Musharraf, *In the Line of Fire: A Memoir*, 215–217; and Hassan Abbas, *Pakistan's Drift into Extremism: Allah, the Army and America's War on Terror* (New York: Routledge, 2005), 217–218.

59 Owen Bowcott, "Drone Strikes Threatens 50 Years of International, Say UN Rapporteur", *The Guardian*, June 21, 2012. Also, see Murphy, "The International Legality of US Military Cross-Border Operations from Afghanistan into Pakistan", 133.

60 Peter Finn, "Khalid Sheikh Mohammed Killed Daniel Pearl, Report Finds", *The Washington Post*, January 20, 2011.

61 Ben West and Scott Stewart, "Uncomfortable Truths and the Times Square Attack", *Security Weekly*, May 6, 2010, accessed January 12, 2020, https://www.stratfor.com/weekly/20100505_uncomfortable_truths_times_square_attack

62 Ismail Khan and Sabrina Tavernise, "U.S. Consulate in Pakistan Attacked by Militants", *The New York Times*, April 5, 2010, A4.

63 For details of Al-Qaeda in Yemen and its terrorist activities, see Gregory D. Johnsen, *The Last Refuge: Yemen, al-Qaeda and America's War in Arabia* (New York: W.W. Norton & Company, 2013); Barak Mendelsohn, *The al-Qaeda Franchise: The Expansion of al-Qaeda and Its Consequences* (New York: Oxford University Press, 2016); and Mitchell D. Silber, *The Al-Qaeda Factor: Plots Against the West* (Philadelphia: University of Pennsylvania Press, 2012).

Yet it is also a fact that none of these attacks and threats to the US security interests is imputable to the Pakistani or Yemeni state as per the criterion of 'effective control' or 'overall control'.[64] Meanwhile, there is no denying the fact that Al-Qaeda terrorist activities continued to have an *origin* and *demonstratable* link to the Pakistani and Yemeni territories. Given this formidable presence of Al-Qaeda in these states, one may argue that the UN Security Council resolutions have a bearing upon the conduct of states in more than one way. These resolutions not only invoke the right of self-defence for past harms but also call upon the states to fulfil their responsibility towards another state since they ask the states to curb all the means and ways that facilitate terrorism. Likewise, one cannot ignore plenty of Court decisions, such as the *Armed Activities* case, *Israeli Wall opinion*, and *Genocide in Bosnia*, wherein the Court continued to apply the tough criteria in terms of the right of self-defence. The Court finds it difficult to attribute sporadic violent acts by the non-state elements to a state in the absence of 'effective control' of the state and the standard of 'armed attack'. It could either reassess the legality of the UN Security Council resolutions or reframe its legal argument. However, it has not taken any such an initiative thus far.[65]

Furthermore, it is submitted that these two institutions adopt different procedural approaches to reach their respective conclusions. The UN Security Council does not hear the state in question directly while fixing the responsibility for a particular violation of obligations. In contrast, the Court takes detailed circumstances of any case into account before coming to a conclusion.[66] The practice of the Court is thus legally more crucial for setting legal precedents and making devising sound legal argumentation. Given these factual discussions, it is observed that the application of direct causation seems problematic to claim the necessity of self-defence in Pakistan and Yemen to curb the threat of terrorism. The fact of the presence of Al-Qaeda and the security threat it poses, however, remains an issue residing beyond the contours of direct causation of harm in instances where the state is not involved in crime. Nonetheless, the direct relation of any such harm to the state territory is quite *evident*.

Imminence of a security threat

In the absence of a prior 'armed attack' and missing of the evidence of state responsibility, the US still has justification to cross the border to attack terrorists in Pakistan and Yemen: that is imminence of a security threat. This is asserted implicitly by Article 51 of the UN Charter.[67] The UN Secretary General's High

64 Murphy, "The International Legality of US Military Cross-Border Operations from Afghanistan into Pakistan", 129–132; Shah, *Islamic Law and the Law of Armed Conflict*, 132–133; and Shah, *International Law and Drone Strikes in Pakistan*, 42–43.

65 Bowett, "The Impact of Security Council Decisions on Dispute Settlement Procedures", 98.

66 Ibid.

67 However, there remain differences over institutional approaches and state policies in dealing with the law of self-defence. For a detailed analysis of these two distinct approaches, see Monica

Level Panel of Threats, Challenges and Change recognised the right of a state to defend against an *imminent* attack.[68] It is important to underline that, given the current century terrorism, this report does not subscribe to the policy of self-defence against a *temporally* remote threat.[69] It, instead, notes the importance of customary international law as a procedural frame to meet the requirement of imminence. Yet one needs to be mindful of the fact that during the time of the *Caroline* case, the scope of "the right of self-preservation and the doctrines of necessity of self-defence" was not fully settled in the law.[70] But the UN Charter established the primacy of the law of self-defence, divorcing the right of self-preservation.

Furthermore, some legal scholars believe that the UN Charter framework does not comprehend a conflict beyond states.[71] This remains, however, a minority view. As there is no explicit provision in the Charter which forbids the use of force against terrorists in instances of self-defence. The recent practice to interpret the UN Charter suggests that terrorist attacks may also trigger the right of self-defence.[72] Indeed, the cross-border conflict between the US and Britain in 1837 was an instance of the use of force involving state and non-state armed elements.[73] This very incident defined and set out the limits of use of force in self-defence. However, given the importance of this customary law, the states are reluctant to accept limitation of the law to assess the issue of the imminence of a security threat. They prefer to make individual assessments of the enemy intentions and military manoeuvres to repel an impending armed attack.[74] The states seek to lower the threshold of imminence in instances of use of force against terrorism.[75] In this backdrop, the strict limits set in the *Caroline criteria* remain a difficult standard to meet. It is truer in cases of pre-emptive use of force.[76]

Hakimi and Josef K. Cogan, "The Two Codes on the Use of Force", *European Journal of International Law* 27, no. 2 (2016): 257–291.

68 "A More Secure World", paras. 139 and 188.

69 Ibid., paras. 189 and 191.

70 Gardam, *Necessity, Proportionality and the Use of Force by States*, 149; Brownlie, *Principles of Public International Law*, 733.

71 For details, see Aiden Warren and Ingvild Bode, *Governing the Use-of-Force in International Relations: The Post-9/11 US Challenge to International Law* (Hampshire: Palgrave Macmillan, 2014), 29–31; and Murphy, "The International Legality of US Military Cross-Border Operations from Afghanistan into Pakistan", 126.

72 Andrew C. Orr, "Unmanned, Unprecedented and Unresolved: The Status of American Drone Strikes in Pakistan Under International Law", *Cornell International Law Journal*, 44 (2011): 739. For further details, see Raul A. Pete Pedrozo, "Use of Unmanned Systems to Combat Terrorism", *International Law Studies* 87, no. 1 (2011): 221; and Wilmshurst, "The Chatham House Principles of International Law on the Use of Force in Self-Defence", 970.

73 Orr, "Unmanned, Unprecedented and Unresolved: The Status of American Drone Strikes in Pakistan Under International Law", 740.

74 Dinstein, *War, Aggression and Self-Defence*, 215–216; and McDougal and Feliciano, *Law and Minimum Public World Order*, 231–240.

75 Amos N. Guiora, "Targeted Killing: When Proportionality Gets All Out of Proportion", *Case Western Reserve Journal of International Law* 45, no. 1 (2012): 243.

76 Doyle, *Striking First*, 14–15; and Michael Walzer, *Just and Unjust Wars: A Moral Argument with Historical Illustrations*. 4th ed. (New York: Basic Books, 2006), 74–75.

In terms of time continuum, there may be various scenarios informing the imminence of a security threat. Some may appear more imminent than others. At times it can be the cost of inaction which tempts the threatened state to initiate armed recourse to self-defence while sometimes it is the fleeting opportunity of targeting which compels a state to launch an attack.[77] It is a matter of *subjective* military choices and political priorities of decision-makers to decide upon the pre-emptive use of force.[78] In any case, pre-emptive action ought to be initiated against a security threat that is *irretrievably* set the course to harm. Yet, due to the limitations of sources of judgement, it is submitted that any precise intelligence of the impending terrorist strike may remain tenuous. Similarly, legitimate questions shall arise concerning a terrorist group which carried out terrorism in the past and intends to harm again. In this context, the condition of imminence might be read against the evolving security circumstances.[79]

The discussions now turn to the factual explanations against the legal justifications informing the application of imminence of security threat in Pakistan and Yemen. At the outset, given the US conduct, one may assume that the political and military logic of the 'war on terror' is driven by the notion that the use of force shall follow the terrorists wherever they are spotted. Certainly, terrorists continue operating from within Pakistan and Yemen. Their intentions to harm the US and its nationals abroad are quite clear. To hunt down them, combat drones emerge as an ever-ready weapon. The former CIA Chief Leon Panetta hence suggested that combat drones are the only viable tool to kill Al-Qaeda leaders. They would follow these terrorists in Yemen, Somalia, and other Middle Eastern states. "We

77 For details, see McDougal and Feliciano, *The International Law of War: Transnational Coercion and World Public Order*, 231–238. Further on, thrashing out the criteria for justifying imminence of a security threat, US State Department Legal Advisor Brian Egan noted that imminence of a security threat involves:

> [T]he nature and immediacy of the threat; whether the anticipated attacks is a part of a concerted pattern of continuing armed activity; the likely scale of the attack and the injury, loss, or damage likely to result therefrom in the absence of a mitigating action;---. The absence of specific evidence of where an attack will take place or the precise nature of an attack does not preclude a conclusion that an armed attack is imminent for purposes of the exercise of the right of self-defence, provided that there is a reasonable and objective basis for concluding that an armed attack is imminent.

Speech by Brian Egan, Legal Advisor to US State Department, ASIL Meeting April 4, 2016, accessed January 12, 2020, https://www.lawfareblog.com/state-department-legal-adviser-brian-egans-speech-asil

78 David Kretzmer, "The Inherent Right to Self-Defence and Proportionality in Jus Ad Bellum", *European Journal of International Law* 24, no. 1 (2013): 248; and Stuart Casey-Maslen, "The Use of Armed Drones", in *Weapons under International Human Rights Law*, ed. Stuart Casey-Maslen (New York: Cambridge University Press, 2014), 402.

79 Ashley S. Deeks, "Taming of the Doctrine of Pre-emption", in *The Oxford Handbook of the Use of Force in International Law*, ed. Marc Weller (Oxford: Oxford University Press, 2015), 672–673.

can't let them escape. We can't let them find hiding places", he emphasised.[80] Thus, the US leadership believes that it has the right to hunt down the leaders of Al-Qaeda and its associated forces due to the *continuous* threat they pose.[81]

In 2002, the Bush administration attempted to recalibrate the requirement of imminence to the new realities of the international security environment. According to it, given the manifest ability of terrorists, it is imperative to take into account their intentions and capability to inflict damage at a scale which is no way less than the state actors, it outlined.[82] Subsequently, different US administrations also justified their counter-terror operations outside the areas of active hostilities within the framework of self-defence. As the former Legal Adviser to the US government, Harold Koh, in his speech at the American Society of International Law, underlined, the US is locked into an armed conflict with Al-Qaeda, Taliban, and their associated forces. Therefore, it "may use force consistent with its inherent right to self-defence under international law", he suggested.[83] Here, the Legal Adviser categorically refers to 'the inherent right of self-defence', which can be construed as an implicit call for pre-emptive self-defence. Such a conclusion was reached due to the facts that the US is at war with "a nimble and determined enemy that cannot be underestimated",[84] for Al-Qaeda and its associated forces are still plotting to kill Americans. The disruption and destruction of Al-Qaeda and its affiliates is the top priority of the US.[85] Hence, an Al-Qaeda perpetrated security threat remains an *imminent* threat for the US.

Given this policy, the launch of combat drones and their operational dynamics was shrouded by secrecy in the beginning. To address this issue and respond to the ever-growing calls for openness and transparency, the Obama administration thrashed out detailed policy guidelines. The policy laid down that the armed measures will only be employed in the safety and security of the US nationals abroad. And terrorists will be targeted in instances "only when capture is not feasible and no other reasonable alternatives exist to address the threat effectively".[86]

80 "Remarks of Director of Central Intelligence Agency, Leon E. Panetta, at the Pacific Council on International Policy", *CIA*, May 18, 2009, accessed January 22, 2020, https://www.cia.gov/news-information/speeches-testimony/directors-remarks-at-pacific-council.html
Panetta, Director's Remarks at the Pacific Council on International Policy, 2009.

81 Brennan, "The Ethics and Efficacy of the President's Counterterrorism Strategy".

82 "The National Security Strategy of the US", 2002, 12–16. Moreover, for further details of the Bush administration's response towards the new realities, see Warren and Bode, *Governing the Use-of-Force in International Relations: The Post-9/11 US Challenge to International Law*, 64–75.

83 Koh, "The Obama Administration and International Law".

84 Attorney General Eric Holder Speech at the Northwestern University School of Law.

85 Ibid. For further details of analysis, see Warren and Bode, *Governing the Use-of-Force in International Relations: The Post-9/11 US Challenge to International Law*, 83–90; and Pardiss Kebriaei, "The Distance between Principle and Practice in the Obama Administration's Target Killing Programme: A Response to Jeh Johnson", *Yale Law & Policy Review* 31, no. 1 (2012): 151–172.

86 White House, "Fact Sheet: US Policy Standards and Procedures for the Use of Force in Counterterrorism Operations Outside the United States and Areas of Active Hostilities", May 23, 2013, accessed January 13, 2020, https://www.whitehouse.gov/the-press-office/2013/05/23/fact-sheet-us-policy-standards-and-procedures-use-force-counterterrorism

Lethal force shall only target those senior leaders of the terrorist organisations, who remains committed conducting terrorist attacks.[87] Besides the target shall be a legitimate one and posing an 'imminent threat'.[88]

When a state decides to use force against an impending attack, it is important to ascertain that such an attack is 'imminent' and the information employed to ascertain the imminence is beyond any *reasonable doubt*.[89] Given this backdrop, the label of terrorism is itself a framework which may potentially reshape and redefine the limits of *imminence*. At least, one can assume this in the context of the prevalent understanding of terrorism, which informs the US decision-making and policy choices. The practice of pre-empting terrorism illustrates that the requirement of imminence is overstretched to accommodate the instances of operational preparedness of terrorists as credible evidence of a looming security threat.[90] In these circumstances, the territorial integrity of the target state is merely an instance of diplomatic dispensation.[91] Yet there can be legitimate concerns about the safety and security of Americans residing in Pakistan and Yemen. Hence, the proximity of terrorists to its citizens may compel the US to treat this scenario as an instance of imminent security threat.

Legal scholars, however, emphasise that the standard of imminence should mean that lethal force is the last resort against a substantive security threat, which the host state failed to quell.[92] In this context, the use of combat drones becomes problematic as they do not give a warning or time to surrender.[93] Perhaps the operational easiness makes the use of combat drones detrimental to uphold the principle of last resort. In effect, it undermines the limits on the necessity of the threshold of pre-emptive use of force.[94] The question of last resort becomes even more problematic in the absence of other means of warfare, like soldiers. And so, the target state is directly jumping to the last resort without entertaining the other options of surrender and capture of terrorists. Presumably, the use of combat drones is predicated upon the notion that terrorists are not ready to surrender.

87 Ibid. (emphasis added)

88 Ibid.

89 Warren and Bode, *Governing the Use-of-Force in International Relations: The Post-9/11 US Challenge to International Law*, 74.

90 Ibid. Also, see Brooks, "Drones and the International Rule of Law", 94; and den Hole, "Anticipatory Self-Defence Under International Law", 99.

91 Anderson, "Rise of the Drones: Unmanned Systems and the Future of War", 4.

92 Wilmshurst, "The Chatham House Principles of International Law on the Use of Force in Self-Defence", 971.

93 The famous incidence of the killing of TTP leader Baitullah Mehsud while sleeping is a case in point here.

94 Brunstetter and Braun, "State of the Union: A Decade of Armed Drones", 89. To the contrary, Christian J. Tams and James G. Devaney stress that a state under threat is not required to exhaust all means of peaceful settlement of any given dispute. Rather she needs to choose only those tools which can be 'effective'. Tams and Devaney, "Applying Necessity and Proportionality to Anti-Terror Self-Defence", 96.

Indeed, this is an extreme measure to counter-terrorism that potentially creates a fog around the legal categories of warfare. Thus, it is submitted that the limit of last resort may also become ineffective when the criterion of the imminence of a security threat is compromised. Perhaps, pre-emptive self-defence is tactically more lucrative against terrorists than states, as terrorists, unlike states, do not pay heed to the deterrent value of laws and power.[95]

Besides, the blurring of boundaries between pre-emption and prevention becomes another aspect of the discourse on pre-emption in the face of counter-terrorism. The chief of the International Law Office of the US Army suggested that drone strikes are permissible in Pakistan as a measure of 'preventive use of force'.[96] He did not back this conclusion with any clear legal justification for preventive use of force within contemporary and customary international laws. Earlier within the realm of state practice, the US 'quarantine' measures against Cuba to stop the entry of Soviet nuclear missiles had failed to convince the majority of states.[97] In this context, failing to prove the evidence of an impending 'armed attack', the US government did not even mention Article 51 for once.[98] Similarly, the majority of states rejected the expansive logic of the Israeli preventive armed attack against the Iraqi nuclear reactor in 1981.[99] One may assume that such attempts to expand the meanings of pre-emption to the adobe of prevention military operations do not contribute to upholding the rule of law among states,[100] whereof some states are supposed to be less responsible when they are framed into the security calculus of other states.

Also, the Court emphasised in the *Israeli Wall Advisory Opinion* that the right of self-defence is subject to the imminence of an impending security threat. The mere presence of terrorists in a state, therefore, does not fulfil the criteria of imminence.[101] However, what to make of terrorists, the sworn enemy of a state? For instance, as is the case of Al-Qaeda and the US. Perhaps here the issue of imminence, as it is among states, becomes somewhat slippery, as even the presence of Al-Qaeda terrorists in a state may threaten the lives of the US nationals therein. As explained above, the acts of Al-Qaeda and its associated forces give credence

95 It is worth noting here that deterrence functions relatively well among states because they are deemed to be rational actors in calculating the resort to armed measures for achieving their goals. On the contrary, terrorists are not thought to be rational actors and prefer to jump to violence to achieve their objectives. For details, see Mark Totten, *First Strike* (New Haven, CT: Yale University Press, 2010), 172, 183, and 186.

96 Chris Jenks, "Law from Above: Unmanned Aerial Systems, Use of Force, and the Law of Armed Conflict", *North Dakota Law Review* 85, no. 3 (2009): 671.

97 Wright, "The Cuban Quarantine", 546; and Shaw, *International Law*, 1130.

98 For details, see David A. Sadoff, "A Question of Determinacy: The Legal Status of Anticipatory Self-Defence", *Georgetown Journal of International Law* 40, no. 2 (2009): 563–564.

99 Ibid., 569–570.

100 Harold H. Koh, "Preserving American Values: The Challenge at Home and Abroad", in *The Age of Terror: America and the World after September 11*, ed. Strobe Talbott and Nayan Chanda (New York: Basic Books, 2001), 155.

101 *Israeli Wall Opinion*, 62–63 at para. 140.

to such fears. Though Pakistan and Yemen introduced safety measures to ensure security, they fell short of the security standards Americans continued to insist on. The interplay of security assurances, perceptions, and security threats played an important role in constructing the notion of imminence while the US is determined to eliminate such a security threat before it causes harm.

The notion that the status and scope of the movement of a terrorist defines the limits of a battlefield is also problematic.[102] Operationally, the use of force against terrorists in Pakistan and Yemen display this reality wherein the opportunity to strike is equated with the imminence of security threat.[103] The US believes in this context while it is leading rethinking—the international community is following. As the US re-defines the traditional concept of imminence, the intentions and capabilities of terrorists impose such conditions to rethink the imminence.[104] On the contrary, one may argue that perhaps combat drone attacks remain an *isolated practice* of counter-terrorism which sits closer to *lex ferenda*.[105] Such a state practice cannot be construed as a sign of emerging customary norm. This is because most of the states do not corroborate the said practice. The question shall arise, however, as to whether their acquiescence could be taken as consent to this effect. For such a norm to become a customary rule, a consistent and juridically conscious state practice shall serve a better signpost.

Indeed, the US justifications for the necessity of self-defence remain rather problematic when assessed against the *Caroline* criteria. These justifications conform, however, to the pre-Charter norm of self-preservation, wherein the states chose to use force, most often, to satisfy the calculus of power. And such a calculus dictated the accumulation of power by destroying others rather than paying heed to laws.[106] Before situating the necessity of self-defence certainly, it is also submitted that any measure of pre-emptive use of force is inherently complex to comprehend and assess legally. This is because an act of pre-emption is active self-defence which depends on the satisfaction of numerous legal principles subject to the circumstantial and factual evidence. It is also because such a phenomenon seeks justification as a defensive attack against "an impending unjustified attack".[107] At the core, however, it will remain a counter-play of intentions and perceptions. This challenge becomes daunting when the state invoking the right

102 "International Humanitarian Law and the Challenges of Contemporary Armed Conflicts", 31st International Conference of the Red Cross and Red Crescent, 2011, 10–11.

103 Statement by David E. Glazier, "Rise of the Drones II: Unmanned Systems and the Future of War", 2010.

104 John O. Brennan, "Strengthening Our Security by Adhering to Our Values and Law", *Speech at Harvard Law School*, 16 September 16, 2011, accessed January 13, 2020, www.whitehouse.gov /the-press-offi ce/2011/09/16/remarks-john-o-brennan-strengthening-our-security-adhering-ou r-values-an

105 Marie Aronsson, "Remote Law-Making? American Drone Strikes and the Development of Jus Ad Bellum", *Journal on the Use of Force and International Law* 1, no. 2 (2014): 283.

106 For details, see McDougal and Feliciano, *The International Law of War: Transnational Coercion and World Public Order*, 210–215; and Jennings, "The Caroline and McLeod Cases", 82–99.

107 Shue and Rodin, *Pre-emption: Military Action and Moral Justification*, 3.

of self-defence does not have contagious borders with the adversary. In such an instance, the security of the nationals abroad rather than the territorial security of the state becomes the priority.

It is also important to note that in his long correspondence after the *Caroline* incident, the US Secretary of State tried to convince his British counterpart that the mere fact of having hostile intentions and roaming along the border of Canada cannot give the British forces any right to launch a cross-border attack. Thus, the concept of imminence must be studied under the given temporal and geographical circumstances. In contemporary times, terrorism does not seem to be succeeding to reshape the requirement of imminence.[108] Yet, at least, terrorism has contributed to change the perceptions of the victim states towards the requirements of imminence.[109]

The right to use force even in the absence of attributability of terrorist attacks against a state is gaining acceptance.[110] Any kind of tangible support to the terrorists by the host state, such as training, equipping, and instructing or providing sanctuary, may entail state responsibility. Negligence and toleration, however, may not lead to the forfeiting of an obligation and, therefore, may be punishable through the use of force.[111] It is also argued that in the absence of any direct state link to a terrorist security threat, states may find forcible intrusions into the territory of other states less objectionable if and when the use of force is limited to the security threat.[112] It may widen the misunderstandings regarding the legal discourses and operational realities, on the one hand, and the doctrinal approaches and dynamics of threat perception, on the other hand.[113] This is because the attribution of state responsibility is not established and yet the terrorist security threat is linked to a state.

To conclude, it is argued that the circumstantial experience of states vis-à-vis terrorism can influence their understanding of the use of force. Those who came under attack shall have reasons to entertain an inflated sense of fear and insecurity as terrorists may target those states again and again, and these states shall, due to their advanced technologies, chase down terrorists more frequently and effectively. In times of hyper-personalisation of the security threats and available high-tech response mechanisms, there are chances that the perceptions of *jus ad bellum* among states may undermine the legitimacy of any measure of

108 Noam Lubell, "The Problem of Imminence in an Uncertain World", in *The Oxford Handbook of the Use of Force in International Law*, ed. Weller, 707–708.

109 Kretzmer, "The Inherent Right to Self-Defence and Proportionality in Jus Ad Bellum", 266.

110 Kimberley N. Trapp, "Can Non-State Actors Mount an Armed Attack?" in *The Oxford Handbook of the Use of Force in International Law*, ed. Weller, 690; and Lindsay Moir, "Action against Host States of Terrorist Groups", in *The Oxford Handbook of the Use of Force in International Law*, ed. Weller, 731.

111 Cassese, *International Law*, 471–472.

112 Hakimi and Cogan, "The Two Codes on the Use of Force", 285.

113 Bethlehem, "Principles Relevant to the Scope of a State's Right of Self-Defence against an Imminent or Actual Armed Attack by Non-State Actors", 774.

force employment.[114] In these contexts, the necessity of self-defence shall continue to be a fluid notion. After all, it only took 19 Al-Qaeda terrorists to kill 3,000 Americans in a mere instant. Indeed, this memory has the adequate potential to endure and shape the threat perception and response of the US administrations.

Proportionality of counter armed measures

Along with necessity, proportionality helps in balancing the doctrine of pre-emption since it is 'the essence of self-defence'.[115] It protects the "subjective interests of the wrongdoer against the over-reaction" as well as it seeks to regulate the "nature and intensity" of the retaliatory violence against the wrongdoer.[116] It is easy to locate and explain it in the *jus in bello*. Its understanding and interpretation, however, in *jus ad bellum* framework is admittedly difficult.[117] This is because self-defence is the main premise of proportionality in *jus in bello*, while in *jus ad bellum* it is pre-emption: a hypothetical scenario of security threat. In this context, strategic calculus of force employment informs and assesses scenario of the target elimination against the lives saved and losses averted. In this calculus, however, the use of combat drones adds another layer of complexity when balancing the consequences against gains of armed intervention.

It is important to mention here that given the lack of literature and conceptual coherence, the following discussion of proportionality shall draw upon analogies from *jus in bello* to build and evaluate this principle within the doctrinal delineations of pre-emptive self-defence.

In the legal literature, opinions vary for judging the proportionality against the legitimacy of ends of force employment and/or concerning the gravity of an impending security threat that it seeks to counter.[118] It is because the idea of pre-emptive self-defence premised on the notion of taking the enemy by surprise and knocking it down before it launches a violent attack. In principle, therefore, proportionality is assessed in the context of an actual force employment and a potential danger of losses. It demands an incremental and bottom-up response: where the arrest is possible, do not injure; where injury to the point of incapacitation is possible, do not kill; and where the killing of the specific enemy is possible and serves the purpose of the force employment, do not kill *indiscriminately*. Indeed, states cannot embark on a forcible recourse "to extract an 'eye' when a 'tooth'

114 Kennedy, *Of War and Law*, 156.

115 Brownlie, *International Law and the Use of Force by States*, 279.

116 Enzo Cannizzaro, "The Role of Proportionality in the Law of International Countermeasures", *European Journal of International Law* 12, no. 5 (2001): 890.

117 Ibid., 889–916.

118 For details of different legal treatments of proportionality, see Gardam, *Necessity, Proportionality and the Use of Force by States*, 8–9; Doyle, *Striking First*, 10; Brownlie, *International Law and the Use of Force by States*, 261; Olivier Corten, *The Law Against War: The Prohibition on the Use of Force in Contemporary International Law* (Oxford: Hart Publishing Ltd., 2010), 470; Cannizzaro, "The Role of Proportionality in the Law of International Countermeasures", 891; Cassese, *International Law*, 355; and Dinstein, *War, Aggression and Self-Defence*, 184.

would be sufficient to neutralize an attack".[119] This emphasis on a calculated counter armed measure is suggestive of the fact that in the context of pre-emption, a use of violent force depends *equally* upon the lawfulness of the recourse to make such a choice as well as its actual conduct.

Within the self-defence framework, moreover, it is emphasised that necessity and proportionality are "two sides of the same coin".[120] Proportionality is an important element in understanding the correlation between the action and its intended purpose.[121] The criterion to assess proportionality, thus, involves the appreciation of *status* and *circumstances* of a given deadly force. In this context, the element of status underlines the material understanding of the target, which includes individuals, physical infrastructure, and their relevance to the security threat projection. It depicts a tangible dimension of the element, whereas the circumstances relate to both tangible and non-tangible understanding of proportionality. On one hand, the element of circumstances involves the military value calculus of the force employment, while on the other hand, it takes into account the resultant damages. In this context, the decision-makers have to decide how much damage and degradation of the enemy capabilities is necessary to seek the objectives as well as the justification of any dose of armed force.

Continuous combat function

In the early 2000s, the bordering regions of Pakistan and Afghanistan did not have strict security infrastructure to check the cross-border movements. There were a few security and custom check posts on the main roads linking both the states. A continuous flow of people across the border was a routine. In the context of Afghanistan, due to the history of external invasions and civil wars, the bordering regions became a hub for terrorists. That is why it is not surprising that the Taliban regime in Afghanistan had lots of sympathisers on the Pakistani side of the bordering areas.[122] Closer cross-border relations and a lack of security had made it easier for the Al-Qaeda terrorists to sneak into Pakistan, after the launch of the US military operation in 2001.[123] After crossing into Pakistan, Al-Qaeda terrorists hid near the bordering regions and then slipped into the settled areas.

Due to the loss of operating base in Afghanistan and closer links with the tribesmen in Pakistan, it was easy for Al-Qaeda to reside and operate from the

119 Sadoff, "A Question of Determinacy: The Legal Status of Anticipatory Self-Defence", 527.

120 *Yearbook of the International Law Commission*, 1980, 69 at para. 121.

121 Ibid.

122 Gilles Dorronsoro, "The Transformation of the Afghanistan-Pakistan Border", in *Under the Drones: Modern Lives in the Afghanistan-Pakistan Borderlands*, ed. Shehzad Bashir and Robert D. Crews (Cambridge, MA: Harvard University Press, 2012), 36.

123 Shah, *International Law and Drone Strikes in Pakistan: The Legal and Socio-Political Aspects*, 1–6; Ziring, *Pakistan: At the Crosscurrent of History*, 318; and Rohan Gunaratna and Anders Nielsen, "Al-Qaeda in the Tribal Areas of Pakistan and Beyond", *Studies in Conflict & Terrorism* 31, no. 9 (2008): 775–807.

bordering areas of South and North Waziristan. It also established rudimentary training infrastructure in these areas. While still being in Pakistan, Al-Qaeda continued to express its intentions to attack the US security interests in the region and beyond.[124] Its operational capability and access to the US security interests was, in no way, the same as it was during the pre–September 11 times. The US intelligence agencies monitored movements and communications of the Al-Qaeda leaders. The continuous presence of combat drones above them also proved to be a strict operational limitation as a number of drone attacks followed the lead of targets by tracing their communications with the outside world.[125] The case of Al-Qaeda in Yemen, moreover, was not any different as well. Their leaders and fighters continued their search for targeting US security interests and nationals.

In this backdrop, it is argued that though the loss of primary bases in Afghanistan dented the operational capability of Al-Qaeda, its intentions and motives did not change. Al-Qaeda terrorists continued to perform a *combat function* to implement the larger goals of their destructive ideology. To eliminate those fulfilling combat functions, the principle of proportionality underlines that any dose of violent force should outweigh the perceived losses of civilian and military lives, which it intends to safeguarded.[126] There are methods to balance the possible damages and intended benefits.[127] Though they comprise the robust checklist, they are not a legal remedy. The sophistication of method itself, however, cannot be a guarantor of the legality of counter armed measures. It is imperative, therefore, that the targeting state gather adequate information about those who fulfil combat functions. Also, it must figure out ways to avoid harming civilians.[128] To satisfy the functionality test, it is imperative to target those objects and individuals (belligerents) having a direct relationship to the capabilities of the adversary.[129]

124 Zahid Hussain, *Frontline Pakistan: The Struggle with Militant Islam* (London: I.B. Tauris & Co. Ltd., 2007), 119–130.

125 This information was substantiated through an interview with a local informant. The interviewee informed that after such incidents people are afraid of using any satellite communication channels in the region. Meanwhile, data shared by the CIA operative Edward Snowden reveals that the CIA intensively coordinates with the National Security Agency (NSA) for getting intelligence about the suspected terrorists in tribal areas of Pakistan. The NSA has effectively 'draped a surveillance blanket over' tribal areas of Pakistan and keeps a complete track of suspected targets through monitoring their all sources of communication with the outside world. For further details, see Greg Miller, Julie Tate and Barton Gellman, "Documents Reveal NSA's Extensive Involvement in Targeted Killing Program", *The Washington Post*, October 17, 2013.

126 Michael N. Schmitt, "Autonomous Weapon Systems and International Humanitarian Law: A Reply to Critics", *Harvard National Security Journal Features* (2013): 19. Also, see Megret, "The Humanitarian Problem with Drones", 1296; John Forge, "Proportionality, Just War Theory and Weapons Innovation", *Science and Engineering Ethics* 15, no. 1 (2009): 25–38.

127 For further details of the concept, see "Briefing: Joint Targeting Cycle and Collateral Damage Methodology", Defense Intelligence Agency General Council, November 10, 2009, accessed January 10, 2019, https://www.aclu.org/files/dronefoia/dod/drone_dod_ACLU_DRONES_JOINT_STAFF_SLIDES_1-47.pdf

128 Guiora, "Targeted Killing: When Proportionality Gets All Out of Proportion", 252.

129 Charles Garraway, "The Changing Character of the Participants in War: Civilization of Warfight-

Functionality test and targeting practices

For being virtually absent from the local territory, the US devised the criteria of 'patterns of life' to launch the drone strikes. The drone operators, while sitting in the US, collected the surveillance data about the targets and their terrorist-like conduct. Given the cultural and social customs in the target areas, one may assume that such a targeting criterion cannot be effective. For instance, in the case of Pakistan, the people of the target areas are almost identical to Afghans in their appearance. As a customary practice, they also carry weapons like in case of terrorists. Being a tribal society, the case is not much different in Yemen as well. These given conditions make the chances of *mistaken identity* higher. Numerous incidents of drone violence underscore this point.[130] Later this practice was further formalised through employing the targeting strategy of 'signature strikes'. It came under consideration during times of the Bush administration.[131] The Obama administration operationalised the 'signature strikes' to hunt down terrorists in Pakistan and Yemen. This relaxation in targeting criterion resulted in 53 drone strikes in Pakistan during the first year alone. During the second year, however, the number jumped to an all-time high of 128 drone attacks. It caused the maximum number of fatalities in a given year.[132]

In contrast to the US practice, under an objective criterion to uphold proportionality, any direct role of the targeted individuals in hostilities is evaluated through the pattern of *distinctively dangerous behaviour*. In this context, acts like taking up weapons and explosives with demonstratable intent to take part in hostilities like planting them can lead to the performance of functions of hostility.[133] But, given the US drone practice, even the people residing around areas frequented by the Al-Qaeda leaders are "probably up to no good".[134] These unintended targets are accounted for terrorists, until and unless it is proven that they are innocent civilians.[135] The fate of civilians, in this context, is tied to the destiny of Al-Qaeda

ing and the Concept of 'Direct Participation in Hostilities'", *International Law Studies* 87 (2009): 180–181.

130 For details, see the section below.

131 "Living under Drones: Death, Injury and Trauma to Civilians from US Drone Practice in Pakistan", International Human Rights and Conflict Resolution Clinic, Stanford Law School and Global Justice Clinic, New York University School of Law, 2012, 12.

132 For details, see the data compiled and made available by the Bureau of Investigative Journalism. Meanwhile, Gregory S. McNeal disputes the methods to count the civilian killings and believes that most of the times, the killings are exaggerated. For details, see McNeal, "Are Targeted Killings Unlawful? A Case Study in Empirical Claims without Empirical Evidence", in *Targeted Killings, Law and Morality in an Asymmetrical World*, ed. Claire Finkelstein, Jens D. Ohlin and Andrew Altmann (Oxford: Oxford University Press, 2012), 326–346.

133 Lewis, "Drones and the Boundaries of Battlefield", 310–311; and Kristina Benson, "Kill 'em and Sort It Out Later": Signature Drone Strikes and International Humanitarian Law", *Global Business & Development Law Journal* 27 (2014): 30–31.

134 Jo Becker and Scott Shane, "Secret 'Kill List' Proves a Test of Obama's Principles and Will", *The New York Times*, 29 May 2012, A1.

135 Ibid.

leaders in a given area of drone operation. Only the migration and relocation of these leaders from that particular area may spare the lives of civilians.

The question of combat roles also becomes complicated when we study the use of combat drones against the 'suspected militants' in an area having a mix up of civilians and militants, thus forming entangled identities.[136] In this context, however, the US Department of Defence in its latest Law of War Manual emphasises to adopt methods to spare the lives of civilians. For instance, it suggests striking the target at a time when there are fewer chances of civilians to be hurt.[137] On the contrary, as per the US drone practice, 'signature strikes' involve "the decontextualisation of the killing from the broader conflict by focusing upon the claimed characteristics of the person killed".[138] The targeted person in this sort of calculus is a legitimate target not because of his capability to harm but due to his unusual conduct at a given time and in a given area.[139] "[B]eing targeted is therefore an indicator that one has been primarily determined to be an illegitimate political subject rather than an important one" such a calculus underscores.[140]

The criterion to carry out the so-called 'signature strikes', thus, inflates the limits of the legal standards of proportionality. Reports suggest that sometimes the drone operators are not certain about the presence of a high-value target at the location of a drone strike, yet they launch attack due to certain conduct of the individuals below.[141] For instance, it is reported that when "three guys doing jumping jacks" are spotted in tribal areas of Pakistan, the pattern is associated with that of a militant training camp. It amounts to the manipulation of the notion of the pattern of behaviour.[142] On other occasions, the 'signature strike' criterion was inflated to the point that it categorised all the military-age men at a location as legitimate targets.[143]

136 Breau and Aronsson, "Drone Attacks, International Law and Recording of Civilian Causalities of Armed Conflict", 285.

137 "Department of Defense, Law of War Manual", Office of Journal Council, Department of Defense, Washington, June 2015, updated December 2016, 7.

138 Kyle Grayson, "Six Theses on Target Killing", *Politics* 32, no. 2 (2012): 125; Christian Enemark, "Drones, Risk, and Perpetual Force", *Ethics & International Affairs* 28, no. 3 (2014): 373; and Joseph Pugliese, "Prosthetics of Law and the Anomic Violence of Drones", *Griffith Law Review* 20, no. 4 (2011): 943–944.

139 Grayson, "Six Theses on Target Killing", 125; and Leila Sadat, "Second Annual Catherine B. Fite Lecture: Drone Wars and the Nuremberg Legacy", *Studies in Transnational Legal Policy* 45, no. 9 (2012): 35–36.

140 Grayson, "Six Theses on Target Killing", 125; and Pardiss Kebriaei, "The Distance Between Principle and Practice in the Obama Administration's Targeted Killing Program: A Response to Jeh Johnson", *Yale Law & Policy Review* 31 (2012): 166.

141 Charlie Savage, *Power Wars: Inside Obama's Post-9/11 Presidency* (New York: Little, Brown and Company, 2015), 442–444.

142 Ibid., 443.

143 Kristina Benson, "Kill 'em and Sort It Out Later': Signature Drone Strikes and International Humanitarian Law", *Global Business & Development Law Journal* 27 (2014): 31; and Daniel Byman, "Why Drones Work? The Case for Washington's Weapon of Choice", *Foreign Affairs* 92, no. 4 (2013): 36.

Besides, the purpose of labelling 'combatants' as 'terrorists' is itself telling here. Perhaps through this act the US government lifts the status of suspects in the battle zone to terrorists and then to combatants using 'patterns of life' categories since common people were targeted for merely being around the suspected militant compounds, carrying arms in public, and travelling in long convoys.[144] For instance, on one occasion, drone operators spotted a group of people having an ostensibly terrorist-like pattern of behaviour and launched the strike.[145] As a result of this strike, the US claimed to have killed 20 terrorists. But the locals and Pakistani state officials contested these claims. Investigations later revealed that the drone strike killed around 38 local elders and four Pakistani Taliban participating in a 'jirga'[146] to settle a local dispute.[147] Similarly, another drone attack against a religious seminary in the Bajaur Agency of Pakistan killed at least 69 students. In this instance, the actual target was the head of the seminary alleged to have close links to Al-Qaeda. The intended target survived the attack.[148] In the case of Yemen, likewise, a convoy of vehicles in the desert was sometimes misconstrued as the movement of terrorists. A drone attack against one of the convoys that happened to be a marriage procession killed numerous innocent civilians.

In these contexts, the prime target, the senior Al-Qaeda leader of a drone strike, fulfils the requirement of 'continuous combat function', but the killing of those who happened to be around such a target does not fully satisfy the *combat functionality* test. Such uses of force amount to undermining the criteria. Instances of back-to-back, or as they are popularly known 'double tap', attacks against some targets attending the funeral processions and wedding ceremonies also pose a challenge for the functionality test.[149] Reports suggest that the frequency of such attacks in certain areas was so high that nearly every other attack accounted for was 'double tap' in nature.[150] Within one year more than 50 civilians were killed as a result of 'double tap', and they were only providing rescuing services at the site of a drone strike.[151] During 2010 and 2011, the combat functionality tests were

144 Savage, *Power Wars: Inside Obama's Post-9/11 Presidency*, 443.

145 Scott Shane, "Contrasting Reports of Drone Strikes", *The New York Times*, August 11, 2011, A1.

146 *Jirga* is a local term which denotes the assembly of local elders convened to settle disputes among the tribal people.

147 An interview with a local informant. Also, see Savage, *Power Wars: Inside Obama's Post-9/11 Presidency*, 443–444.

148 Chris Woods, "The Day 69 Children Died", *The Express Tribune*, August 12, 2011. Estimates in the Daily Situation Report from the area, however, records 81 deaths, including that of 80 children.

149 For further details, see Chris Cole, Mary Dobing, and Amy Hailwood. "Convenient Killing: Armed Drones and the 'Playstation' Mentality". *The Fellowship of Reconciliation*, London, 2010, 8.

150 "Living under Drones: Death, Injury and Trauma to Civilians from US Drone Practice in Pakistan", 74–76.

151 Chris Woods and Christina Lamb, "Drone Strikes in Pakistan: CIA Tactics in Pakistan Include Targeting Rescuers and Funerals", *The Bureau of Investigative Journalism*, February 4, 2012, accessed January 12, 2020, https://www.thebureauinvestigates.com/2012/02/04/obama-terror-drones-cia-tactics-in-pakistan-include-targeting-rescuers-and-funerals/. Moreover, for detailed

so inflated that even the US military asked the CIA to show restraint.[152] In this backdrop, it is noted that though the killing of legitimate targets such as leaders of Al-Qaeda fulfils the combat function in an instance of pre-emptive self-defence, the killing of those who happened to be around a target does not meet the standard of continuous combat function.

Threshold of harm

The second element underpinning the principle of proportionality relates to the combat strength and circumstances of the intended targets. Customary norms stressed that any measure of the use of force must be *kept within the limits* of its necessity. They require that the intervening state show that it took every possible step to sort out the *innocent from the guilty* and the option of incapacitating the enemy was fully measured before killing him.[153] The US *Commander's Handbook of Law of Naval Operations* lays down that the principle of proportionality requires "the use of force be in all circumstances limited in intensity, duration, and scope to that which is reasonably required to counter the attack or threat of attack and to ensure the continued safety of U.S. forces".[154] It is assumed, however, that the operationalisation of this principle remains a difficult task because the standard application of the principle of proportionality varies with the change in the legal framework within which it is applied and evaluated. Among all the relevant legal frameworks, it gets stricter treatment within pre-emptive self-defence. Loss of innocent lives is hardly tolerated here. Civilians with no link to combat (in this context security threat) cannot be targeted as part of any military operation.[155]

In addition to this, those indirectly part of an armed conflict can also not be targeted. These include persons and organisations providing welfare, financial, and political aid to the fighting forces.[156] To evaluate the principle of proportionality, there are two methodological approaches to measure the gravity of threshold of harm. The first one considers the overall damage caused by a given dose of violence, whereas the second one "implies a technique of destructuring the response into a series of single measures, the proportionality of which must be determined

---

coverage of collateral damage of drone strikes, see in Marjorie Cohn, ed., *Drone and Targeted Killing: Legal, Moral and Geopolitical Issues* (Massachusetts: Olive Branch Press, 2015); and Brian G. Williams, *Predators; The CIA's Drone War on al Qaeda* (Washington, DC: Potomac Books, 2013). This fact is also corroborated through the study of a particular incident of 'double tap' by the author in an interview with a local informant.

152 Adam Entous, Siobhan Giorman, and Julian E. Barnes, "U.S. Tightens Drone Rules", *The Wall Street Journal*, November 4, 2011.

153 Jennings, "The Caroline and McLeod Cases", 89. (emphasis added)

154 Andrew R. Thomas and James C. Duncan, eds., *Annotated Supplement to the Commander's Handbook on the Law of Naval Operations* 73 (Washington: US Naval War College, 1999), para. 4.3.2.

155 Geneva Conventions III, Article 3.

156 Ryan Goodman, "The Detention of Civilians in an Armed Conflict", *American Journal of International Law* 103, no. 48 (2009): 52–53.

autonomously concerning the function accomplished by each".[157] Stressing upon the importance of overall damage, the Court in the *Oil Platforms* case pointed out that it could not ignore the fact of the use of force in its entirety while deciding upon the principle of proportionality of armed counter-measures.[158] In an operational sense, any pre-emptive force employment "requires a consideration of such matters as the geographical and destructive scope of the response, the duration of the response, and the selection of means and methods of warfare", among others.[159] In this context, it is also important to note that unlike Islamic law and natural law's conduct of hostilities that stems from the right of self-preservation appealing to some lofty ideological goals, positive law puts strict limits of proportionality. State practice during the UN Charter era bears testimony to this transformational fact, wherein any disproportionate use of force met with severe criticism by other states.[160]

One may argue that the threshold of harm allows legitimate 'incidental' loss of civilian lives as a consequence of an attack, which most of the time can be justified as unavoidable collateral damage. It does not, however, permit *excessive* civilian damage.[161] Furthermore, regarding the language and intent of the laws of the threshold, they speak of the proportionality in a 'prospective' sense of the unfolding situation.[162] It is maintained that such an understanding can be useful in evaluating sporadic incidents of violence in a limited time period. The application of this yardstick against a perpetual armed conflict, such as the 'war on terror',[163] shall consider the accumulative as well as individually distinctive impacts of the use of force. In turn, this may help in understanding whether there is an emerging pattern of excessive use of force along horizontal and vertical coordinates.

The threshold of harm also takes into account the choice of weapons. It is emphasised, however, that a weapon of war does not become illegal by the dint of its specific characteristics. Instead, its use under certain circumstances informs the judgment of legality and illegality.[164] Presumably, the characteristics of combat

157 Cannizzaro, "The Role of Proportionality in the Law of International Countermeasures", 896.

158 *Case Concerning Oil Platforms*, 41–42 at para. 77.

159 Gardam, *Necessity, Proportionality and the Use of Force by States*, 162.

160 Ibid., 162–167.

161 Laurie R. Blank, "After 'Top Gun': How Drone Strikes Impact the Law of War", *University of Pennsylvania Journal of International Law* 33, no. 3 (2012): 696 (emphasis in original); and Kenneth Anderson, "Predators Over Pakistan", *Weekly Standard* 15, no. 24 (2010): 30–33.

162 Blank, "After 'Top Gun': How Drone Strikes Impact the Law of War", 696. Schmitt, "Fault Lines in the Law of Attack", 277 and 293; and Joseph Holland, "Military Objective and Collateral Damage: Their Relationship and Dynamics", *Year Book of International Humanitarian Law* 7 (2004): 35 and 47.

163 Pardiss Kebriaei, "The Distance between Principle and Practice in the Obama Administration's Targeted Killing Program: A Response to Jeh Johnson", *Yale Law & Policy Review* 31 (2012): 161.

164 *Threat or Use of Nuclear Weapons*, Advisory Opinion, 23 at paras. 41–44. For a more general discussions on the role of technology in proportionality, see Chamayou, *A Theory of the Drone*, 15–17.

drones should have a bearing upon the outcomes of the use of force, wherein the careful usage of these weapons in counter-terror operations can *supposedly* help in making it proportionate and legitimate.[165] In fact, it is the confidence in the technological precision of combat drones which compels the US to claim that it is fully committed to uphold the principle of proportionality in Pakistan and Yemen. The US claimed that it does not carry out an attack "that may be expected to cause incidental loss of civilian life, injury to civilians, damage to civilian objects, or a combination thereof, that would be excessive in relation to the concrete and direct military advantage anticipated".[166] Yet it does not share any meaningful data about the effectiveness of combat drones as well as how these attacks are fulfilling the requirement of proportionality.[167]

Threshold of harm and targeting practices

In terms of their technological prowess, the combat drones are useful in accessing areas that are otherwise difficult for the soldiers to reach. The inaccessibility of the targeted area, however, also makes the assessment of the loss of lives a challenging task as it is difficult to be certain about the total number of drone attacks, let alone the actual numbers of resultant damages. This difficulty is serious in the case of Yemen, where the combat drones and fighter jets, sometimes, fire missiles simultaneously. It is imperative, therefore, to consult multiple sources of data to make any meaningful inferences. Similarly, in the case of Pakistan, the New America Foundation documents that the country suffered 414 drone attacks between June 2004 and December 2018. Of these, a whopping 353 were under the Obama administration alone. In 2010, 128 drone strikes were recorded. Between 2,366 and 3,702 terrorists and civilians perished in these drone attacks. Among these, 245 to 300 were confirmed civilians.[168] In the case of Yemen, the US launched around 232 drone strikes from November 2002 to December 2018, killing between 1,201 and 1,593 terrorists and civilians. Among these, 100 to 130 were civilian deaths.[169] Highlighting the difficulties in recording

165 Louis Henkin, "Use of Force: Law and U.S. Policy", in *Might V. Right: International Law and the Use of Force*. 2nd ed., ed. Loius Henkin et al. (New York: Council on Foreign Relations Press, 1991), 37 and 50. Also, see Tarcisio Gazzini, "A Response to Amos Guiora: Pre-Emptive Self-Defence Against Non-State Actors", *Journal of Conflict & Security Law* 13, no. 1 (2008): 25–32.

166 Harold H. Koh, "The Obama Administration and International Law", March 25, 2010; and Attorney General Eric Holder Speech at the Northwestern University School of Law, March 5, 2012.

167 It is important to note here that the Obama administration did share data on the killings out of drone attacks inside Pakistan, Somalia, and Yemen. But this data only covers the time period of Obama presidency. Moreover, it did not involve country specific figures. Therefore, it is difficult to know the actual number of killings of civilians in Pakistan or Yemen separately.

168 "America's Counterterrorism Wars", *The New America Foundation*, accessed January 12, 2019, https://www.newamerica.org/in-depth/americas-counterterrorism-wars/

169 Ibid. It is worth mentioning here that data compiled by the New America Foundation is relatively moderate in comparison to two other sources of detailed drone attacks and killings estimations, namely the Bureau of Investigative Journalism and the *Long War Journal*. In comparison to the

losses, Columbia Law School, New York University Law School, and Stanford Law School reports underscore that to reach any certain conclusion out of the data is difficult. Furthermore, these reports conclude that for the US government, all the military-age persons are terrorists and, thus, are counted under the same category.[170]

Such conclusions are further corroborated by the US government; when the US government notes that most among those killed in drone attacks are terrorists, it imparts credence rather inadvertently to the impression that it does count military-age persons as terrorists. The Obama administration estimates suggest that across Pakistan, Yemen, Somalia, and Libya 416 drone strikes left between 64 and 116 civilians dead, whereas around 2,500 terrorists were killed in these attacks. In contrast to this, when considering the alternative sources for estimating the number of casualties due to drone strikes, it is revealed that the total number of civilian deaths reported by the US government is even less than the number of children killed in Pakistan, let alone the total number of civilian deaths in the country.[171] Furthermore, even the most conservative estimates of the *Long War Journal* note that 212 civilians died during this period, whereas the Bureau of Investigative Journalism recorded 325 civilian deaths.[172] James Clapper, the Director of national intelligence, contested that the US government in comparison to other organisations has better resources to count and assess the damages. These include, among others, better sources of intelligence about all stages of a drone strike, video observations, human intelligence assets, open-source reporting from the local areas, signals, and geospatial intelligence.[173] In these contexts, one can assume that the belief of the US government tells one story about the threshold of harm while the investigations and conclusions of various research reports narrate another.

It seems that the US government banks confidence on the technological prowess of the combat drones and skills of their operators. Those who dig down the aftermath of a drone attack, however, do not support the US claims. For instance, Human Rights Watch investigated 6 drone attacks in Yemen carried out during

New America Foundation, the *Long War Journal* concludes lesser overall and civilian deaths while the Bureau of Investigative Journalism suggests more overall as well as civilian deaths. For a detailed comparison of different data collection sources, see "Civilian Casualties & Collateral Damage", *LAWFARE*, accessed, January 12, 2020, https://www.lawfareblog.com/civilian-casualties-collateral-damage

170 For details, see "Counting Drone Strike Deaths"; and "Living Under Drones: Death, Injury and Trauma to Civilians from US Drone Practices in Pakistan"; and Hugh Gusterson, *Drone: Remote Control Warfare* (London: The MIT Press, 2016), 97–98. Moreover, for a detailed comparison of different reports on the drone killings, see Ritika Singh, "Drone Strikes Kill Innocent People: Why Is It So Hard to Know How Many?" *New Republic*, October 25, 2013.

171 According to Daily Situation Report, the total number of children killed is 175 to 197.

172 Karen DeYoung and Greg Miller, "White House Releases its Count of Civilian Deaths in Counterterrorism Operations under Obama", *The Washington Post*, July 1, 2016.

173 Christopher J. Fuller, *See It/ Shoot It: The Secret History of the CIA's Lethal Drone Program* (New Haven, CT: Yale University Press, 2017), 214.

the Obama presidency and concluded that at least 57 out of the total 82 persons killed in these attacks were civilians.[174] In another instance, when the US government claimed to have killed the Al-Qaeda members involved in planning to attack the US embassy in Yemen, the Human Rights Watch investigations proved that 12 innocent civilians died because of that drone strike.[175]

In the case of Pakistan, likewise, the data compiled out of the Daily Situation Report shows that the majority among those assassinated were local civilians.[176] It is worth mentioning here that the said report categorises the killings in locals and non-locals. Given the precedents and patterns of terrorism, the link of non-locals to Al-Qaeda is easy, but establishing any connection between local civilians and Al-Qaeda is questionable. Among non-locals, moreover, it is estimated that around 61 senior leaders of Al-Qaeda died in Pakistan.[177] At the same time, some estimates suggest that one out of seven drone strikes in Pakistan killed an Al-Qaeda leader.[178] In this context, perhaps most of those killed are either low-level foot soldiers or innocent civilians. In 2009 alone, Pakistani officials recorded that drone strikes killed 700 civilians.[179] The US government, however, claimed that during May 2008 and May 2010, only 30 civilians died.[180] Certainly, the senior Al-Qaeda leadership remains a security threat for US security interests and individuals abroad. Questions abound, in this context, to satisfy the legal criteria of the threshold of harm while pursuing the elimination of senior Al-Qaeda leaders.

The perceptions of locals, which are formulated through their interactions with victims of drone attacks, also downplay the effectiveness of drone strikes in killing Al-Qaeda terrorists. A survey by the New American Foundation pointed out that more than half of the locals in areas of drone strikes in Pakistan believed that civilians remained the main victims of drone attacks.[181] The successive drone strikes following the killing of Baitullah Mehsud, the leader of the Pakistani Taliban, killed between 207 and 321 unintended persons deemed to be civilians.[182]

174 Letta Tayler, "Between a Drone and Al-Qaeda: The Civilian Cost of US Targeted Killing in Yemen", (New York: Human Rights Watch, 2013), 10.

175 "A Wedding That Became a Funeral", *Human Rights Watch*, 2014, accessed January 20, 2020 http:// www.hrw.org / reports / 2014 / 02 / 19 / wedding-became-funeral

176 These numbers range from 1,600 to 2,000. Data compiled by the author via the Daily Situation Report. This report is official document of the Pakistani government.

177 Bill Roggio, "Senior al Qaeda, Taliban, and Allied Jihadist Leaders Killed in US Airstrikes in Pakistan, 2004–2016", *The Long War Journal*, 2016, accessed January 19, 2019 http://www.longwarjournal.org/pakistan-strikes-hvts

178 Peter Bergen and Katherine Tiedemann, "Washington's Phantom War: The Effects of the U.S. Drone Program in Pakistan", *Foreign Affairs* 90, no. 4 (2011): 12.

179 Ibid.; and Ann Rogers and John Hill, *Unmanned: Drone Warfare and Global Security* (New York: Pluto Press, 2014), 10.

180 Hill, *Unmanned: Drone Warfare and Global Security*, 13.

181 Ibid., 14.

182 For details, see Jane Mayer, "The Predator War: What are the Risks of the C.I.A.'s Covert Drone Program?" *The New Yorker*, October 26, 2009, 45.

Though Mehsud was a high-value target, the killing of a large number of civilians for the sake of one terrorist raises some serious questions. This proves that the ratio of the killing of high-value terrorists to that of civilians is very low. More precisely, some estimates note that it is only 2 per cent of those killed.[183] This, in turn, suggests that the majority of those killed were not leaders of Al-Qaeda and its associated forces but were low-key terrorists immersed in violent activities against their respective governments.[184] Given these estimates, one may safely assume that the destruction caused by the combat drones to hunt down terrorist leadership stretches the limits of the threshold of harm.[185] It raises questions regarding whether it is meant to kill the terrorist leadership plotting to cause harm to the US and its nationals abroad.[186]

Thus, the US drone attacks are problematic given the *Caroline* standards of proportionality, which emphasise to take utmost care to spare the lives of innocents. However, contexts do matter and the principle of proportionality "must be assessed within the context of particular facts and circumstances", and under no circumstance, can conclusions "be drawn *in abstracto*".[187] So when the US launches a drone strike in circumstances of 'near certainty' of the presence of an intended target in a given area, it emerges that perhaps it does not pay much heed to the surroundings of an intended target as well as the amount of explosive used. Indeed, the precision ability of the combat drones to strike down the intended target cannot be doubted. It was accurate on certain occasions when used carefully, and thorough intelligence was calibrated before launching a strike, the killing of the Taliban leader Waliur Rehman, is an instructive case in this regard. A single missile fired by the combat drone did the perfect job of killing the terrorist in a house without damaging the surrounding houses and persons.[188]

Furthermore, data compiled from the Daily Situation Report suggested that around 30 per cent of drone attacks in Pakistan were on target, killing between one to five terrorists. In this backdrop, one may assume, however, that the drone attacks against targets located within innocent civilians speak more to the choices and decisions of the combat drone operators.

183 For details of different estimates, see Neta C. Crawford, *Accountability for Killing: Moral Responsibility for Collateral Damage in America's Post-9/11 Wars* (New York: Oxford University Press, 2013), 124–133; and Medea Benjamin, "War on Demand: The Global Rise of Drones", Rosa Luxemburg Stiftung, New York, 2013, 5.

184 Micah Zenko, "Reforming U.S. Drone Strikes Policies", Council on Foreign Relations Special Report No. 65, 2013, 10. For details, see Noam Lubell and Nathan Derejko, "A Global Battlefield? Drones and Geographical Scope of Armed Conflict", *Journal of International Criminal Justice* 11 (2013): 83.

185 Sadat, "America's Drone Wars", 233.

186 Ibid., 230; and Megret, "The Humanitarian Problem with Drones", 1312.

187 Robert P. Barnidge, Jr., "A Qualified Defense of American Drone Attacks in Northwest Pakistan under International Humanitarian Law", *Boston University International Law Journal* 30 (2012): 440.

188 An interview with a local informant.

To meet the threshold of harm concerning drone attacks, the US laid down standards. Explaining them, a CIA lawyer said that if bin Laden happened to be in a situation with one child, most of the lawyers would give a go-ahead response for the attack, but if he happened to be in a school, many lawyers would not consent to such an attack, due to the prospect of disproportionate damage to the civilian lives.[189] On the contrary, the actual application of this standard fell short of the target many times. The combat drones hit the high-value targets in religious seminaries, funeral processions, and wedding ceremonies. Thus the killing of various innocents was a necessary means to achieve the death of the intended target.[190] It is, in fact, the killing of a terrorist which determines the objectives.[191] This may be the reason that the former CIA chief John Brennan remarked that the drone strikes cause zero civilian casualties.[192] This certainty in claims must be seen in the context of the ratio of unintended killings out of drone strikes, which ranges from 50 to 1 and in case of civilians to militants 20 to 1.[193] Therefore, former President Obama conceded that the civilian killings remain a challenge in combat drone campaigns. He maintained, however, that there is a wide difference between the estimates of the US government and others.[194] Yet the US did not share complete facts and figures of the combat drone killings. The maintenance of the strict secrecy is itself a violation of the norm of proving the proportional effect of the counter-measures as in cases of war in self-defence, the burden of proof always lies with those who choose to wage war and claim its legality and justice.[195] It is emphasised, therefore, that any use of force "must be overt".[196]

One may also argue that within the positivist discourse of law, the killing of civilians is not easily tolerable. The test of proportionality, therefore, becomes stringent when the target is located among civilians.[197] In this context, the notion of 'war on terror' is itself fraught with the risk of expanding the use of force in self-defence. By categorising a counter-terror campaign as war, one has expanded the self-defence measures in temporality and spatiality to 'near infinity'.[198] It presumes that war ends with the elimination of the terrorist threat. However,

189 Mayer, "The Predator War: What are the Risks of the C.I.A.'s Covert Drone Program?" 45.

190 Steinhoff, *On the Ethics of War and Terrorism*, 42.

191 Sarah Kreps and John Kaag, "The Use of Unmanned Aerial Vehicles in Contemporary Conflicts: A Legal and Ethical Analysis", *Polity* 44, no. 2 (2012): 278; and Guiora, "Target Killing: When Proportionality Gets All Out of Proportion", 241.

192 For details, see Scott Shane, "C.I.A. Is Disputed on Civilian Toll in Drone Strikes", *The New York Times*, August 12, 2011, A1.

193 Richard Murphy, "Responses to the Ten Questions", *William Mitchel Law Review*, 37, no. 5 (2011): 5063.

194 "Remarks by the President at the National Defence University", 2013.

195 Crawford, "Just War Theory and the U.S. Counterterror War", 7.

196 Kenneth Anderson, "Predators Over Pakistan", *Weekly Standard* 15, no. 24 (2010): 30–33.

197 Vogel, "Drone Warfare and the Law of Armed Conflict", 127.

198 Crawford, "Just War Theory and the U.S. Counterterror War", 16; and Radsan and Murphy, "The Evolution of Law and Policy for CIA Targeted Killing", 451.

Al-Qaeda–perpetrated terrorism is an ideology of global *jihad* as well as a tactic. So, linking a counter-terror campaign to ideology undermines the threshold of harm.

It is vital to hold the ends firmly to pre-empt terrorism in an era of the revolution in warfare technologies.[199] The exaggerated confidence in technology may dislocate ends and limits; the precision technology cannot 'determine the proportionality' of counter armed measures in pre-emption against an adversary living and operating among the civilians.[200] In a similar vein, the confidence in the accuracy of drone attacks runs the risk of making a value judgment. Perhaps, it may make it harder to take account of the facts.[201] The US drone practice also underlines that the tendency to address security threats using remote control warfare technologies can make the conflicts timeless military campaigns.

The laws of war, moreover, require states not to create a 'state of war'. The right of self-defence is subject to the strict measure of proportionate use of force. The limit of proportionality is rarely observed when a state creates a 'state of war'.[202] In the context of the 'war on terror', the fact of the endurance of combat drones contributes to expanding the space and state of war.[203] Such an expansion would not have been problematic if it did not result in the indiscriminate killings. Unlike the soldiers, combat drones can wait a bit longer while hovering over an intended target. On the contrary, as explained earlier, the failure to eliminate any certain target in one strike is giving way to expanding the bounds of time, space, and damage—the essential conditions for the justification of proportionality of measures.[204] This practice, potentially, puts the drone operators in a 'play-station' frame of mind, prone to killing innocents.[205]

Above all, the application of proportionality is bound to become problematic where drone attacks eliminate would-be terrorists. In this scenario, hypothetical gains are squared against the actual losses.[206] The number of fatalities shows that once the legitimacy of the target is loosely selected, then the chance of

199 Walzer, *Just and Unjust Wars*, 120.

200 Kreps and Kaag, "The Use of Unmanned Aerial Vehicles in Contemporary Conflicts: A Legal and Ethical Analysis", 261.

201 Ibid., 274–277; and Sharkey, "Automating Warfare: Lessons Learned from the Drones", 151–152.

202 Greenwood, "The Concept of War in Modern International Law", 289. Meanwhile, Jordan Paust notes that the losses of civilian lives is not indiscriminate when assessed against the backdrop of other available alternative means of warfare like cruise missiles and manned fighter jets. For further details, see Paust, "Self-Defense Targetings of Non-state Actors and Permissibility of U.S. Use of Drones in Pakistan", 274–277.

203 Sharkey, "Automating Warfare: Lessons Learned from the Drones", 151.

204 Williams, "Distant Intimacy: Space, Drones, and Just War", 95; and Vogel, "Drone Warfare and the Law of Armed Conflict", 133.

205 Philip Alston, "Report of the Special Rapporteur on extrajudicial, summary or arbitrary executions", presented to the Human Rights Council, 14th session, May 28, 2010, p. 25. For further details and to understand about the videogame analogy of drone killings, see Pugliese, "Prosthetics of Law and the Anomic Violence of Drones", 940–941.

206 Brooks, "Drones and the International Rule of Law", 95.

"significant collateral damage is inevitable".[207] In past, there have been instances of disproportionate use of force among the warring parties. Sometimes, the inherent asymmetry between the adversaries gave way to the use of disproportionate force. On other occasions, the strategic rationale drove the choice to inflict maximum damage to deter the enemy and keep her away from choosing the recourse to force in future. In the case of counter-terrorism, however, these logics do not stand the test of the nature and character of the conflict because terrorists prefer to fight a long-drawn conflict and deterrence loses value. The use of disproportionate force to pre-empt, thus, does not fit well into the rationality of conduct.

Pre-emption and Islamic and natural laws

In contrast to the strict limits set in positive law, the requirements of necessity and proportionality, in this context, may fulfil the criteria of the Islamic and natural legal discourses on the use of force in pre-emption. This is because these discourses not only consider the seriousness of a security threat but also keep in view the past behaviour, disparity in power, difference in religious ideology, and the opportunity cost of striking first. Indeed, these discourses appeal more to the norm of self-preservation than to the right of self-defence.[208] Also, there is no precondition of 'armed attack' in the Islamic and natural laws of nations.[209] These discourses also back the political security and geographical expansionist claims of the invading powers and set aside the strict legal limits of the necessity of self-defence. One may assume that such an understanding and reasoning was due to the fact of contemporary circumstances, wherein wars out of differences over religious ideology, control over natural resources, and honour were common among the adversaries. The expansionist wars around Medina and taking over of the New World by the Spanish under the pretext of humanising the local populations bear testimony to this fact.

As a normative practice, both the Islamic and natural laws supported the use of force to tackle the hindrance in the spread of the divine message. It also shows the supremacy of one's divinity over the other as one reason, among many others,

207 Guiora, "Targeted Killing: When Proportionality Gets All Out of Proportion", 238.

208 For details of Islamic legal discourse, see Khadduri, *War and Peace in the Law of Islam*, 200–238; Martin, "The Religious Foundations of War, Peace and Statecraft in Islam", 95–106; Donner, *The Early Islamic Conquests*, 10–55; Watt, *Muhammad at Medina*, 75–145; Afsaruddin, "Views of *Jihad* Throughout History", 90–112; Neff, *War and the Law of Nations*, 39–55; Firestone, *Jihad: The Origin of Holy War in Islam*, 53–64; and Bonner, *Jihad in Islamic History: Doctrines and Practice*, 20–34. Whereas for details inside the natural law discourse, see Grotius, *The Rights of War and Peace*, Book I, 150–263; Scott, *The Spanish Origin of International Law: Francisco de Vitoria and His Law of Nations*, 195–220; Szabo, *Anticipatory Action in Self-Defense: Essence and Limits under International Law*, 29–64: and Ballis, *The Legal Position of War: Changes in its Practice and Theory from Plato to Vattel*, 13–45.

209 Alder, *The Inherent Right of Self-Defence in International Law*, 20. Also for details of sixteenth- and seventeenth-century European wars on religious differences, see Chesterman, *Just War or Just Peace?*, 10–15.

to wage war against the adversaries, whereas positive law divorced this reasoning altogether and set the physical harm as the only reason to initiate self-defence. Furthermore, the status of proportionality in the Islamic and natural legal discourses does not inform us much about any certain limits on the collateral damage. Again, perhaps it is because of the context of the development of these discourses since there was not much emphasis on the proportionality of counter armed measures, especially during the early era of the origin of Islamic legal discourse on the use of force. It was because of two fundamental reasons: first of all, the battlefield used to be a place outside the residential areas; second, maximum damage was a common norm in contemporary times to inflict severe injuries, so that the enemy may not adopt the course of war again. In effect, this practice led to the blurring of boundaries between self-defence and preventive self-defence.[210] In contrast to this normative practice though, the Prophet Muhammad commanded Muslims to spare women, children, and old men in wars. The killing of all military-age men, however, was a norm under Islamic law.[211] Similarly, natural law initially did not focus on proportionality. Later-day natural law theorists, however, did criticise the outsized violence in wars, especially in the backdrop of religious wars in Europe.[212] In this context, it is submitted that though we see traces of norms on proportionality, certain and detailed principles remain absent from both the discourses.

In these contexts of the past norms and practices, these are the precision weapons which can help uphold the principles of military necessity and proportionality of armed measures. Earlier, militaries were required to destroy large complexes to shut down a factory because they lacked precision weapons, but today they only need to target a few key buildings.[213] The evolution in precision technology demands the replacement of the goalposts to make the idea relevant and effective in seeking the legality of force employment as a self-defence measure. In an instance of pre-emption, these goalposts ought to be stricter. The advantage of technology should translate to relieving the miseries of targets. Thus far, the US drone strikes have served many tactical objectives of the campaign. For example, the US government is no more worried about the terrorists' detention because it effectively killing them rather than capturing them.[214] The cost, however, in terms of losses of innocent lives in Pakistan and Yemen is disproportionate. Indeed, the

210 For details, see Muhammad C. Bassiouni, *The Shari'a and Islamic Public Law in Times of War and Peace* (New York: Cambridge University Press, 2014), 165–179; and Ahmad Al-Dawoody, *The Islamic Law of War: Justifications and Regulations* (New York: Palgrave MacMillan, 2011), 11–42.

211 Yamani, "Humanitarian International Law in Islam: A General Outlook",189; Sheikh W. al-Zuhili, "Islam and International Law", *International Review of the Red Cross* 87, no. 858 (2005): 281–282; and Karima Bennoune, "As-Salamu-Alaykum? Humanitarian Law in Islamic Jurisprudence", *Michigan Journal of International Law* 15 (1994): 625–626.

212 Grotius, *The Rights of War and Peace*, Book III, 1472–1474.

213 Buster C. Glosson, "Impact of Precision Weapons on Air Combat Operations", *Airpower Journal* (1993): 4–10.

214 Byman, "Why Drones Work? The Case for Washington's Weapon of Choice", 34.

recourse to pre-emption through the use of combat drones underlines that until and "unless the two laws, the pre-war and the in-war, move in close harmony with one another, the apparent exigencies of in-war law tend to trump pre-war law as soon as the going gets rough".[215]

To conclude, it is emphasised that the discussions surrounding the pre-emption of terrorism raise some difficult questions over the use of force in self-defence against an enemy who crosses border and resides in the neighbouring state. Pursuing security threats across the border leads to the change of the context of force employment: that is, from the self-defence to pre-emptive self-defence. In this context, can the armed measures be extended to the level of total elimination of Al-Qaeda and its associated forces? After all, the group perpetrated violence in the past and provided justifications for self-defence. In addition, the discussions accentuate the fact that there remain serious contextual disparities between the case of the US drone attacks in Pakistan and Yemen and the *Caroline* incident. The rebels fighting inside Canada had very specific goals, with temporal and geographical constraints. Al-Qaeda and its associated forces do not believe in the limits of territory and time frame. Despite these contextual differences, one cannot disprove the sanctity of innocents in any event of pre-emption.

Summary

By extensively deploying analogical reasoning, this chapter constructed and interpreted the primary and subsidiary principles of the doctrine of pre-emption. As drawing upon the analogies from *jus in bello*, treaty law and *Caroline* criteria (customary law), these discussions thoroughly analysed the theoretical and empirical discourse on pre-emptive self-defence in the face of the terrorist threat to the security of states. These explanations are important in the sense that the previous studies related to these subjects did not endeavour to build and explain the discourse on the drone through the doctrinal framework of pre-emption. As most of the time, the focus was on self-defence and its primary and subsidiary principles. Also, this chapter established once again why the Islamic law and natural law frameworks, unlike the positive law, fall short in understanding, interpreting, and explaining the doctrine of pre-emption.

Bibliography

"A Wedding That Became a Funeral". *Human Rights Watch*, 2014. Accessed January 20, 2020. http:// www.hrw.org/reports/2014/02/19/wedding-became–funeral

Abbas, Hassan. *Pakistan's Drift into Extremism: Allah, the Army and America's War on Terror*. New York: Routledge, 2005.

Afsaruddin, Asma. "Views of *Jihad* Throughout History". In *International Law and Islamic Law*. Edited by Mashood A. Baderin, 97–101. Hampshire: Ashgate Publishing Company, 2008.

215 Geoffrey Best, *War and Law since 1945* (New York: Oxford University Press, 1997), 244–245.

Al-Dawoody, Ahmad. *The Islamic Law of War: Justifications and Regulations*. New York: Palgrave MacMillan, 2011.

al-Zuhili, Sheikh W. "Islam and International Law". *International Review of the Red Cross* 87, no. 856 (2005): 269–283.

Anderson, Kenneth. "Predators Over Pakistan". *Weekly Standard* 15, no. 24 (2010): 30–33.

Aronsson, Maric. "Remote Law-Making? American Drone Strikes and the Development of Jus Ad Bellum". *Journal on the Use of Force and International Law* 1, no. 2 (2014): 273–298.

"Attorney General Eric Holder Speech at Northwestern University School of Law". March 5, 2012. Accessed January 20, 2019, http://www.justice.gov/opa/speech/attorney-general-eric-holder-speaks-northwestern-university-school-law

Baer, Rober. "Finding Bin Laden Raises Questions about Pakistan's Complicity". *The New York Time*, May 2, 2011. Accessed January 10, 2020 http://content.time.com/time/world/article/0,8599,2069012,00.html

Ballis, William. *The Legal Position of War: Changes in its Practice and Theory from Plato to Vattel*. The Hague: Martinus Nijhoff, 1937.

Balz, Dan. "Obama Says He Would Take Fight to Pakistan". *The Washington Post*, August 2, 2007, A1.

Barnidge, Jr. Robert P. "A Qualified Defense of American Drone Attacks in Northwest Pakistan under International Humanitarian Law". *Boston University International Law Journal* 30 (2012): 409–447.

Bassiouni, Mahmoud C. "Legal Control of International Terrorism: A Policy-Oriented Assessment". *Harvard International Law Journal* 43 (2002): 83–103.

Bassiouni, Muhammad C. *The Shari'a and Islamic Public Law in Times of War and Peace*. New York: Cambridge University Press, 2014.

Beard, Jack M. "America's New War on Terror: The Case for Self-Defence under International Law". *Harvard Journal of Law & Public Policy* 25 (2001): 559–590.

Becker, Jo and Scott Shane. "Secret 'Kill List' Proves a Test of Obama's Principles and Will". *The New York Times*, 29 May 2012, A1.

Benjamin, Medea. *War on Demand: The Global Rise of Drones*. New York: Rosa Luxemburg Stiftung, 2013.

Bennoune, Karima. "As-Salamu-Alaykum? Humanitarian Law in Islamic Jurisprudence". *Michigan Journal of International Law* 15 (1994): 605–643.

Benson, Kristina. "Kill 'em and Sort It Out Later:" Signature Drone Strikes and International Humanitarian Law". *Global Business & Development Law Journal* 27 (2014): 17–51.

Bergen, Peter L. and Daniel Rothenberg, eds. *Drone Wars: Transforming Conflict, Law, and Policy*. New York: Cambridge University Press, 2015.

Bergen, Peter L. and Katherine Tiedemann. "Washington's Phantom War: The Effects of the U.S. Drone Program in Pakistan". *Foreign Affairs* 90, no. 4 (2011): 12–17.

Bergen, Peter L., David Sterman and Melissa Salyk-Virk. "America's Counterterrorism Wars". *The New America Foundation* (last updated 2020). Accessed January 12, 2020, https://www.newamerica.org/in-depth/americas-counterterrorism-wars/

Best, Geoffrey. *War and Law Since 1945*. New York: Oxford University Press, 1997.

Blank, Laurie R. "After 'Top Gun': How Drone Strikes Impact the Law of War". *University of Pennsylvania Journal of International Law* 33, no. 3 (2012): 675–718.

Blum, Gabriella and Phillip Heymann. "Law and Policy of Target Killing". *Harvard National Security Journal* 1 (2010): 145–170.

Bonner, Michael. *Jihad in Islamic History: Doctrines and Practice*. Princeton: Princeton University Press, 2006.

Bowcott, Owen. "Drone Strikes Threatens 50 Years of International, Say UN Rapporteur". *The Guardian*, June 21, 2012.

Bowett, Derek W. *Self-Defence in International Law*. Manchester: Manchester University Press, 1958.

Bowett, Derek W. "The Impact of Security Council Decisions on Dispute Settlement Procedures". *European Journal of International Law* 5, no. 1 (1994): 89–101.

Brennan, John O. "Strengthening Our Security by Adhering to Our Values and Law". Speech at Harvard Law School, September 16, 2011. Accessed January 13, 2020, www.whitehouse.gov/the-press-offi ce/2011/09/16/remarks-john-o-brennan-strengthening-our-security-adhering-our-values-an

Brennan, John O. "The Ethics and Efficacy of the President's Counterterrorism Strategy". Washington: Woodrow Wilson Center, April 30, 2012. Accessed January 10, 2020, https://www.wilsoncenter.org/event/the-efficacy-and-ethics-us-counterterrorism-strategy

"Briefing: Joint Targeting Cycle and Collateral Damage Methodology". Defense Intelligence Agency General Council. November 10, 2009. Accessed January 10, 2019 https://www.aclu.org/files/dronefoia/dod/drone_dod_ACLU_DRONES_JOINT_STAFF_SLIDES_1-47.pdf

Brooks, Rosa. "Drones and the International Rule of Law". *Ethics & International Affairs* 28, no.1 (2014): 83–103.

Brownlie, Ian. *Principles of Public International Law*. 7th ed. Oxford: Oxford University Press, 2008.

Brunstetter, Daniel and Megan Braun. "From *Jus Ad Bellum* to *Jus Ad Vim*: Recalibrating Our Understanding of the Moral Use of Force". *Ethics & International Affairs* 27, no. 1 (2013): 87–106.

Byman, Daniel. "Why Drones Work? The Case for Washington's Weapon of Choice". *Foreign Affairs* 92, no. 4 (2013): 32–43.

Cannizzaro, Enzo. "The Role of Proportionality in the Law of International Countermeasures". *European Journal of International Law* 12, no. 5 (2001): 889–916.

Case Concerning Military and Paramilitary Activities in and against Nicaragua (Nicaragua vs. United States of America), ICJ Reports, 1986.

Case Concerning Oil Platforms (Islamic Republic of Iran vs. United States of America), ICJ Reports, 2003.

Casey-Maslen, Stuart. "The Use of Armed Drones". In *Weapons under International Human Rights Law*. Edited by Stuart Casey-Maslen, 382–408. New York: Cambridge University Press, 2014.

Cassese, Antonio. *International Law*. 2nd ed. Oxford: Oxford University Press, 2005.

Chamayou, Gregoire. *A Theory of the Drone*. Translated by Janet Lloyd. New York: The New Press, 2015.

"Civilian Casualties & Collateral Damage". Lawfare. Accessed, January 12, 2020, https://www.lawfareblog.com/civilian-casualties-collateral-damage

Cohn, Marjorie, ed. *Drone and Targeted Killing: Legal, Moral and Geopolitical Issues*. Massachusetts: Olive Branch Press, 2015.

Cole, Chris, Mary Dobing and Amy Hailwood. *Convenient Killing: Armed Drones and the 'Playstation' Mentality*.London: The Fellowship of Reconciliation, 2010.

Colonomos, Ariel. "Preventive War a l' Americaine: In the Fog of Norms". In *War, Torture and Terrorism: Rethinking the Rules of International Security*. Edited by Anthony F. Lang, Jr. and Amanda R. Beattie, 85–102. New York: Routledge, 2008.

Corten, Olivier. *The Law Against War: The Prohibition on the Use of Force in Contemporary International Law*. Oxford: Hart Publishing Ltd., 2010.

Corten, Olivier. "The 'Unwilling or Unable' Test: Has it Been, and Could it be, Accepted"? *Leiden Journal of International Law* 29, no. 3 (2016): 777–799.

Crawford, Neta C. "Just War Theory and the U.S. Counterterror War". *Perspectives on Politics* 1, no. 1 (2003): 5–26.

Crawford, Neta C. *Accountability for Killing: Moral Responsibility for Collateral Damage in America's Post-9/11 Wars*. New York: Oxford University Press, 2013.

Crenshaw, Martha. "Will Threats Deter Nuclear Terrorism"? In *Deterring Terrorism: Theory and Practice*. Edited by Andreas Wenger and Alex Wilner, 136–163. Stanford, California: Stanford University Press, 2012.

Day, Stephen W. *Regionalism and Rebellion in Yemen: A Troubled National Union*. New York: Cambridge University Press, 2012.

Deeks, Ashley S. "Unwilling or Unable': Toward a Normative Framework for Extraterritorial Self-Defence". *Virginian Journal of International Law* 52, no. 3 (2012): 483–549.

Deeks, Ashley S. "Taming of the Doctrine of Pre-emption". In *The Oxford Handbook of the Use of Force in International Law*. Edited by Marc Weller, 661–668. Oxford: Oxford University Press, 2015.

DeYoung, Karen and Greg Miller. "White House Releases Its Count of Civilian Deaths in Counterterrorism Operations under Obama". *The Washington Post*, July 1, 2016.

Dinstein, Yoram. *War, Aggression and Self-Defence*. 4th ed. Cambridge: Cambridge University Press, 2005.

Donner, Fred M. *The Early Islamic Conquests*. Princeton: Princeton University Press, 1981.

Dorronsoro, Gilles. "The Transformation of the Afghanistan-Pakistan Border". In *Under the Drones: Modern Lives in the Afghanistan-Pakistan Borderlands*. Edited by Shehzad Bashir and Robert D. Crews, 30–44. Cambridge, MA: Harvard University Press, 2012.

Doyle, Michael W. *Striking First: Pre-emption and Prevention in International Conflict*. Edited by Stephen Macedo. Princeton: Princeton University Press, 2008.

El Dahan, Maha and Mohammad Ghobari. "Yemeni Parliament in Non-Binding Vote Against Drone Attacks". *Reuters*, December 15, 2013. Accessed January 10, 2020, https://www.reuters.com/article/us-yemen-drones/yemeni-parliament-in-non-binding-vote-against-drone-attacks-idUSBRE9BE0EN20131215

Emmerson, Ben. "Report of the Special Rapporteur on the Promotion and Protection of Human Rights and Fundamental Freedoms While Countering Terrorism". *UN Document A/68/389*, September 18, 2013.

Enemark, Christian. "Drones, Risk, and Perpetual Force". *Ethics & International Affairs* 28, no. 3 (2014): 365–381.

Entous, Adam, Siobhan Giorman and Julian E. Barnes. "U.S. Tightens Drone Rules". *The Wall Street Journal*, November 4, 2011.

Fair, Christine C. and Ali Hamza. "From Elite Consumption to Popular Opinion: Framing of the US Drone Program in Pakistani Newspapers". *Small Wars & Insurgencies* 27, no. 4 (2016): 578–607.

Finn, Peter "Khalid Sheikh Mohammed Killed Daniel Pearl, Report Finds". *The Washington Post*, January 20, 2011.

West, Ben and Scott Stewart. "Uncomfortable Truths and the Times Square Attack". *Security Weekly*, May 6, 2010. Accessed January 23, 2020, https://www.stratfor.com/weekly/20100505_uncomfortable_truths_times_square_attack

Firestone, Reuven. *Jihad: The Origin of Holy War in Islam*. Oxford: Oxford University Press, 1999.

Forge, John. "Proportionality, Just War Theory and Weapons Innovation". *Science and Engineering Ethics* 15, no. 1 (2009): 25–38.

Franck, Thomas. *Recourse to Force: State Action Against Threats and Armed Attacks*. Cambridge: Cambridge University Press, 2004.

Fuller, Christopher J. *See It/ Shoot It: The Secret History of the CIA's Lethal Drone Program*. New Haven: Yale University Press, 2017.

Gardam, Judith. *Necessity, Proportionality and the Use of Force by States*. Cambridge: Cambridge University Press, 2004.

Garraway, Charles. "The Changing Character of the Participants in War: Civilization of Warfighting and the Concept of 'Direct Participation in Hostilities'". *International Law Studies* 87 (2009): 178–186.

Gazzini, Tarcisio. "A Response to Amos Guiora: Pre-Emptive Self-Defence Against Non-State Actors". *Journal of Conflict & Security Law* 13, no. 1 (2008): 25–32.

"George W. Bush Address to the Nation." Washington, September 20, 2001. Accessed January 22, 2020, http://www.presidentialrhetoric.com/speeches/09.20.01.html

The Geneva Conventions, 1949 and Additional Protocols 1974.

Glazier, David E. "Rise of the Drones II: Unmanned Systems and the Future of War". Hearing before the Subcommittee on National Security and Foreign Affairs, Committee on Oversight and Government Reforms, House of Representatives, 111th Congress, 2nd Session, Serial No. 111-120, April 28, 2010.

Glosson, Buster C. "Impact of Precision Weapons on Air Combat Operations". *Airpower Journal* 7 (1993): 4–10.

Goodman, Ryan. "The Detention of Civilians in an Armed Conflict". *American Journal of International Law* 103 (2009): 46–74.

Grayson, Kyle. "Six Theses on Target Killing". *Politics* 32, no. 2 (2012): 120–128.

Grotius, Hugo. *The Rights of War and Peace*. Book I. Edited by Richard Tuck. Indianapolis: Liberty Fund Inc., 2005.

Grotius, Hugo. *The Rights of War and Peace*. Book III. Edited by Richard Tuck. Indianapolis: Liberty Fund Inc., 2005.

Guiora, Amos N. "Targeted Killing: When Proportionality Gets All out of Proportion". *Case Western Reserve Journal of International Law* 45, no. 1 (2012): 235–257.

Gunaratna, Rohan and Anders Nielsen. "Al-Qaeda in the Tribal Areas of Pakistan and Beyond". *Studies in Conflict & Terrorism* 31, no. 9 (2008): 775–807.

Gusterson, Hugh. *Drone: Remote Control Warfare*. Cambridge, MA: The MIT Press, 2016.

Hakimi, Monica and Josef K. Cogan. "The Two Codes on the Use of Force". *European Journal of International Law* 27, no. 2 (2016): 257–291.

Henkin, Loius. "Use of Force: Law and U.S. Policy". In *Might V. Right: International Law and the Use of Force*. 2nd ed. Edited by Loius Henkin, Stanley Hoffmann, Jeane J. Kirkpatrick and Allan Gerson, 37–70. New York: Council on Foreign Relations Press, 1991.

Henriksen, Anders. "*Jus ad Bellum* and American Targeted Use of Force to Fight Terrorism around the World". *Journal of Conflict & Security Law* 19, no. 2 (2014): 211–250.

Holland, Joseph. "Military Objective and Collateral Damage: Their Relationship and Dynamics". *Year Book of International Humanitarian Law* 7 (2004): 38–78.

Hussain, Zahid. *Frontline Pakistan: The Struggle with Militant Islam*. London: I.B. Tauris & Co. Ltd., 2007.

"International Humanitarian Law and the Challenges of Contemporary Armed Conflicts". ICRC Report, 2011.

Jenks, Chris. "Law from Above: Unmanned Aerial Systems, Use of Force, and the Law of Armed Conflict". *North Dakota Law Review* 85, no. 3 (2009): 649–671.

Jennings, Robert Y. "The Caroline and McLeod Cases". *American Journal of International Law* 32, no. 1 (1938): 82–99.

Johnsen, Gregory D. *The Last Refuge: Yemen, al-Qaeda and America's War in Arabia*. New York: W.W. Norton & and Company, 2013.

Kebriaei, Pardiss. "The Distance between Principle and Practice in the Obama Administration's Target Killing Programme: A Response to Jeh Johnson". *Yale Law & Policy Review* 31 (2012): 151–172.

Khadduri, Majid. *War and Peace in the Law of Islam*. Baltimore: The Johns Hopkins Press, 1955.

Khan, Ismail and Sabrina Tavernise. "U.S. Consulate in Pakistan Attacked by Militants". *The New York Times*, April 5, 2010, A4.

Koh, Harold H. "Preserving American Values: The Challenge at Home and Abroad". In *The Age of Terror: America and the World after September 11*. Edited by Strobe Talbott and Nayan Chanda, 143–169. New York: Basic Books, 2001.

Koh, Harold H. "The Obama Administration and International Law". Speech at Annual Meeting of the American Society of International Law, Washington, March 25, 2010. Accessed January 10, 2020 http://www.state.gov/s/l/releases/remarks/139119.htm

Kreps, Sarah and John Kaag, "The Use of Unmanned Aerial Vehicles in Contemporary Conflicts: A Legal and Ethical Analysis". *Polity* 44, no. 2 (2012): 260–285.

Kretzmer, David. "The Inherent Right to Self-Defence and Proportionality in Jus Ad Bellum". *European Journal of International Law* 24, no. 1 (2013): 235–282.

Kretzmer, David. "US Extra-Territorial Actions Against Individuals: Bin Laden, Al Awlaki and Abu Khattalah". In *The Use of Force in International Law: A Case-Based Approach*. Edited by Tom Ruys, Olivier Corten and Alexandra Hofer, 760–782. Oxford: Oxford University Press, 2018.

Kroenig, Matthew and Barry Pavel. "How to Deter Terrorism". *The Washington Quarterly* 35, no. 2 (2012): 21–36.

Larson, Kurt and Zachary Malamud. "The United States, Pakistan, the Law of War and the Legality of Drone Attacks". *The Journal of International Business & Law* 10, no. 1 (2011): 1–22.

Legal Consequences of a Wall in the Occupied Palestinian Territory, Advisory Opinion, ICJ Reports, 2004.

Legality of the Threat or Use of Nuclear Weapons, Advisory Opinion, ICJ Reports, 1996.

Lewis, Michael W. "Drones and the Boundaries of Battlefield". *Texas International Law Journal* 47, no. 2 (2012): 293–315.

"Living under Drones: Death, Injury and Trauma to Civilians from US Drone Practice in Pakistan". International Human Rights and Conflict Resolution Clinic, Stanford Law School and Global Justice Clinic, New York University School of Law, 2012.

Lowe, Vaughan, Adam Roberts, Jennifer Welsh and Dominik Zaum, eds. *The United Nations Security Council and War: The Evolution of Thought and Practice Since 1945*. New York: Oxford University Press, 2008.

Lubell, Noam. "The Problem of Imminence in an Uncertain World". In *The Oxford Handbook of the Use of Force in International Law*. Edited by Marc Weller, 697–719. Oxford: Oxford University Press, 2015.

Lubell, Noam and Nathan Derejko. "A Global Battlefield? Drones and Geographical Scope of Armed Conflict". *Journal of International Criminal Justice* 11, no. 1 (2013): 65–88.

MacDougal, Myres S. "The Soviet-Cuban Quarantine and Self-Defense". *American Journal of International Law* 57, no. 3 (1963): 597–604.

Mannes, Aaron. *Profile in Terror: The Guide to Middle East Terrorist Organizations*. New York: Rowman & Littlefield Publishers, 2004.

Marra, William C. and Sonia K. McNeil. "Understanding 'The Loop': Regulating the Next Generation of War Machines". *Harvard Journal of Law & Public Policy* 36, no. 3 (2013): 1139–1185.

Martin, Richard C. "The Religious Foundations of War, Peace and Statecraft in Islam". In *Just War and Jihad: Historical and Theoretical Perspectives on War and Peace in Western and Islamic Traditions*. Edited by James T. Johnson and John Kelsay, 91–119. New York: Greenwood Press, 1991.

Mayer, Jane. "The Predator War: What are the Risks of the C.I.A.'s Covert Drone Program"? *The New Yorker*, October 26, 2009.

McDougal, Myres S. and Florentino P. Feliciano. *Law and Minimum Public World Order*. New Haven: Yale University Press, 1961.

McDougal, Myres S. and Florentino P. Feliciano. *The International Law of War: Transnational Coercion and World Public Order*. Dordrecht: Martinus Nijhoff Publishers, 1994.

McNeal, Gregory S. "Are Targeted Killings Unlawful? A Case Study in Empirical Claims without Empirical Evidence". In *Targeted Killings, Law and Morality in an Asymmetrical World*. Edited by Claire Finkelstein, Jens D. Ohlin and Andrew Altmann, 326–346. Oxford: Oxford University Press, 2012.

Mendelsohn, Barak. *The al-Qaeda Franchise: The Expansion of al-Qaeda and Its Consequences*. New York: Oxford University Press, 2016.

Miller, Greg, Julie Tate and Barton Gellman, "Documents Reveal NSA's Extensive Involvement in Targeted Killing Program". *The Washington Post*, October 17, 2013.

Miller, Gregory D. "Terrorist Decision-Making and the Deterrence". *Studies in Conflict & Terrorism* 36, no. 2 (2013): 132–151.

Moir, Lindsay. "Action against Host States of Terrorist Groups". In *The Oxford Handbook of the Use of Force in International Law*. Edited by Marc Weller, 720–736. Oxford: Oxford University Press, 2015.

Murphy, Sean D. "The Doctrine of Preemptive Self-Defence". *Villanova Law Review* 50, no. 3 (2005): 699–748.

Murphy, Sean D. "The International Legality of US Military Cross-Border Operations from Afghanistan into Pakistan". *International Law Studies* 85 (2009): 109–139.

Murphy, Richard. "Responses to the Ten Questions". *William Mitchel Law Review* 37, no. 5 (2011): 5062–5070.

Musharraf, Pervez. *In the Line of Fire: A Memoir*. London: Simon & Schuster, UK Ltd., 2006.

Office of Journal Council, Department of Defense. *Law of War Manual*. Washington, June 2015, updated December 2016.

Orr, Andrew C. "Unmanned, Unprecedented and Unresolved: The Status of American Drone Strikes in Pakistan Under International Law". *Cornell International Law Journal* 44, no. 3 (2011): 729–752.

"Pete" Pedrozo, Raul A. "Use of Unmanned Systems to Combat Terrorism". *International Law Studies* 87, no. 1 (2011): 217–269.

Pincus, Walter. "Missile Strike Carried out with Yemeni Cooperation". *The Washington Post*, November 6, 2002, A10.

President George W. Bush. *The National Security Strategy of the United States*. Washington: The White House, 2002.

"President Says Saddam Must Leave Within 48 Hours". White House, Washington. March 17, 2003. Accessed January 10, 2020 http://georgewbush-whitehouse.archives.gov/news/releases/2003/03/20030317-7.html

Pugliese, Joseph. "Prosthetics of Law and the Anomic Violence of Drones". *Griffith Law Review* 20, no. 4 (2011): 931–961.

"Remarks of Director of Central Intelligence Agency, Leon E. Panetta, at the Pacific Council on International Policy". *CIA*. May 18, 2009. Accessed January 22, 2020, https://www.cia.gov/news-information/speeches-testimony/directors-remarks-at-pacific-council.html

"Remarks by the US President at the National Defence University". Washington, May 23, 2013. Accessed January 30, 2020, https://www.whitehouse.gov/the-press-office/2013/05/23/remarks-president-national-defense-university

Rinehart, Christine S. *Drones and the Targeted Killing in the Middle East and Africa: An Appraisal of American Counterterrorism Policies*. New York: Lexington Books, 2016.

Rogers, Ann and John Hill. *Unmanned: Drone Warfare and Global Security*. New York: Pluto Press, 2014.

Roggio, Bill. "Senior al Qaeda, Taliban, and Allied jihadist Leaders Killed in US Airstrikes in Pakistan, 2004–2016". *The Long War Journal*, 2016. Accessed January 19, 2019 http://www.longwarjournal.org/pakistan-strikes-hvts

Roy, Kaushik. *Military Manpower, Armies and Warfare in South Asia*. New York: Routledge, 2013.

Ruys, Tom. *'Armed Attacks' and Article 51 of the UN Charter: Evolutions in Customary Law and Practice*. Cambridge: Cambridge University Press, 2010.

Sadat, Leila N. "Second Annual Catherine B. Fite Lecture: Drone Wars and the Nuremberg Legacy". *Studies in Transnational Legal Policy* 45, no. 9 (2012): 27–38.

Sadoff, David A. "A Question of Determinacy: The Legal Status of Anticipatory Self-Defence". *Georgetown Journal of International Law* 40, no. 2 (2009): 523–571.

Savage, Charlie. *Power Wars: Inside Obama's Post-9/11 Presidency*. New York: Little, Brown and Company, 2015.

Schmitt, Michael N. "Counter-terrorism and the Use of Force in International Law". *International Law Studies*, 76 (2002): 7–73.

Schmitt, Michael N. "Responding to Transnational Terrorism under Jus Ad Bellum: A Normative Framework". In *International Law and Armed Conflict: Exploring the Faultlines, Essays in Honour of Yoram Dinstein*. Edited by Michael N. Schmitt and Jelena Pejic, 157–198. Leiden: Martin Nijhoff Publishers, 2007.

Schmitt, Michael N. "Autonomous Weapon Systems and International Humanitarian Law: A Reply to Critics". *Harvard National Security Journal Features* (2013): 1–19.

Scott, James B. *The Spanish Origin of International Law: Francisco de Vitoria and His Law of Nations*. Oxford: The Clarendon Press, 1934.

Shah, Niaz A. *Islamic Law and the Law of Armed Conflict: The Armed Conflict in Pakistan*. New York: Routledge, 2011.

Shah, Sabir. "Top Al-Qaeda Leaders Captured or Killed on Pakistani Soil". *The News*, May 3, 2011.

Shah, Sikander A. *International Law and Drone Strikes in Pakistan: The Legal and Socio-Political Aspects*. Oxon: Routledge, 2015.

Shane, Scott. "Contrasting Reports of Drone Strikes". *The New York Times*, August 11, 2011, A1.

Shane, Scott. "C.I.A. is Disputed on Civilian Toll in Drone Strikes". *The New York Times*, August 12, 2011, A1.

Shue, Henry and David Rodin, eds. *Preemption: Military Action and Moral Justification*. New York: Oxford University Press, 2007.

Silber, Mitchell D. *The Al-Qaeda Factor: Plots Against the West*. Philadelphia: University of Pennsylvania Press, 2012.

Singh, Ritika. "Drone Strikes Kill Innocent People: Why Is It So Hard to Know How Many"? *New Republic*, October 25, 2013.

"Statement of Admiral Michael Mullen, U.S. Navy Chairman Joint Chiefs of Staff before the Senate Armed Services Committee on Afghanistan and Iraq". Washington, September 22, 2011.

"Speech by Brian Egan, Legal Advisor to US State Department". American Society of International Law Meeting, April 4, 2016. Accessed January 12, 2020, https://www.lawfareblog.com/state-department-legal-adviser-brian-egans-speech-asil

Tams, Christian J. and James G. Devaney. "Applying Necessity and Proportionality to Anti-Terror Self-Defence". *Israel Law Review* 45, no. 1 (2012): 91–106.

Tayler, Letta. "Between a Drone and Al-Qaeda: The Civilian Cost of US Targeted Killing in Yemen". New York: Human Rights Watch, 2013.

Terrorist Threat to the Americas. *Twenty-fourth Meeting of Ministers of Foreign Affairs, OEA/Ser.F/II.24 RC.24/RES.1/01*. Washington, September 21, 2001. Accessed January 20, 2020, http://www.oas.org/oaspage/crisis/rc.24e.htm

The Secretary General. *A More Secured World: Our Shared Responsibility*. New York: United Nations, 2004.

Thomas, Andrew R. and James C. Duncan, eds. *Annotated Supplement to the Commander's Handbook on the Law of Naval Operations*. Vol. 73. Washington: US Naval War College, 1999.

Totten, Mark. *First Strike*. New Haven, Conn.: Yale University Press, 2010.

Trapp, Kimberly N.. "Back to Basics: Necessity, Proportionality, and the Right of Self-Defence Against Non-State Terrorists Actors". *International & Comparative Law Quarterly* 56, no. 1 (2007): 141–156.

Trapp, Kimberley N. "Can Non-State Actors Mount an Armed Attack"? In *The Oxford Handbook of the Use of Force in International Law*. Edited by Marc Weller, 679–698. Oxford: Oxford University Press, 2015.

Tsagourias, Nicholas. "Self-Defence against Non-State Actors: The Interaction between Self-defence as a Primary Rule and Self-Defence as Secondary Rule". *Leiden Journal of International Law* 29, no. 3 (2016): 801–825.

UN Security Council Resolutions 1269, 1368, and 1373.

UNSC Rep. of the Sect. General, UN Documents, S/2010/394, July 26, 2010.

Van den hole, Leo. "Anticipatory Self-Defence under International Law". *American University International Law Review* 19, no. 1 (2003): 69–106.

Vogel, Ryan J. "Drone Warfare and the Law of Armed Conflict". *Denver Journal of International Law & Policy* 39, no. 1 (2010): 101–138.

Walzer, Michael. *Just and Unjust Wars: A Moral Argument with Historical Illustrations*. 4th ed. New York: Basic Books, 2006.

Warren, Aiden and Ingvild Bode. *Governing the Use-of-Force in International Relations: The Post-9/11 US Challenge to International Law*. Hampshire: Palgrave Macmillan, 2014.

Watkin, Kenneth. *Fighting at the Legal Boundaries: Controlling the Use of Force in Contemporary Conflict*. New York: Oxford University Press, 2016.

White House. "Fact Sheet: US Policy Standards and Procedures for the Use of Force in Counterterrorism Operations Outside the United States and Areas of Active Hostilities".

May 23, 2013. Accessed January 13, 2020, https://www.whitehouse.gov/the-press-office/2013/05/23/fact-sheet-us-policy-standards-and-procedures-use-force-counterterrorism

Williams, Brian G. *Predators; The CIA's Drone War on al Qaeda*. Washington: Potomac Books, 2013.

Williams, John. "Distant Intimacy: Space, Drones, and Just War". *Ethics & International Affairs* 29, no. 1 (2015): 93–110.

Wilmshurst, Elizabeth. "The Chatham House Principles of International Law on the Use of Force in Self-Defence". *International & Comparative Law Quarterly* 55, no. 4 (2006): 963–972.

Woods, Chris. "The Day 69 Children Died". *The Express Tribune*, August 12, 2011.

Woods, Chris and Christina Lamb. "Obama Terror Drones: CIA Tactics in Pakistan Include Targeting Rescuers and Funerals". *The Bureau of Investigative Journalism*, February 4, 2012. Accessed January 12, 2020, https://www.thebureauinvestigates.com/2012/02/04/obama-terror-drones-cia-tactics-in-pakistan-include-targeting-rescuers-and-funerals/.

Woodward, Bob. *Obama's Wars*. London: Simon & Schuchter, 2010.

Wright, Quincy. "The Cuban Quarantine". *American Journal of International Law* 57, no. 3 (1963): 546–565.

Yamani, Ahmad Z. "Humanitarian International Law in Islam: A General Outlook". *Michigan Yearbook of International Legal Studies* 7 (1985): 189–215.

Yasmeen, Samina. "Unexpectedly at Center Stage: Pakistan". In *Global Responses to Terrorism: 9/11, Afghanistan and Beyond*. Edited by Mark Buckley and Rick Fawn, 188–201. New York: Routledge, 2003.

Zenko, Micah. "Reforming U.S. Drone Strikes Policies". Council on Foreign Relations, Special Report No. 65, January, 2013.

Ziring, Lawrence. *Pakistan: At the Crosscurrent of History*. Oxford: Oneworld Publications, 2003.

6 What future for the pre-emption of terrorism through drones?

After detailed discussions on the doctrinal contours of pre-emptive self-defence, its general practices, and interpretations in the context of non-state violence as well as its specific application in the cases of Pakistan and Yemen, this chapter spreads out the findings of this study to analyse the broader unfolding landscape of pre-emptive use of force to hunt down terrorists through the use of combat drones. To accomplish this task, different pieces of the puzzle that jointly formulate the doctrine of pre-emption are put together. In contrast to the citation practices in the previous chapters, however, the focus on footnotes this time will be kept to a possible minimum.

Contemporary world and drones

Combat drones are rapidly emerging as an *essential* tool of contemporary warfare. Their effectiveness in striking down the intended targets in areas difficult to access for the soldiers and fighter jets is marvellous. They help in achieving the objectives of warfare even without the fear of loss of human lives on one end of the violent spectrum. It seems, thus, that states prefer to rapidly build as well as deploy combat drones in warring and war-preparedness scenarios, in contrast to other violent aerial technology alternatives like long-range missiles and fighter jets. This is happening when the contemporary practices in the non-state security threat projection realm show that terrorism as a violent tactic is here to stay, and so the usage of combat drones to hunt down these terrorists. Estimates suggest that in the post–September 11, 2001, era, despite the fact of serious counter-terror military operations by the US and its allies, the events and threat of terrorist violence have increased. In the absence of any permanent territorial base to operate, terrorists belonging to Al-Qaeda and its affiliated groups have spread around the world. They are adopting new circumstances and operational constraints. As underlined by a recent US State Department Report, the terrorist threat remains formidable even in the backdrop of numerous counter-terror successes in recent years.[1]

1 United States Department of State, "Country Reports on Terrorism 2018", Washington, 2019. For a detailed description of the spread of terrorism in recent years, see Williamson, *Terrorism, War and International Law*, 29–34.

To respond to this reality, around 101 states are employing drones of various kinds. During the previous decade alone, the drone proliferation recorded a 58 per cent jump.[2] Among those having drones, 22 states are already in possession of combat drones,[3] and, thus far, around 10 states have employed combat drones to carry out counter-terrorism operations in various roles, ranging from surveillance to combat. Similarly, 30 more states are in the process of acquiring combat drones for military purposes.[4] Around eight countries have deployed combat drones for counter-terror attacks and surveillance in Syria alone. These include Iran, Turkey, Russia, Italy, Britain, Syria, Iraq, and the US. However, 21 states continue to use drones in Afghanistan. Overall, the US strides far ahead of its other competitors when it comes to deploying combat drones in warfighting and preparedness missions around the globe. Currently, she is using combat drones, in addition to Iraq and Syria, in Afghanistan, Yemen, Pakistan, Somalia, West Africa, the Sahel, the Korean Peninsula, Philippines, and Eastern Europe.[5] In recent months, France has also stepped up its fight against terrorism in the Sahel, wherein combat drones once more remain an essential weapon and a frontline force application to kill terrorists before they embark on the course to hurt French national security interests.

Emerging centrality of the 'unwilling or unable' formula?

The ensuing era after the September 11, 2001 terrorist attacks is marked by plenty of shifts in understanding as well as interpretive practices of states invoking laws of war in self-defence. Hours after the terrorist attacks, the US government attributed the attacks to Al-Qaeda based in Afghanistan and demanded that Afghanistan hand over Al-Qaeda leadership. Any failure to act upon this demand shall make Afghanistan liable for the terrorist attacks and consequences.[6] The US government, meanwhile, also brought up this case before the UN Security Council. The Security Council, in its numerous resolutions, called upon Afghanistan to apprehend Al-Qaeda leaders. Any failure to do so shall amount to forfeiting of its international duty towards the victim state. Herein, we see that the Security Council and the US government did not prefer to debate the fact of the attribution of these terrorist attacks to the Afghan government. In fact, the presence of Al-Qaeda leadership on Afghan territory at the time of the terrorist attack amounted to implicating the state for the harm caused. In this particular context,

2 Dan Gettinger, "The Drone Databook", The Center for the Study of the Drone at Bard College, New York, 2019, viii.

3 Michael C. Howortiz, Joshua A. Schwartz, and Mathew Fuhrmann, eds., "Who's Prone to Drone? A Global Time-Series Analysis of Armed Uninhabited Aerial Vehicle Proliferation", 2, accessed February 2, 2020, https://ssrn.com/abstract=3422313

4 Gettinger, "The Drone Databook", xii–xiii.

5 Ibid.

6 Peter V. Jakobsen, "Coercive Diplomacy: Countering War-Threatening Crises and Armed Conflicts", in *Contemporary Security Studies*, ed. Alan Collins. 4th ed. (Oxford: Oxford University Press, 2016), 282.

there can arise a question as to whether the US government was not interested in fixing state responsibility as it did not recognise the Taliban regime as a legitimate Afghan government.

Anyhow, in this context, numerous legal scholars did treat it as an instance of a 'constitutional moment', with a potential to alter the course of *jus as bellum*.[7] This potential speaks of the trend in displacing the importance of attributing the harm to the state as a primary requirement in the recourse to the use of force. Such an assessment of the state practice, however, now underlines the fact that pre-emptive self-defence against non-state violent actors is perhaps emerging as a separate category of laws of recourse to war, whereof justificatory formulas like 'unwilling or unable' and 'harbouring' are taking primacy over other subsidiary norms enshrined in the 'state responsibility and complicity' frameworks. We notice that, after the September 11, 2001 terrorist attacks, Russia against Chechen rebels in Georgia, Israel against Hezbollah in Lebanon, Turkey against Kurd rebels in Iraq, and Columbia against Fuerzas Armadas Revolucionrias de Columbia (FARC) rebels in Ecuador deployed the 'unwilling or unable' formula to launch armed attacks.[8] More recently, likewise, the US government in its letter to the Security Council to reason the use of force to target Islamic State and Al-Qaeda in Syria was categorical in pitching its arguments for launching pre-emptive attacks inside another state with the help of the 'unwilling or unable' formula. It stated that despite the fact of clear evidence of the functioning of terrorists from Syrian territory, it seems Syria is not willing and able to curtail this security threat.[9] Likewise, India, while invoking the right of self-defence to pre-empt an imminent terrorist attack emanating from the Pakistani territory, also deployed the 'unwilling or unable' formula.[10]

These instances point towards the evolving understanding of states to situate the 'unwilling or unable' formula at the centre of the legal argumentation for the legality of their claims to hunt down terrorists inside the territory of other states. It is noteworthy, in this context, that they make no attempt to directly implicate or attribute the terrorist threat to the state. Perhaps, they assume that the presence of terrorist threat is itself evidentiarily sufficient to prove that the host state lacks the *political will* and *ability* to eliminate the security threat on its own. And thus, as per Article 3(f) of the Definition of Aggression, wherein "the action of a State in allowing its territory,—to be used by [another] State for perpetrating an act of aggression against the third State",[11] the host state may lack legitimacy in propel-

7 Slaughter and Burke-White, "An International Constitutional Moment", 1–21; Turner, "Operation Iraqi Freedom: Legal and Policy Considerations", 765–796; and Lietzau, "Old Laws, New Wars: Jus ad Bellum in an Age of Terrorism", 384–455.

8 Deeks, "Unwilling or Unable: Toward a Normative Framework for Extra-territorial Self-Defense", 486–491.

9 Letter from the Permanent Representative of the United States of America to the United Nations addressed to the Secretary-General, UN Doc S/2014/695, September 23, 2014.

10 "Full Text: Indian Government's Statement on Surgical Airstrike in Pakistan", *India Today*, February 26, 2019.

11 "Definition of Aggression", Annex to GA Res. 3314 (XXIX) of December 14, 1974.

ling claims of territorial sovereignty in an instance of the use of force to neutralise the security threat.

(Re)visiting the *Caroline* case

In any discourse analysis, it is imperative to contextualise a legal text to interpret and infer its meaning. Such an understanding, however, also raises the question that if laws are context-specific, then how can they be applied across times?[12] In this backdrop, can a change of context impede the attempts to fully unlock and interpret a legal text? To answer this question, it is important to understand that the law formulation context will not always perfectly repeat as it is to understand and interpret laws. Yet understanding the law-formulating context is vital to appreciate the essence and contours of the enacted law in different contexts. The importance of the *Caroline* case, in this sense, to understand and interpret the right of (pre-emptive) self-defence is, therefore, vital. This is because, though it set the legal parameters to regulate the use of force among states, the said episode of violent engagement was between state and non-state violent actors. For framing arguments, revisiting the circumstantial delineations of this case shall help in better understanding the legal issues and challenges of our times, which are also, obviously, marked by the exchange of violence between the state and the non-state actors.

The cross-border movements of the US citizens,[13] supporting the Canadian rebels during the ongoing insurgency, created serious tensions between the British and US governments. The British government, in its diplomatic correspondence, put across the point that by not being *able* to stop the cross-border movements of its nationals, the US government is forfeiting its important legal *duty* towards a neighbour at peace with her. Such a duty, the British government underlined, is set down in contemporary international legal principles of 'neutrality' and 'non-interference'.[14] The US government endorsed these principles and conceded that her citizens have no right to participate in cross-border violence.[15] In this context, the setting down of these rudimentary principles, which were later on, sufficiently, explained in the frameworks of 'state responsibility' and 'state complicity', was an important step towards invoking and fixing the responsibility of states for violent acts of their citizens.

In this backdrop, of course, to ascertain and appreciate the customary legal importance of the *Caroline* criteria while it is important to take into account the circumstances of laying down the criteria, one cannot, nonetheless, solely rely

12 Martti Koskenneimi, "Imagining the Rule of Law: Rereading the Grotian 'Tradition'", *European Journal of International Law* 30, no. 1 (2019): 19–20.

13 The factual details and its legal relevance are explained in the Chapters 2 and 3. The current discussions only cover its legal contours in the backdrop of contemporary security dynamics and debates.

14 Charles G. Earles, *The Impact of International Law on British Foreign Policy to the United States, 1836-1846*, PhD Dissertation submitted at Sidney Sussex College, UK, 2018, 117–118.

15 Webster to Fox, *Diplomatic Correspondence*, Vol. III (British Foreign Office, 1841), 1269.

on the criteria set in the 1830s and ignore state practices afterwards.[16] To counter an impending security threat, the crossing of an international border, squarely, makes the test of the use of force tough to negotiate with as well as subject to the fulfilling of numerous requirements of state responsibility, necessity, and proportionality of armed self-defence measures. Understanding and (re)framing these requirements in view of contemporary means of assault and violence is essential. And such an understanding, according to the numerous international law scholars, should not ignore the changes in the means of delivery and the lethal potential of modern weaponry.[17] We cannot ignore, moreover, the ability of terrorists to launch massive attacks rather than, as in the context of the *Caroline* case, engage in only sporadic border skirmishes. In a similar vein, we should also put the principles of the *Caroline* criteria in the context of an environment where terrorists are, essentially, thwarting the efforts of host states to stop them from using its territory and people to inflict harm on other states.

Examining the (state) unwillingness

Indeed, in its entirety, the 'unwilling or unable' test is not part of any contemporary treaty law.[18] Nonetheless, there is no denying the fact that this test has been an important source and precursor to fixing state responsibility for harmful acts, as well as to ascertain the principle of due diligence among states.[19] In the context of the existent scenario, we understand that due to its *already* manifest ability to do harm, a security threat posed by terrorists compels the victim states to adopt *active* armed measures to forestall such security threats. The scale of terrorist violence, and its permeating presence across numerous states, is a message for the host states to take effective counter-terrorism measures. Perhaps also due to the fact of the presence in digital space and usage of social media by the terrorists, today it is, somewhat, inconceivable to think that a host state does not know about their presence on its territory. Normative changes and regulative evolution in the present era, thus, bind states not to tolerate the presence of terrorists in their respective territorial jurisdictions and wait for any actual harm to be attributed. It is because of the fact that international terrorist groups, such as Al-Qaeda, Islamic State, Boko Haram, etc., have already committed acts of terrorism in multiple states and against the citizens of numerous states.

In addition, numerous Security Council resolutions, which are legally binding, have called upon states to be vigilant against the threat of international terrorism and help the international community in curbing this security threat through all necessary and available means. Among these resolutions, 1333, 1368, and 1373 are the salient ones. These resolutions reemphasise and reinforce the already

16 Ruys, *'Armed Attack' and Article 51 of the UN Charter*, 515.

17 Ibid., 320–322.

18 Corten, "The 'Unwilling or Unable' Test: Has it Been, and Could it Be, Accepted?" 780.

19 *The Corfu Channel Case*, 22.

laid down obligations under the frameworks of *state responsibility* and *state complicity*. In this context, now a state cannot, reasonably, claim that it is unaware about its obligations towards other states when terrorists are present in its territorial jurisdiction. Hence, any negligence in curbing terrorism may amount to a willful act of a state, underpinning the *unwillingness* to fulfil its responsibility and, thus, leading to the state being considered complicit in case of any harm by the terrorists.[20]

Yet before any attempt to link the state to the terrorist threat, one cannot ignore the Court ruling in the *Armed Activities* case that a lack of political will to act or, for that matter, inaction on the part of the host state against terrorists itself was not tantamount to toleration of terrorists on its territory.[21] This, in turn, means that a lack of political will shall not, automatically, put a host state in the crosshairs for failure to use force against the terrorist threat on its territory. In this backdrop, therefore, it seems that the fact of the presence of a security threat on a territory does not normatively make the question of first fixing state responsibility and attributability pertinent.[22] The Chatham House Principles,[23] Bethlehem Principles,[24] and Leiden Policy Recommendations[25] point towards this emerging state understanding vis-à-vis the terrorist threats. In contrast to this, there are also numerous voices inside the legal fraternity challenging any shift in the law which affects or displaces the importance of state responsibility, complicity, and attributability.[26] Anyhow, in the opinion of the present author, state unwillingness may spare the host state from any direct harm while countering terrorism on its territory; it may not end up guaranteeing territorial sovereignty. At least, that is what we can already see in view of the emerging state practice.

20 Kimberly N. Trapp, *State Responsibility for International Terrorism: Problems and Prospects* (Oxford: Oxford University Press, 2011); and Becker, *Terrorism and the State: Rethinking the Rules of State Responsibility*.

21 *Armed Activities Case*, 104, para 301.

22 For details, see Christian Marxsen and Anne Peters, "Dilution of Self-Defence and its Discontents", in *Self-Defence Against Non-State Actors*, Vol. 1, ed. Mary E. O' Connell, Christian J. Tams, and Dire Tladi (Cambridge: Cambridge University Press, 2019), 6–7; and Deeks, "Unwilling or Unable: Toward a Normative Framework for Extra-territorial Self-Defense", 495.

23 Wilmshurst, "Chatham House Principles of International Law on the Use of Force by States in Self-Defence", 969.

24 Bethlehem, "Self-Defense against an Imminent or Actual Armed Attack by Nonstate Actors", 776 (principle 11).

25 Nico Schrijver and Larissa van den Herik, "Leiden Policy Recommendations on Counter-Terrorism and International Law", Leiden University, 2010, 42, accessed January 12, 2020, https://openaccess.leidenuniv.nl/bitstream/handle/1887/42298/LeidenPolicyRecommendations1April 2010 .pdf

26 Corten, "The 'Unwilling or Unable' Test: Has It Been, and Could It Be, Accepted?" 777; Craig Martin, "Challenging and Refining the 'Unwilling or Unable' Doctrine", *Vanderbilt Journal of Transnational Law* 52 (2019): 387–461; Jutta Brunnee and Stephen Toope, "Self-Defence against Non-State Actors: Are Powerful States Willing but Unable to Change International?", *ICLQ* 67 (2018): 263–285; and Mary E. O' Connell, "Self-Defence, Pernicious Doctrines, Peremptory Norms", in *Self-Defence Against Non-State Actors*, Vol. 1, ed. Connell, Tams and Tladi, 224–227.

Interpreting the (state) inability

With regard to the September 11 terrorist attacks and the question of attribution of responsibility for these attacks, not only the Security Council but also the OAS and NATO took a quite expansive view of state responsibility. These multi-lateral organisations interpreted the fact of the presence of Al-Qaeda on Afghan soil as a justification to launch military action against the state,[27] and the presence of Al-Qaeda and its claim to inflict harm as tantamount to the state inability to curb the danger. Later, to assess the inability of a state, the loss of its own territory to terrorists was set as an indicator that the state in question shall be, effectively, unable to curtail the terrorist threat.[28] Conversely, there are those who believe that a mere loss of certain parts of territory may also not be conflated with the loss of state jurisdiction over its territory[29] and that the state must be given the opportunity to eradicate the danger originating from its territorial jurisdiction.

Meanwhile, we also know that in comparison to the analysis of the unwilling state, the interpretation of state inability is more convoluted, for it is essentially an interplay of plenty of variables related to the military strength of the state as well as the challenge of the terrorist threat it strives to quell.[30] We know that it is an obvious fact that states in their capability to ward off security threats are not equally powerful. As an effect, presumably, the terrorists would prey upon the weaker states more frequently to assemble, train, and plan attacks against other states. In the post–September 11 period, the cases of Libya, Iraq, Syria, Somalia, Yemen, Pakistan, Niger, Mali, Nigeria, and Afghanistan are illustrative ones. While, on the one hand, such a vulnerability induces the terrorists to flock to the weaker states, on the other hand, it invites foreign military interventions more easily due to the fact of disparity in state military prowess between the host state and the victim state. In this context, the easiness of militarily striking a state involved in harbouring terrorists can potentially give way to lowering the threshold of the legal necessity in view of pre-emption. Thus, state inability is double jeopardy in terms of violations of the rights of a state.

With regard to interpretive practices, the Court was categorical in its judgement in the *Diplomatic and Consular Staff* case that, given the fact of the availability of resources at its disposal to fulfil certain obligations, if a state chooses not to initiate action, it violates certain rules of state responsibility.[31] Another possible scenario is when states initiate action against terrorists, but the terrorist threat, which threatens the state security of other states, remains present. These are cases of fighting terrorist dangers in weaker states, wherein we see that the war against terrorism is continuing for decades. In this context, as was the case with

27 Jinks, "State Responsibility for the Acts of Private Armed Groups", 90.

28 Ruys, *'Armed Attack' and Article 51 of the UN Charter*, 544.

29 For details of such scenarios, see Terry D. Gill and Kinga Tibori-Szabo "Twelve Key Questions on Self-Defense against Non-State Actors", *International Law Studies* 95 (2019): 497.

30 Gill and Tibori-Szabo "Twelve Key Questions on Self-Defense against Non-State Actors", 497.

31 *Diplomatic and Consular Staff Case*, 33–34, para 68.

state unwillingness, while state inability may shield the host state from any direct harm from foreign military intervention, it may, however, not end up protecting her territorial sovereignty.

Changing conception of 'imminence' of security threats

In present times, the advent of modern weaponry, burgeoning non-state violence, and changing state practices have brought the debate about the criterion of 'imminence' within the framework of pre-emption to the fore.[32] Characteristically, in comparison to states, terrorists pose a different kind of security threat. During the past two decades, numerous terrorist attacks against the technologically advanced Western states lay bare the fact that detecting the movements and violent onslaught of terrorists is difficult. Mechanisms of early warning and detection of hostile movements, which help in evaluating the security threat posed by a state adversary, may not help in discovering an imminent terrorist attack. In addition to this, even if the impending terrorist attack is detected, the response time is too short of engaging in an armed encounter to neutralise the security threat. In this backdrop, while on the one hand pre-emptive strike-through drones becomes an obvious choice for the states, on the other hand, such a choice entails plenty of legal questions to square off the choice of such a course against the legal necessity and prudence of it.

Arguably, the criterion of 'imminence' has different meanings and scope for different states. Those who are facing the threat of terrorism or already fighting such a threat shall have different calculus to gauge 'imminence'. To the contrary, those who did not face the threat of terrorism themselves and rather can be a target of foreign military intervention due to the presence of terrorists on their soil shall have a different understanding of 'imminence'. Such states would not endorse the idea that the mere presence and intentions of terrorists to strike a state amounts to fulfilling the criteria of imminence. For in such a scenario, they would be the victim of the use of force on their soil though directed against terrorists. In this backdrop, we see that despite the fact of overly restrictive applications of the laws related to self-defence against violent non-state actors by the Court, understanding and interpretive practices regarding the customary rules seem to be evolving rapidly under the dictates of new security threats.[33]

The issue of benchmarking the state practice in ascertaining the norm formation and crystallisation regarding the pre-emption of imminent terrorism is a delicate one. Understandably, in any event of the use of pre-emptive force against an imminent terrorist threat, the states would find it safe not to condemn such acts of other states because the issue is of terrorism. Their silence, however, may be taken as acquiescence, which, according to the opinion of the present author, may be out

32 Franck, "What Happens Now?" 619.

33 Ruys, *'Armed Attack' and Article 51 of the UN Charter*, 531–532.

of political calculus most of the time.[34] Moreover, terrorists, unlike states, do not have any ideological allies and friends in the international system that will support them and condemn any act of pre-emptive use of force. In effect, we see either the support of pre-emptive self-defence against the terrorist threat or wilful silence, except in the case of a state whose territory is struck in the process. In this regard, Israeli pre-emptive military actions in Syria, Iraq, and Lebanon, the US killing of Iranian military leader in Baghdad, and Indian military action in Pakistan in recent months, are instructive.

In the case of Israel, though, it is targeting alleged terrorists around multiple states; there is no condemnation of her acts at the international level except by the Iranian government, whose interests are being struck directly and frequently. Similarly, the case of Indian pre-emptive use of military force against the alleged terrorist camps inside Pakistani territory in February 2019 suggests that there are only two kinds of responses at the international level: those who supported the pre-emptive armed measure and those who kept quiet. And, of course, Pakistan was quick to condemn the military action as a blatant violation of its state sovereignty.

In these contexts, the question of the relevance of time-period also arises, which should be focused or ignored for ascertaining the fact of the customary norm origin and stabilisation.[35] During the Cold War period, though states engaged in pre-emption, there was no chance of getting it approved by the Security Council due to the fact of the prevailing ideological politics between the two blocks.[36] However, in present times, owing to the change in the treatment of pre-emption by the Security Council, which is kind of a muted response, as well as the increased frequency of its use, the number of such incidents has increased manifold. The treatment of the issue of terrorism by the Security Council in its numerous resolutions and by other regional organisations and existent state practice, in conduct and otherwise, suggests that the threat of terrorism shall entail a different understanding of imminence from the host and the victim state with regard to state security threat perceptions. Presumably, terrorists remain committed to inflicting harm and waiting for the opportunity to attack. Hence, given the opportunity to strike, states shall wait at their own peril to be struck the first blow by terrorists. The norm of the imminence of a security threat, in this context, remains in flux. Also, it seems to be caught up between the *conduct* of numerous states and the *wilful political acquiescence* of others. In the realm of policy debates, moreover,

34 This claim is further substantiated by the recent trends in state practice following the killing of Iranian military leader in a US drone attack in Baghdad. According to the data compiled by Mehrnuch Anssari and Benjamin Nußberger after the US drone attacks, most of the states remained silent. While the US allies supported the attack, and Iranian allies condemned it. For details, see Anssari and Nußberger, "Compilation of States' Reactions to U.S. and Iranian Uses of Force in Iraq in January 2020", Just Security, January 22, 2020, accessed January 28, 2020, https://www.justsecurity.org/68173/compilation-of-states-reactions-to-u-s-and-iranian-uses-of-force-in-iraq-in-january-2020/

35 Murphy, "The Doctrine of Pre-Emptive Self-Defence", 27.

36 Ibid.

it is obvious that the imminence of a terrorist threat shall have different meanings for different states. Powerful but victim states, due to their advanced means of surveillance and intelligence gathering tools, shall be able to see the security threat much in advance, in comparison to weaker states. The temptation to scramble means of redress, on the part of powerful states, therefore, shall also be overwhelming. This is what we are witnessing in the case of the practices of powerful states like the US, Israel, India, Turkey, Britain, and France.

Challenges to interpret and fulfil proportionality

Indeed, when proportionality remains the cornerstone of any measure of the use force, in an instance of pre-emption, however, it serves as the central pillar. At the same time, while the principle of proportionality is easy to apply and ascertain in an instance of self-defence, it turns out to be an extremely difficult undertaking in view of its assessment in a pre-emptive self-defence episode. This is because the doctrine of pre-emption is *essentially an elemental interplay of the necessity and proportionality* of an armed self-defence measure. In effect, it has no *jus ad bellum* and *jus in bello* distinction. To put it simply, the recourse to the use of force cannot be reasonably separated from the actual employment of any dose of violent force. Hence, the lawfulness of one element underpins the legality of the other and vice versa. In the context of drone practices, however, this complexity further multiplies.

The use of force employed through drones poses a unique challenge for the principle of proportionality, as the drone operators engage in the use of force without any fear of their safety and security. Such an edge in killing the adversary with zero loss of lives demands that the losses on the other end of the spectrum also be proportionate to the expected security threat. Given this expectation, however, it should subtract the security threat they (terrorists) pose to those, employing the deadly force. Indeed, any loss of civilian lives, in an event of the pre-emptive use of force through combat drones, poses a serious challenge for the principle of proportionality. However, there is also no denying the fact that in view of the war between drones and terrorists, the application of the norm of discrimination between terrorists and civilians is far more difficult in comparison to that between civilians and soldiers, as terrorists, unlike soldiers, wear no uniforms and do not travel on signature vehicles. Instead, they live, commute, and launch attacks while sharing the same space as civilians.

In the backdrop of the fact of zero loss of or threat to life on one end of the spectrum, there arises a scenario that a high-value target is spotted among the civilians, the very target, whom drone operators were struggling to locate since months. Now if the operators wait too long and let him separate himself from the civilians, then there is a chance that he will slip away once again. While being at large, he will continue planning terrorist attacks and may kill numerous civilians. In such a scenario, the drone operators have to make judgement calls while balancing the cost of inaction against immediate action. Hence, given the chance of hunting down the high-value terrorist, the question of the scale of damage he can inflict on civilians still remains. Is the killing of a few civilians along with the intended target legitimate? However, such an exceptional scenario may not serve as a common *norm* in taking down the high-value terrorist targets every time they are spotted among civilians. Otherwise, the opportunity to strike down terrorists among civilians shall end up as a disregard for the losses of actual civilian lives in an attempt to hypothetically calculate the lives of civilians saved. Of course, a no cost-benefit analysis would fulfil the evidentiary formula, which gives primacy to the scenarios of saving of hypothetical losses of lives in one state over the actual innocent killings in another state.

By dint of technological advancements drone operators have the luxury of time and technological means to remain focused on the target while waiting for the civilians to move out of the target area. In practice, however, we see by analysing the numerous cases above that targeting of high-value terrorists on the basis of human intelligence as evidence while travelling alongside civilians or hiding inside a building has caused serious losses of the civilian lives, who happened to be in close proximity at the time of the attack. Perhaps, relying on multiple sources of evidence, along with more patience on the part of drone operators, could spare civilian lives in the process of targeting the terrorists. This in turn also helps in addressing and fulfilling the criteria of proportionality when availing this exceptional window of pre-emptively targeting the terrorists lawfully.

Due to its ability to access and target terrorists in an otherwise inaccessible area, killings through combat drones also pose a serious evidentiary challenge. As explained in the previous chapter, among all the sources of fatality counting, nowhere have two sources reached the same conclusions about the number of deaths. This divide is even more serious when two governmental sources put across their estimates. In any case, however, no one denies the fact of civilian loss of lives. Situating these facts in a larger frame and for the sake of understanding the discourse, it is also important to view the turn towards hi-tech semi-autonomous weapons to kill terrorists despite the fact of their consequences for the civilian populations around the target. However, the emergent targeting discourse in the post–World War II world suggests that saving the lives of soldiers is more important than saving those of civilians.[37] In present times, the losses of civilian lives in Afghanistan, Iraq, Syria, Yemen, and Somalia bear testimony to this existent fact. So, when in an instance of pre-emptive drone attack the security of an operator (soldier) is 100 per cent guaranteed, then it is quite reasonable to *expect* and *demand* that it should translate into balancing out the standard of protecting the lives of civilians.

Bibliography

Anssari, Mehrnuch and Benjamin Nußberger. "Compilation of States' Reactions to U.S. and Iranian Uses of Force in Iraq in January 2020". Just Security, January 22, 2020.

37 Kennedy, *Of War and Law*, 89. For the emerging trend, see Henderson, *The Contemporary Law of Targeting: Military Objectives, Proportionality, and Precautions in Attack under Additional Protocol I* (Leiden: Martinus Nijhoff Publishers, 2009), 158–159.

Accessed January 28, 2020, https://www.justsecurity.org/68173/compilation-of-states-reactions-to-u-s-and-iranian-uses-of-force-in-iraq-in-january-2020/

Becker, Tal. *Terrorism and the State: Rethinking the Rules of State Responsibility*. Oxford: Hart Publishing, 2006.

Bethlehem, Daniel. "Self-Defense against an Imminent or Actual Armed Attack by Nonstate Actors". *American Journal of International Law* 106, no. 4 (2012): 770 777.

Brunnee, Jutta and Stephen Toope. "Self-Defence against Non-State Actors: Are Powerful States Willing but Unable to Change International"? *International & Comparative Law Quarterly* 67 (2018): 263–285.

Case Concerning Armed Activities on the Territory of Congo (Democratic Republic of Congo vs. Uganda), Judgement, ICJ Reports, 2005.

Corten, Olivier. "The 'Unwilling or Unable' Test: Has it Been, and Could it be, Accepted"? *Leiden Journal of International Law* 29, no. 3 (2016): 777–799.

Deeks, Ashley S. "Unwilling or Unable": Toward a Normative Framework for Extraterritorial Self-Defence". *Virginian Journal of International Law* 52, no. 3 (2012): 483–549.

"Definition of Aggression." Annex to GA Res. 3314 (XXIX), December 14, 1974.

Earles, Charles G. *The Impact of International Law on British Foreign Policy to the United States, 1836–1846*, PhD Dissertation submitted at Sidney Sussex College, UK, 2018.

Franck, Thomas M. "What Happens Now? The United Nations after Iraq". *American Journal of International Law* 97, no. 3 (2003): 607–620.

Gettinger, Dan. "The Drone Databook". The Center for the Study of the Drone at Bard College, New York, 2019.

Gill, Terry D. and Kinga Tibori-Szabo. "Twelve Key Questions on Self-Defense against Non-State Actors". *International Law Studies* 95 (2019): 467–505.

Henderson, Ian. *The Contemporary Law of Targeting: Military Objectives, Proportionality, and Precautions in Attack under Additional Protocol I*. Leiden: Martinus Nijhoff Publishers, 2009.

Howortiz, Michael C., Joshua A. Schwartz and Mathew Fuhrmann, eds. "Who's Prone to Drone? A Global Time-Series Analysis of Armed Uninhabited Aerial Vehicle Proliferation". Accessed January 2, 2020, https://ssrn.com/abstract=3422313

Jakobsen, Peter V. "Coercive Diplomacy: Countering War-Threatening Crises and Armed Conflicts". In *Contemporary Security Studies*. 4th ed. Edited by Alan Collins. Oxford: Oxford University Press, 2016.

Jinks, Derek. "State Responsibility for the Acts of Private Armed Groups". *Chicago Journal of International Law* 4, no. 1 (2003): 83–95.

Kennedy, David. *Of War and Law*. Princeton: Princeton University Press, 2006.

Koskenneimi, Martti. "Imagining the Rule of Law: Rereading the Grotian 'Tradition'". *European Journal of International Law* 30, no. 1 (2019): 17–52.

Letter from the Permanent Representative of the United States of America to the United Nations addressed to the Secretary-General, UN Doc S/2014/695, September 23, 2014.

Lietzau, William K. "Old Laws, New Wars: Jus ad Bellum in an Age of Terrorism". *Max Planck United Nations Yearbook* 8 (2004): 384–455.

Martin, Craig. "Challenging and Refining the 'Unwilling or Unable' Doctrine". *Vanderbilt Journal of Transnational Law* 52 (2019): 387–461.

Marxsen, Christian and Anne Peters. "Dilution of Self-Defence and its Discontents". In *Self-Defence Against Non-State Actors*, Vol. 1. Edited by Mary E. O' Connell, Christian J. Tams and Dire Tladi, 1–7. Cambridge: Cambridge University Press, 2019.

Ministry of External Affairs. "Full Text: Indian Government's Statement on Surgical Airstrike in Pakistan". *India Today*, February 26, 2019.

Murphy, Sean D. "The Doctrine of Preemptive Self-Defence". *Villanova Law Review* 50, no. 3 (2005): 699–748.

O' Connell, Mary E. "Self-Defence, Pernicious Doctrines, Peremptory Norms". In *Self-Defence Against Non-State Actors*, Vol. 1. Edited by Mary E. O' Connell, Christian J. Tams and Dire Tladi, 174–257. Cambridge: Cambridge University Press, 2019.

Ruys, Tom. *'Armed Attacks' and Article 51 of the UN Charter: Evolutions in Customary Law and Practice*. Cambridge: Cambridge University Press, 2010.

Schrijver, Nico and Larissa van den Herik. *Leiden Policy Recommendations on Counter-terrorism and International Law*. Leiden University, 2010. Accessed January 12, 2020 https://openaccess.leidenuniv.nl/bitstream/handle/1887/42298/LeidenPolicyRecommendations1April 2010.pdf

Slaughter, Anne-Marie and William Burke-White. "An International Constitutional Moment". *Harvard International Law Journal* 43, no. 1 (2002): 1–21.

The Corfu Channel Case (United Kingdom and Northern Ireland vs. People's Republic of Albania), ICJ Reports, 1949.

Trapp, Kimberly N. *State Responsibility for International Terrorism: Problems and Prospects*. Oxford: Oxford University Press, 2011.

Turner, Robert F. "Operation Iraqi Freedom: Legal and Policy Considerations". *Harvard Journal of Law & Public Policy* 27 (2004): 765–796.

United States Department of State. "Country Reports on Terrorism 2018". Washington, 2019.

United States Diplomatic and Consular Staff in Tehran (United States of America vs. Iran), Judgement, ICJ Reports, 1980.

Webster to Fox. *Diplomatic Correspondence*, Vol. III. British Foreign Office, 1841.

Williamson, Myra. *Terrorism, War and International Law: The Legality of the Use of Force Against Afghanistan in 2001*. Surrey: Ashgate Publishing Limited, 2009.

Wilmshurst, Elizabeth. "The Chatham House Principles of International Law on the Use of Force in Self-Defence". *International & Comparative Law Quarterly* 55, no. 4 (2006): 963–972.

7 Conclusion

By analysing the doctrine of pre-emption within the frame of different legal traditions, this study underlines that overtime doctrinal understanding, as well as scope, was put subject to numerous justificatory conditions and constraints. Indeed, it depicts the element of progress in international law to make the *jus ad bellum* coherent and determinate. The role of the natural and Islamic law of nations remains of foundational character. It informed and then transposed the idea of pre-emptive self-defence into positive international law. The norm of self-preservation, in its various manifestations, drove this transition. Once set down inside positive international law, various subsidiary norms form the justificatory framework for the lawful execution of pre-emption. Although these requirements, at times, gave way to serious tensions among different interpretive discourses, their importance in stabilising this inherently unstable doctrine is incomparable. In the past, moreover, any engagement with the right of self-defence to counter an impending security threat set a relatively stable discourse. The entry of terrorism in the realm of security threats in the post–September 11 world, however, posed a serious challenge to the justificatory frameworks and their established denotation in positivism. These legal categories include, among others, 'self-defence', 'armed attack', 'necessity', and 'proportionality'.[1]

With regard to the non-state violence, the ability of terrorists to launch 'armed attack' led to many questions. Within the realm of interpretive discourse, while the Court was adamant in not treating the sporadic and low gravity non-state violent attacks as an armed attack, the Security Council after September 11 chose to move past this material barrier and declared that a violent non-state attack may also unravel the right of self-defence. Nevertheless, questions arise about the status and role of the Security Council in setting legal precedents. In this backdrop, however, it has been argued that *jus ad bellum* "requires interpretation and judgment in order to apply it to real world situations. These interpretations and judgments are aided by historical precedents and established standards, but they are

1 Brooks, "Drones and the International Rule of Law", 83.

not strictly determined by them" in all circumstances.[2] Indeed, international law evolves through state practice and, thus, perhaps it is only state practice which mirrors responses to the real-world security threats. Where one can assume that such a response is a time-bound necessity, the emergence of legal norms out of this necessity, however, is not time-dependent.

In present times, the security threats driven by international terrorism have effectively created certain and stable threat perception norms among states. So, when states feel vulnerable, time becomes the essence of negotiating this security challenge. In this context, the need for pre-empting terrorist security threat is overwhelming. As noted above, states, therefore, find it easy to employ pre-emptive self-defence to eliminate a security threat without indulging in the legal controversies of *armed attack, gravity of the use of force, and effective control.* Yet such a choice to tackle a terrorist threat on the territory of another state entails various justificatory requirements for availing this exceptional legal remedy. This is, primarily, due to the fact of the nature and character of violent actors in this sort of use of force equation. As in the context of a pre-emptive strike against terrorists, the fulfilment of the criterion of *necessity* and *proportionality* is more difficult to meet in comparison to state-specific force employment. In addition to this, such complexity arises due to the dense nature of the doctrine of pre-emptive self-defence. Unlike the traditional self-defence, ancillary principles of pre-emptive self-defence are less coherent and elaborative. It is because pre-emption is characteristically a one-way force employment and, therefore, sets strict limits around the targeting of an intended target.

In these contexts, presumably, questions about the willingness or ability of the host state also compound the recourse to arms. Certainly, powerful states have more capacity and yearning to launch pre-emptive strikes inside the territory of weaker states as a matter of policy choice to counter an existent or brewing security threat. Any failure, however, to fulfil the customary law criteria of proportionality may raise questions about the role of law in creating a more stable order and respect for state sovereignty rather than being a tool to delineate the relationship between security and politics. As explained in this study, the necessity of self-defence cannot be a substitute for the requirement of proportionality in any instance of pre-emptive self-defence. To the contrary, due to their exceptional nature, both of these principles in unison inform about the character and legal status of this sort of use of force. To respond to contemporary terrorist violence, empirical evidence highlights the fact of disproportionate and civilian-targeted violence as an emerging tendency. We see, therefore, that "in vast areas of security, self-defence, and the use of force, the US government has in recent years left a huge deficit as to how its actions constitute a coherent statement of international law".[3]

2 Peter Asaro, "On Banning Autonomous Weapon Systems: Human Rights, Automation, and Dehumanization of Lethal Decision-Making", *International Review of the Red Cross* 94, no. 886 (2012): 705.

3 Anderson, "Predators Over Pakistan", 30–33.

Perhaps, we are reaching these conclusions against the background of the paradoxical nature of the legal framework applied to study the issue of drone attacks in Pakistan and Yemen. After all, questions shall arise out of an instance of pre-emptive self-defence. Any argumentation to expose the fact of disproportionality takes into account the actual loss of lives, which such a use of force inflicts, in comparison to the presumed protection of humans thereof. Whereas the intervening state shall justify the loss of civilian lives, out of a pre-emptive force employment against terrorists, with the help of a fictional number of prevented losses on the other end of the spectrum. Nonetheless, one needs to be mindful of the fact that the deployment of combat drones to pre-empt terrorism creates heightened expectations that civilian lives shall be spared. After all, the drone operators cannot complain about the pressure of time and battlefield fatigue and stress. Their losses, in any case, shall be zero, and they shall not face any danger to their lives even after killing the terrorists. Therefore, they could easily wait a bit longer to let the *innocents* move away from the *guilty*. But when they target the guilty and kill innocent people in large numbers, these are matters of policy choices and entail responsibility for the loss of civilian lives. These choices can undermine the legality of pre-emptive self-defence, the exceptional right they are availing to *kill first*.

One notices that, at times, the precision of combat drones did translate to pinpointing of the intended targets. In these instances, this practice saved many innocents. Indeed, this could have become a broader practice creating a more favourable atmosphere to uphold the principle of proportionality set down by the *Caroline criteria*. Inversely, we see that the US drone attacks ripped open the complex interplay between the opportunity of targeting and the prudence of waiting. Understandably, there are serious contextual differences between the Caroline case and the US drone campaign in Pakistan and Yemen. Al-Qaeda and its associated forces continue to express their willingness to harm US interests and civilians. Terrorists remain at large in the vicinity of the US nationals in various states. Yet it has been argued that a "state has absolute, but not unlimited, right and obligation to protect its civilian population".[4] Easiness as well as cost-free killing should not give way to the crossing of the thin line between lawful and unlawful use of force in self-defence—under the assumptions of the perceived severity of security threats. It may enhance asymmetry and squeeze out the principle of reciprocity from the institution of war. It is submitted, thus, that over-reliance on the technological advancements in fighting the contemporary security threats and relaxation of long-established principles of *imminence*, *necessity*, and *proportionality* may make it harder to address security threats.[5]

In addition, as explained throughout this study, with regard to combat drones, it is natural to assess the collateral damage caused by them against higher legal

4 Guiora, "Targeted Killing: When Proportionality Gets All Out of Proportion", 256.

5 Guiora, "The Legal and Ethical Limits of Technological Limits of Warfare: Introduction", 1223; and Kreps and Kaag, "The Use of Unmanned Aerial Vehicles in Contemporary Conflicts: A Legal and Ethical Analysis", 261 (emphasis added).

standards of proportionality.[6] Consequently, this is what makes the legality of the US drone strikes contestable. As explained in the chapter on empirical evidence, within the pre-emptive self-defence framework, the proportion of civilian deaths is hard to reconcile with the intended targets: terrorists. In view of the existent security environment, however, it is argued that while the institution of warfare is evolving, it is creating anomalies of various kinds along the way. It is knocking around the boundaries of temporality and geography. A very restricted and time-bound doctrine of pre-emptive self-defence is creating a 'state of war'. It remains to be seen, however, if drone practice in lieu of pre-emption would create any new norm of customary international law, as there is no manifest widespread state practice with a belief of the norm as *opinio juris*. Yet there are chances that, due to its usefulness as a counter-terror framework, the doctrine of pre-emption may end up providing "powerful states an almost unlimited licence to use force".[7] It can, meanwhile, help awaken states to the realities of the contemporary security environment: an environment marked by the normative transitions in the conceptions of state responsibility and state complicity. In such circumstances, the safety of one's own civilians will depend upon securing its territory from infiltration by terrorists, as well as ensuring the security of foreign nationals thereon.

To sum up, it is submitted that as any pre-emptive force employment against terrorism is justified on the idea of killing those who are committed to taking the lives of innocents, instances of attack on terrorists, which itself cause civilian casualties, are unaccounted for. Can the doctrine of pre-emptive self-defence sustain *excessive collateral damage* in the age of terror? Indeed, there are no clear legal answers to this legal conundrum. Perhaps, it seems that the legal order is yet figuring out the scale of the unfolding landscape and assessing the scope of the shift. In these contexts, it is emphasised that only a move away from mere claims of the right of self-defence towards ascertaining its consequences shall better serve the purposes of law as a regulative tool among states. Inside the doctrine of pre-emptive self-defence such a move can moderate the shift and stabilisation of legal order. More focus on the operational elements of this doctrine, therefore, is an essential condition here as the necessity of self-defence only informs about the procedural dimensions. In this situation, however, the *necessity of self-defence* can manage this shift, and the *proportionality of counter armed-measures* help in its stabilisation. The right of self-defence, otherwise, shall retrogress into the realm of the norm of self-preservation—with a severe bearing for the doctrinal discourse of pre-emption as well as the global legal order.

Bibliography

Anderson, Kenneth. "Predators Over Pakistan". *Weekly Standard* 15, no. 24 (2010): 30–33.
Brooks, Rosa. "Drones and the International Rule of Law". *Ethics & International Affairs* 28, no.1 (2014): 83–103.

6 Megret, "The Humanitarian Problem with Drones", 1301.
7 Klabbers, *International Law*, 193.

Frederic, Megret. "The Humanitarian Problem with Drones". *Utah Law Review* 2013, no. 5 (2013): 1283–1319.

Guiora, Amos N. "Targeted Killing: When Proportionality Gets All out of Proportion". *Case Western Reserve Journal of International Law* 45, no. 1 (2012): 235–257.

Guiora, Amos N. "The Legal and Ethical Limits of Technological Limits of Warfare: Introduction". *Utah Law Review* 2013, no. 5 (2013): 1215 1226.

Klabbers, Jan. *International Law*. Cambridge: Cambridge University Press, 2013.

Kreps, Sarah and John Kaag. "The Use of Unmanned Aerial Vehicles in Contemporary Conflicts: A Legal and Ethical Analysis". *Polity* 44, no. 2 (2012): 260–285.

Peter, Asaro. "On Banning Autonomous Weapon Systems: Human Rights, Automation, and Dehumanization of Lethal Decision-Making". *International Review of the Red Cross* 94, no. 886 (2012): 687–709.

Index

www.ingramcontent.com/pod-product-compliance
Lightning Source LLC
LaVergne TN
LVHW021129300926
849160LV00010B/937
* 9 7 8 0 3 6 7 7 0 2 8 5 4 *